Sevenoaks Chronicle

Westerham Courier and Kentish Advertiser incorporating Westerham Herald

No. 4633   FRIDAY SEPTEMBER 20 1968   POSTAGE: Inland 4d. Overseas 5½d.

C000104199

FLOOD HAVOC SWEEPS TOWN, VILLAGES

Families evacuated as raging water leaves trail of devastation

...OS thought to be the worst local disaster since the ...nd world war swept Sevenoaks and surrounding vil... ...the weekend leaving a trail of filth, devastation and ...ak.

...ere swept away and old people trapped in upstairs rooms as swirling ...s hurtled down the Darenth valley from Westerham to Shoreham.

...pewed from blocked drains to ...of muck and mud that roared ...ee on a mile wide sweep down ...rees and shrubs were torn from ...like straws.

...High Street the bridge over ...swept away in the early hours ...aving a 20-foot gap of broken ...raging water. In Brasted and ...people brought out rubber ...small boats but soon aban... ...in the unmanageable torrent.

...m trapped in upstairs rooms in ...Sevenoaks, were rescued by ...water rose to seven feet on ...ghbours rowed in with hot food ...ly women trapped in a bed...

...w Road became a raging river ...roke through from Knole Park ..."breaking" leaving a nine-foot ...all Valley Drive was a quag... ...and the torrent surged into ...d Greatness "like the river

...p torrents

...worst flood for more than ...e waded chest deep to help ...ue belongings as more water ...om hills into blocked streets ...streams into ten-foot deep

...100 families in Chipstead, the ...are, were evacuated to the ...lakes burst their banks and ...houses from back to front ...four feet. Most of a pie... ...n disappeared overnight. A ...greenhouse, kitchen garden, ...om slid 15 feet to the lake

...families from devastated ...found shelter in the parish ..."It was like the blitz." The ...ewett, rector of Chevening, ...enfice service for distressed ...of whom spent the weekend ...d.

...the whole of the village ...nder water. Torrents roaring ...hills turned the street into ..."The water came through ...ave" said one man. Water ...t of 4ft. 6in.

...m a local firm swelled the ...ood Sundridge village and ...over barricades as people ...ct sodden homes

...m 250 yards of Church Road ...er at the worst of the flood ...ed the third step on stair... ...40 and 90 houses had ground ...er and the old stone bridge ...mortal was covered by swirl...

...ning Station two cars were ...oad by a stream in spate and ...ds away in a field of stubble. ...carried an elderly couple to ...ay when their van stuck in ...water on Longford Bridge at ...Earth slips and flooding ...elay to rail travellers. Twenty ...randed in Sevenoaks when ...age train ran into floodwater. ...worked all night on Monday

...in erect a Bailey bridge over the river at Otford. Women on the broken west bank collected milk from a roundsman who braved a broken footplank, all that remained of the old bridge.

...In Riverhead water roared through Marley Tiles's premises, cascaded over the main London Road and ripped through a service station, a bungalow and a cafe on the opposite side.

Ten people from Braintree, Essex, stranded by the floods in Sevenoaks on Sunday, were accommodated at West Heath School. Seats in the Odeon cinema in the town were six inches deep in floodwater at the weekend.

Church attendance fell sharply on Sunday as regular worshippers abandoned attempts to leave homes. The boiler room at Brasted parish church was flooded. The Bishop of Tonbridge, the Rt. Rev. H. D. Halsey, was unable to reach Kemsing on Sunday night where he was due to preach.

Power cut off

Widespread electricity faults affected many villages including Chipstead, Brasted, Ide Hill and Otford. At the Battle of Britain display on Saturday at Biggin Hill an airborne Vulcan bomber was struck by lightning and damaged although it managed to return to base.

Sevenoaks garages were kept busy in the aftermath of the floods bringing in stranded and abandoned cars in Sevenoaks and surrounding districts. Members of the Voluntary Service Unit from Coombe Bank Convent helped distressed families in Chipstead, scrubbing carpets and cleaning floors.

Westerham people described the weekend floods as the worst in living memory. A wide area round Quebec Square was inundated and buildings at the foot of Vicarage and Hosey Hills were badly affected. Flooding built up early in Croydon Road where a great rush of water swept into Rysted Lane.

In spite of everything the mails got through. In vans and on foot postmen covered the whole area and collected letters from more than 100 pillar boxes, many deep in flood water. Only six boxes were left uncollected and these were completely under water.

Even at the height of the flood there was little complaint: no bad temper. Neighbours helped each other, brewed tea, comforted the old and infirm.

An old lady in Shoreham said: "It was like the war. We all helped each other. We had to, didn't we?"

● MORE DRAMATIC photographs and stories about the great flood disaster which swept through town and villages appear in Pages 10, 11, 12, 13, 15, 18 and 28

CHIPSTEAD STORES

A TRACTOR and trailer were used to take some of 102 families who were forced to evacuate their flooded homes in Chipstead, the worst hit Sevenoaks village. Full story in Page Ten, pictures in Page 18

THE BEDROOMS were the only dry places in these houses in Grassy Lane, Sevenoaks, which was probably the worst affected area in Sevenoaks, where the water rose to a depth of 15 feet. Full story in Page 28

RAIN GAUGES OVERFLOWED

WEATHERMEN looked at their gauges in disbelief following Sunday's violent storm, when record rainfall was recorded throughout the district.

West Malling was one of the hardest hit areas in the South East. The R.A.F. meteorological office recorded a fall of 5.18 inches between midnight on Saturday and midnight Sunday.

One inch of rain is equivalent to 22,500 gallons an acre.

Second highest on the water poll was Riverhead with 5.3 inches.

Rainfall figures supplied by the Sevenoaks Urban Council's engineer and surveyor, Mr. Alan Bennett, show that between 9 a.m. on Friday until 10 a.m. on Sunday 4.5 inches of rain fell on the Sevenoaks area.

From 10 a.m. Sunday until 9 a.m. the following Sunday bringing a further 2.3 inches fell, making a total of 6.8 inches.

From Monday of last week to Monday there was an amazing total of 7.9 inches.

Mr. John Newton, of Lester Box Lane, Sevenoaks who has been taking weather records at his home over the past eight years, supplies his own figures.

During the weekend from Saturday to Monday morning, he recorded a total of 7.85 inches.

"These figures, if anything, are rather on the low side as at one point the rainfall gauge had overflowed," said Mr. Hewson. "I kept having to empty my gauge as it only holds two inches."

Closed

We give

SHIELD stamps

Summer Term 2002

Sevenoaks
Preparatory
School

Matthew Essam

Sevenoaks Chronicle

of the

Century

Here is the illustrated story of an attractive Kentish market town in the most remarkable century mankind has ever known. The photographs, many of them taken by *Sevenoaks Chronicle* staff cameramen, help to capture the changing social scene from the primitive shops, the unmetalled roads and the horse and cart to the complex world of machines, computers and environmental issues which dominate our society today. The names of our civic leaders will be instantly recognisable but they are not the true heroes of this century. That honour belongs to the tradesmen, the soldiers, the doctors and many others to whom we owe our health, freedom, comfort and mobility.

Whether you turn these pages for nostalgia, discovery, reference or just fun here is the story of Sevenoaks, researched and written by the former and present editors of the *Sevenoaks Chronicle*.

Bob Ogley and Roger Perkins

Froglets Publications Ltd

Brasted Chart, Westerham,
Kent TN16 1LY
Tel: 01959 562972
Fax: 01959 565365

ISBN 1 872337 26 0

© Bob Ogley &
Roger Perkins

Originated by Froglets Publications Ltd. Scanning by CK Litho, Whitstable. Printed and bound by MPG Book Division, Victoria Square, Bodmin, Cornwall, PL31 1EG

PICTURE ACKNOWLEDGEMENTS
The majority of photographs in this book came from the Chronicle's own archives whose photographers include Alex Watson, Roger Tutt, Mike Knights, Holly Pelling, Clare Kendall, Paul Ellis, Mark Davey, Matt Devine. We are also grateful to the following for the use of their photographs: Gordon Anckorn, Ed Thompson, Sevenoaks Society, Nancy Rosser, David Peacock and Sir David Smithers.

Jacket design Stuart Webber

*This book is dedicated to the memory of the late Victor Froud, editor of the Sevenoaks Chronicle (1959 - 1967) and Sevenoaks News (1967 - 1976). Vic was born in Boughton Monchelsea and moved with his parents to Riverhead before the 1914-18 war. He attended Riverhead primary school, won a scholarship to Sevenoaks School and left with considerable academic and sporting honours, particularly at rugby and cricket. Joining the Sevenoaks Chronicle in 1929 as a cub reporter he enjoyed a long and successful association with the newspaper. Following his retirement in 1976 he became secretary of Sevenoaks Chamber of Trade.
Vic Froud died in 1996.*

Gordon Anckorn is another former Chronicle reporter whose contribution to the history of Sevenoaks, through his remarkable collection of old photographs, is already legendary. Gordon was born at Dunton Green attended the local school and became a pupil at Sevenoaks School during the headship of Geoffrey Garrod. He also joined the Sevenoaks Chronicle in the late 1920s and, apart from a brief spell in London, worked as a reporter in the town for almost 50 years covering many of the town's major stories and taking numerous pictures. He was the newspaper's first Chronicler columnist. Gordon, who was 86 in 1999, lives in Dersingham, Norfolk.

CONTENTS

A special thanks to Sevenoaks Society and the staff of Sevenoaks Library

Four Chronicle front pages are reproduced
on the front and back end papers of this book

This aerial photograph of Sevenoaks was taken in the 1960s before the Tesco and Waitrose supermarket era, before the post office moved to its new site next to the Odeon cinema, before the demolition of the Granada and before the introduction of Suffolk Way, the library and swimming pool. Note the narrow entrance to Buckhurst Lane where the Grey House was to give way to the modern Boots building, the council offices in Argyle Road and the Eardley Road fire station and swimming baths round the corner. Also gone are Buckhurst Lodge, next door to the Granada, the old rugby changing rooms at Knole Paddock, St Nicholas parish hall and the old brewery buildings behind Daws. Now compare this with the modern aerial on pages 158/159.

The Royal Crown Hotel in London Road — coaching stop, social centre and the venue for lavish dinner and dances.

1900: A country market town

IN 1900, Sevenoaks was a small country town of some 8,100 people where, on the third Wednesday of the month — market day — cattle, pigs and sheep pens filled the High Street from the fountain to the old Rose and Crown Inn (opposite Lloyds Bank). There were two, perhaps three motor cars but no motor buses and those who wished to travel further afield either boarded the large horse-drawn carriage on its journey from Rye to London, used the family trap (if they were lucky enough to own one) or walked.

People used their legs frequently to travel long distances. Men walked to work, children walked to school, housewives walked to the shops. Tradesmen used carts, drawn by ponies or even shire horses and clouds of dust would rise from the roads as the rigs bowled along — the drivers almost oblivious to the discomfort of the pedestrian.

The main shopping centre of the town extended from St Nicholas Church to Bank Street, although there were a few new shops towards Blighs Hotel and in the London Road, where the business of S. Young and Son had been established for more than 100 years. Public houses and cafes abounded.

There were two banks in Sevenoaks. The London and County Banking Company (now the Nat West) had moved to its imposing new building at 67 High Street as early as 1874 and, in 1900, Lloyds Bank was just a year old.

The Royal Crown Hotel in the London Road, with its great ballroom, meeting rooms and luxury bars, had been a going concern for many years. By 1900 it was a coaching stop, the social centre of Sevenoaks and the venue for dinners and dances and auction sales which were then increasing in popularity.

Behind the hotel (now the Odeon car park) were beautiful gardens where afternoon teas were served in the summer months. Beyond a small farm, on the slopes of South Park, customers enjoyed uninterrupted views towards Ide Hill.

Major events since the coming of the railway

1862: The South Eastern Railway Company wins approval from Parliament to build a direct line from London to Tonbridge via Orpington and Sevenoaks.

A railway station opens at Bat and Ball with a line to London via Swanley. There are six trains daily each way.

1864: A police station is built in Sevenoaks High Street next to the junction with Seal Hollow Road.

1865: A Congregational Church is built on St John's Hill.

1867: Her Majesty Queen Victoria visits Knole.

The Wednesday cattle market was run by Messrs Cronk and cattle pens were pitched across the road. The Ready Fire Brigade kept their engine and equipment in premises next door to The Chequers and the firemen drilled in the High Street. The horse mail was then stabled in the Rose and Crown Yard opposite Lloyds Bank. Cavalry regiments in full dress were often billetted in the town and local publicans, by law, were compelled to feed the men and stable the horses.

There were seven doctors in practice in Sevenoaks at the turn of the century but few dentists apart from the daunting Dr Seagle, always dressed in a top hat and frock coat, who pitched his wagon in the Market Place each Saturday evening and extracted teeth for 6d. The most popular restaurant was at 132 High Street where Thomas Parris and his two daughters provided lunches and teas. The shop had no back door so the horse had to be led through the shop past the customers and freshly stacked baked loaves (it was also a bakery) to the yard where his stable was situated. Behind him on every journey through the shop ran Miss Paris with a dustpan and brush!

The community life of the town was divided into three distinct classes. The great houses of Knole, Montreal and Wildernesse were occupied by their titled owners and below them in the social scale were the inhabitants of Ash Grove, River Hill, Kippington, Beechmont, Bradbourne, Vine House, Lyle Court, Rockdale, Park Grange, Solefields and many others.

All had indoor staff of maids and cooks with coachmen, gardeners and stable boys working out of doors. Each year, usually in the winter, they would be invited to a servants' ball, organised by the butler and the housekeeper. Tradesmen would

Sevenoaks High Street, looking north, where the road from Tonbridge makes its famous division to London or Dartford. In the High Street Lloyds Bank was well established next to J.Salmon, stationers and steam printers. The area between the fountain (built in 1881) and the bank was fully occupied every third Wednesday with the stock market, believed to have been established since the mid-fifteenth century and then run by Kent and Sussex Farmers. The Chronicle office can be seen on the right with its circulating Sennocke library and next door is the small post office with a public telephone. Notice the tall mast in the market place carrying the wires of the National Telephone Company — the first telegraph pole ever seen in Sevenoaks. Notice also the fountain with just one lamp, the gas lamps and the Sevenoaks Coffee Tavern, yet to give way to a new dominant building housing the Midland Bank.

also be invited and consider it an honour and a privilege to attend.

Lawyers, doctors, church ministers, accountants, schoolteachers, bank managers and the merchants and clerks, who daily travelled to London, lived in the smaller detached villas which were going up on the northern slopes of the town in such places as St Botolphs, Hitchen Hatch and Mount Harry.

Horse-drawn delivery carts were everywhere and Sevenoaks residents were served by a variety of good-humoured, well-mannered tradesmen delivering milk, bread, oil and paraffin. The rag and bone man, the muffin man and the tinker would also call regularly — their bells and cries getting louder as they approached.

A few people in Sevenoaks in 1900 were on the telephone. A tall mast in the market place had been erected in 1898 and this carried a dozen crossbars supporting the wires of the National Telephone Company. The High Street was illuminated by gas lanterns on metal standards and water was supplied from the pumping station on the junction of Weald and Ashgrove Roads. Electricity was a faraway dream.

In 1900 the urban council was six years old, having been created by the Local Government Act of 1894. Its first offices were in the High Street where Naylor's butcher's shop was later established. Cricket was played on the Vine and, during The Week, the ground, fringed by tents, was full of enthusiastic spectators.

While children played in the road with their hoops, spinning tops and kites, adults stood in small groups outside shops — preoccupied with the worrying news from South Africa where Dutch settlers were revolting against the just sovereignity of Queen Victoria.

1868: Tubs Hill railway station opens with a direct line to Charing Cross and Cannon Street.

1873: Holmesdale Cottage Hospital is built at the foot of St John's Hill.

1876: Mortimer Sackville-West is created first Baron Sackville of Knole.

1882: Walthamstow Hall is built.

The fountain at the junction of London Road and the High Street is erected by an anonymous benefactor.

1889: Fort Halstead and Fort Westerham are built as defence against a possible French invasion.

1895: The Long Pond (on today's junction of The Drive and High Street) freezes and is thick with skaters.

Mrs Annie Streeter, headmistress (1894-1922) and one of her youngest teacher, Miss Phoebe Buckwell with the girls of Lady Boswell's in 1903. The school was situated in the London Road (now the Job Centre) and the girls were segregated from the boys by iron railings across the middle of the playground — an arrangement which continued until the 1950s. In the early part of the century Mrs Streeter was very concerned about the girls who stayed away from school during the hop-picking season and then took more time off to collect their meagre wages from the Bligh's office.

Charles Essenhigh Corke, seen here in his studio at 42 London Road, was a pioneer photographer and artist, renowned for his watercolour paintings of Knole. By the turn of the century his shop, studio and fine art gallery were well established in the London Road and attracted many visitors from London. Born and educated in Sevenoaks, Charles passed on his photographic skills to his son Henry who experimented with colour photography and became one of the principal exponents of the subject. He built his own studio.
It was customary for well-off Sevenoaks families to book a photographic "sitting" with the Essenhigh Corkes.

The 'wretched' motor craze
1900-1909

WHEN the editor of the *Sevenoaks Chronicle* arrived at his office, 66 High Street, on the morning of Monday January 1st, 1900, he was not bothered by the significance of the date, nor was his reporter and nor were the people of Sevenoaks. The official start of the last century of the second millennium was still a year away so all celebrations would have to wait. Frank Richards was more concerned with strife, as his editorial that morning made abundantly clear. Strife in the High Courts, strife in the council chamber, strife within the Young Men's Christian Association of Sevenoaks and, most important of all, strife in South Africa.

The Boer War was dragging on, proving to be the longest, the costliest, the bloodiest and the most humiliating conflict that Britain had endured for many years. It was, in Kipling's famous words, giving us "no end of a lesson". Wireless telegraphy messages from Reuters in London allowed Richards to print the latest news from Modder River, the border between the Cape Colony and Orange Free State where local men were encamped with their battalions and from Mafeking and Ladysmith, the two besieged garrison towns. Long reports, more than two columns in length, were accompanied by several local letters. Sergeant Charlie Lees of the 3rd Grenadier Guards wrote to his father in Westerham: *"I have had my rifle shot into fragments out of my hands and my helmet has been shot off my head but I'm still uninjured."* Private George Fletcher told his parents in Bank Street: *"I was unlucky to be wounded at Driefontein. Now in hospital but please don't worry."*

But his parents were worried and so were the people of Sevenoaks. The long weekly reports gave no hope to an early end to the fighting. Ladysmith was relieved in February but, as the winter weeks gave way to spring, there was no sign of relief for Mafeking where the garrison, under the command of Robert Baden Powell, had been under siege from the start of the war. Officers of the West Kent Yeomanry, showing a willingness to help their comrades, offered their services at the front. Col C.E.Warde, Commandant and 36 members of his Regiment were accepted. So was George Anquetil of Ightham, a civilian volunteer and, a month later, so was Lionel Sackville-West of Knole.

On March 2nd a dinner was held at the Royal Crown Hotel, London Road in honour of a further eleven men leaving for South Africa. Corporals Harry Marchant, Harold Marchant and Loveland, Privates Waterman, Zealey, Mitchell, Talmage, Smith, Best, Joy and Twort promised they would do their best for Queen, country and Sevenoaks.

On Sunday May 20th came the news that Mafeking had been relieved. For seven months Colonel Baden Powell, who lived in Speldhurst as a child and went to school in Tunbridge Wells, had led the defence of the little town on the

---

Sidebar

1900

Kippington Church Institute opens at Walnut Tree House, London Road, Sevenoaks.

The Beacon School is removed to Cross Keys and renamed The New Beacon.

Holmesdale Football Club wins the Sevenoaks Charity Competition which is on a league basis. Nine clubs take part.

The name of Halstead railway station changes to Knockholt to avoid confusion with Halstead in Essex.

60 per cent of dwellings in Sevenoaks have no flush toilets. Landlords are ordered to make improvements.

1901

November 15th: James Richard Stanhope has come of age. The heir to Chevening is awakened by the ringing of bells to the delight of all villagers. A ball is held in the evening.

Viscountess Templeton lays the foundation stone for Miss Emily Jackson's new Children's Hip Hospital in Eardley Road, Sevenoaks.

1902

James Stanhope is ordered to join his regiment, The Grenadier Guards in South Africa.

Scores of people turn out to see W.G. Grace, the cricketer, take part in the Automobile Club's reliability trials between Crystal Palace and Folkestone. The great doctor is keen to prove that the motor car is as reliable as the railway as a means of transport.

1903

80 die in Kemsing as the diptheria scourge ravages the village. 80 cases reported in March. All schools in the vicinity of Kemsing are closed.

1903

A new Methodist Church is built next to the free library. Work continues in laying out new roads to be called The Drive and Pembroke Road.

To the delight of shoppers a town clock is erected over Warren's optician's shop in Sevenoaks High Street.

An American millionaire, William Waldorf Astor, has bought the dilapidated 13th century castle at Hever and plans to restore it.

1904

January 1st: Mr W.S. McLelland, JP, chairman of the Sevenoaks Bench dies at his home, The White House, High Street.

Sevenoaks baker, F.H. Brigden of 12 High Street advertises a 2lb loaf for 2°d, thus provoking a "bread war".

railway line to Rhodesia at a cost of 168 British casualties. In its issue of May 25th the Chronicle reported the celebrations.

"One could not but marvel at the effect of the news and the mysterious potency of kinship when added to patriotism. One moment the streets were quiet as only Sevenoaks streets can be at 9 pm and the few pedestrians were sedate as only Sevenoaks people know how to be. Five minutes later order was at an end and the precise Sennockian had disappeared. Thronging thoroughfares, excited, gesticulating, cheering, enthusiastic men, and even women, had taken their place. Mafeking is relieved. The cry spread like wildfire and when, by 10 pm, a confirmatory telegram had been received the town woke up in a manner which has never been excelled."

The Chronicle described the scene. How the rector of St Nicholas, the Rev T.S.Curteis got together his bell ringers, how the spirits of the younger Sennockian ran riot and pandemonium reigned supreme, how trumpets were blown, tin cans beaten and hankerchiefs waved from every window and how an impromptu cavalcade of cheering people marched to the fountain singing *God Save the Queen* and *Rule Britannia - Britons never, never, never shall be slaves.*

Five days later a carnival was held in Sevenoaks to celebrate "the glad tidings" and Quinnell's traction engine led the procession with a float depicting sons of the Empire. The villages, too celebrated with great enthusiasm. A torchlight procession in Seal was initiated by Mr Fuggle and Mr Barham, captain of the fire brigade. A crowd of 200 proceeded to the Wildernesse where a brief but eloquent address was given by the Dowager Lady Hillingdon. At Brasted, a solitary church bell rang throughout Monday

Among the brave men who volunteered to help teach the Dutch farmers a big lesson were eight members of one Riverhead family — and so great was their contribution to the war effort that Queen Victoria wrote a personal note from Windsor Castle with a £5 gift for the family. Caroline Iddenden of Barrow Way, Riverhead, also received a framed commendation which read: "Not only has your husband served with distinction but at the present time six of your sons are in the army while a seventh died not long ago of Enteric."
The gallant soldier family were Sergeant Major James Iddenden of the 14th Hussars and his sons, Harry (Royal Dragoons), James (2nd Field Btn), Francis (9th Btn RA), Edward (21st Lancers), George (14th Hussars) and John (Royal Dragoons).
A seventh son, Albert, aged 16, left the Duke of York's School to join his father's regiment.

1904

March 16th: Canon Burn-Murdoch, vicar of Riverhead and Dunton Green churches for 40 years, dies. As a young man he saw service in India and The Crimea and took part in the Light Brigade's charge at Balaclava. It was largely through his efforts that Holmesdale Cottage Hospital was founded in 1873. At his death aged 76 he was the hospital's honorary secretary and treasurer.

April 8th: The newly-built St Luke's Church in Eardley Road is consecrated by the Bishop of Dover. Pews and pulpit are tranferred from the dismantled "iron church" in Granville Road.

April 8th: The foundation stone is laid to The Retreat, Sevenoaks, where Henry Swaffield has paid for the building of eight cottage almshouses.

October 8th: Twenty cottages are built in Crampton's Road, Sevenoaks by the Sevenoaks Artisans Dwelling Company. This will now be the main road to Otford

William Thompson dies at Kippington House which he bought from the Austens in 1864. He erected the so-called Iron Church on the corner of Granville Road and South Park and, with his sister, paid for the building of St. Mary's Kippington which was consecrated in 1880.

The Holmesdale Cottage Hospital is enlarged to hold 12 beds.

1905

A new Grammar School for Girls opens at Tonbridge with 21 pupils.

A proposal to change the name from Hitchen Hatch Lane to Vine Road is defeated.

Diptheria in Sevenoaks — John Bligh gets the blame

and picturesque effects were obtained by the use of coloured lights placed in the trees along the High Street. At Riverhead, houses and carts were decorated with a liberal display of flags and tri-coloured ribbons.

The glorious news from Mafeking and the tumultuous celebrations which followed must have squeezed many important local issues from the few news pages in the *Chronicle* but when Major Gore Lambarde of Bradbourne Hall, Sevenoaks succeeded in obtaining a High Court injunction restraining Sevenoaks Urban Council from discharging storm water onto his estate, the newspaper was quick to point out that much of the cost of this long drawn-out action had been borne by ratepayers. The urban council, now in its seventh year of existence since the Local Government Act of 1894, was roundly condemned.

The council were quickly back on the attack. Looking for a reason for the outbreak of diptheria, which had claimed many victims, the finger of suspicion fell on the milk supplied by John Bligh of Bligh's Farm. The High Street farmer vigorously defended the purity of his product and was eventually allowed, successfully, to present his case at a council meeting in Argyle Road.

Mr Bligh was a local man. His farm was once known as Bethlehem Farm and the home meadow and oast houses were further to the north; his family had lived in the town for decades. Henry Swaffield, also in the news in those early months of the century, was a newcomer — an influential and wealthy representative of the upper middle class who had moved to Sevenoaks and become involved quickly in the civic life of the town.

Before the turn of the century, Mr Swaffield had leased the Old Market House in the High Street from Lord Sackville, modernised it at his own cost and handed it over to the YMCA. As president of the association it was a tremendous gift.

Alas, all was not well. According to letters published in the *Chronicle*, Mr Swaffield was a man who liked to have his own way and he wanted the YMCA to agree to him nominating a secretary. Controversy broke out and the entire committee of the YMCA resigned so Mr Swaffield offered the lease of the Market House to the urban council, suggesting it should become a public library.

Another facet of his character was revealed at the annual meeting of the UDC when the founder chairman, Admiral Miller, retired. When it came to the election of a new chairman, Mr Swaffield presided as he had often done before. There were six votes for

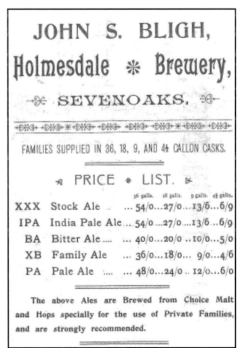

JOHN S. BLIGH,
Holmesdale ✳ Brewery,
SEVENOAKS.

FAMILIES SUPPLIED IN 36, 18, 9, AND 4½ GALLON CASKS.

PRICE LIST.

		36 galls.	18 galls.	9 galls.	4½ galls.
XXX	Stock Ale	54/0	27/0	13/6	6/9
IPA	India Pale Ale	54/0	27/0	13/6	6/9
BA	Bitter Ale	40/0	20/0	10/0	5/0
XB	Family Ale	36/0	18/0	9/0	4/6
PA	Pale Ale	48/0	24/0	12/0	6/0

The above Ales are Brewed from Choice Malt and Hops specially for the use of Private Families, and are strongly recommended.

'How the great London octopus will be arrested'

Mr C.H.B. Ince and six for Mr Swaffield, who then exercised his right to a casting vote and installed himself as the second chairman of the council!

So Henry Swaffield, a prosperous banker who had a strong belief in the merits of private enterprise and a man with a great sense of civic duty, took the reins for the final months of the nineteenth century and what was soon to be the end of the Victorian Age.

It was on Friday January 4th, 1901, that Sevenoaks at last celebrated the closing of "the most remarkable century in history" and welcomed the new one. The *Chronicle* reviewed the past 100 years: *"The introduction of steam revolutionised the industrial life of the country. It shook our commercial fabric to its very foundation, it swept away the picturesque but wearisome post carriage and stage coach, it weakened the barrier of distance..."*

The newspaper also predicted some of the scientific marvels to come. *"Contact with Mars through wireless telegraphy, the ability to cross from Dover to Calais in a vessel which will remain under water for the entire journey, clean healthy towns cleared of the pall of smoke, the arrest of the London octopus in its encroachment on our green nature and the arrival from overseas of English-speaking students to admire our village churches."*

The excitement was short-lived. The huge crowds which gathered outside the *Chronicle* office on the evening of January 22 saw their worst forebodings confirmed as the telegram giving the grim news was pinned in the window. Her Majesty Queen Victoria passed away peacefully at 6.30 pm.

"Sevenoaks assumed an aspect of profound sorrow," the *Chronicle* said in its next issue. *"The gloom was heightened by the solemn tolling of the bells on St Nicholas and St John's Churches. It filled everyone with a deep sense of personal, rather than national, loss. Tradesmen have shown their sympathy by placing shutters before their windows and individuals have donned a sombre attire..."*

For many weeks the events at home overshadowed the war in South Africa but in the same week that 12 additional volunteers responded to an appeal from the War Office, so a contingent of soldiers returned home to a heroes' welcome. The Town Band, the Sevenoaks section of L (cyclist) company and hearty crowds were at the station to greet them.

The stories told by the returning warriors occupied many column inches and no-one took much notice of a magistrates court case in which Mr A.L.Bucknall was

A terrace of homes is completed near the railway station. It will be named Holyoak Terrace.

A new book by the children's author Miss E Nesbit is published. Entitled *The Railway Children* it is inspired by her memories of the men who cut the embankment and dug the long tunnel under the North Downs at Polhill.

Vivienne III, the second largest balloon in Britain soars into the skies from Knole Paddock. It is filled by the local gas company and William Older of Cobden Road is in charge of this operation.

1907

Lime Tree temperance hotel becomes a centre for cycling clubs in the district.

Reckless motorists fined for speeding — at 8 mph!

charged with driving an automobile dangerously. PC Crouch said the defendant drove past a cyclist at a speed of more than 8 mph. Bucknall admitted he was "alarmingly reckless" and fined 10 shillings.

An outing by members of the newly-formed National Democratic Socialists' League to Knole Park was even more shocking to conservative Sevenoaks than the recklessness of automobile drivers. They came on a Sunday from the metropolis and held a series of races in the park followed by a public meeting on the Vine.

"It is our earnest hope", said the *Chronicle, "that our peaceful serenity will not be broken again by these people. We have no sympathy with the socialist movement who show little respect for the Sabbath."*

No peace in Knole Park but peace at last in South Africa. The news came through on the wireless telegraphy on June 7, 1902. *"Never perhaps in the history of the British Empire has an announcement been received with more heartfelt graditude and joy,"* wrote the *Chronicle. "Thanksgiving services will be held in every church in the district. G Company will attend divine service at St Nicholas. The dress will be helmets, tunics, belt and bayonet."*

As Sevenoaks prepared to celebrate the accession to the throne of Edward VII came the news that the King had been taken to hospital for an appendix operation and the coronation was postponed.

Sevenoaks, though, had finalised its plans and the festival programme was already printed so the town decided to go ahead with the revelries. On June 30,

Dr Bury is generally credited as being the owner of the first automobile in Sevenoaks. His Benz Ideal was supplied by Mr Bywater of London Road. The Chronicle wrote: "Upon enquiring we learn that Dr Bury is very pleased with the performance of his new carriage. It does the work of two horses and climbs any hill with ease..."
Here is the doctor on his rounds in Knockholt.

1902, a massive bonfire in Bligh's Meadow was ignited, a dinner for active servicemen was given at the Drill Hall by Capt John Laurie and the St John's Church Lads Brigade were reviewed by Lord Roberts. That was followed, a week later, by a Coronation dinner at the Drill Hall for all Sevenoaks residents over 50 years of age.

As the King recovered, the real coronation was set for August 9 and hundreds of local people travelled to London to see the royal procession. In Sevenoaks, all children were given coronation mugs and 400 people over 60 enjoyed another dinner at the Drill Hall.

For many months Sevenoaks discussed ways of commemorating this coronation year and it was eventually decided by the urban council to plant seven young oak trees on the Vine at the northern end. The ceremony took place on November 28th, 1902.

The *Chronicle* reported: *"The planting of the coronation trees (they were Turkish oaks) showed that the importance of historical association is not allowed to fade from the minds of residents. Sevenoaks is one of the few old Saxon towns in the country which can trace the source from whence its name was derived and can take active steps to keep ever green and fresh that source — the seven oak trees. It may be half a century hence that boys present at this ceremony will recall with pleasure the infinitesimal part they took in planting the trees which will stand for hundreds of years to come."*

With the great Boer War over and a new King presiding over Britain and the Empire, Sevenoaks settled down to enjoy the Edwardian years. Those who occupied the spacious Victorian homes in Upper Sevenoaks and by the side of the Common, in Kippington Park and on the slopes of Mount Harry, lived in style with their servants — parlourmaids, cooks, coachmen, gardeners and stable boys. The biggest house in the town centre was Rockdale where Mr and Mrs Laurie lived with their sons, John and Dyson. The telephone number was Sevenoaks 1.

By 1903 the very wealthy owned a motor car, parked usually in the stable yard. In April of that year the Chronicle complained about the *"unforeseen dangers facing pedestrian and horse in this wretched age of the automobile".*

The *Chronicle* highlighted the complaints. 1: A source of constant danger to the general public. 2: A factor of decadence to the prosperity and attractiveness of the town. 3: An increasing source of expense to ratepayers.

"Reckless driving of these machines causes the nervous to refrain from walking," said the *Chronicle. "Many people are deterred from shopping in the town... and the amount of increased trade resulting from the passage through the town of automobiles is practically nil."*

Although the great motor craze was catching on fast and was possibly here to stay, horse-drawn traffic was still dominant in Sevenoaks. The carriage folk would have been delighted with the opening of alternative routes to the

---

Sevenoaks Chronicle   August 24, 1906

Dr Don Killed in Motor Accident

There have been many accidents recorded with the advent of the motorcar but this is the first fatal one in Sevenoaks.

Dr Don, one of the most popular and successful practitioners, had been visiting patients and was returning to Sevenoaks in an automobile driven by the chauffeur, Stanley Arthur Thurgar, when the car skidded on a freshly watered road, turned turtle and landed in the ditch throwing Dr Don and the driver out.

Although the latter received only slight hurt and was severely shaken, the medical gentleman received fatal injuries.

Arthur Gorbut Don, who was educated at Sevenoaks Grammar School, had no liking for automobiles and just the day before his death told friends he preferred the pony and trap.

railway station for The Drive and Pembroke Roads were both laid out in 1903. With the building of the free library, the new Methodist Church, Cornwall Hall and dozens of "delightful residences" the whole area buzzed with an activity that was a feature of Edwardian Sevenoaks. The opening of the free library in the new road on November 17, 1905, overshadowed all other events of that year.

Lord Avebury was entrusted with the official honours and a large and influential company headed by the benefactors, Andrew Carnegie, who donated £3,000, and Henry Swaffield and such notables as Cr John Laurie and Lord Sackville enjoyed a special luncheon at the Drill Hall. In 1907, Sevenoaks paid their last respects to the rector of 33 years, the Rev Thomas Samuel Curteis, BA, who was best known for his great alterations to St Nicholas' Church. He was to be the fifth and last of his name to be Rector of Sevenoaks. It was in 1877 the Rev Curteis obtained a faculty for alterations from the archbishop's court, took down the galleries, resited the organ and placed the bell ringing chamber halfway up the tower. He closed the east entry into the church and opened up the north door.

The Rev John Rooker who succeeded him later wrote: "Mr Euan Christian, an architect of note, superintended operations. The great west window was thrown

1908

Lionel 2nd Baron Sackville dies. A suit of legitimacy is brought by Henri E. J. B. Sackville West, his illegitimate son by his mistress, Pepita.

A 90-degree heatwave has made this year's August Bank Holiday one of the hottest ever known. Thousands of people arrive by train to picnic in Knole Park.

1909

March 17th: A Battalion of the Guards is moved from London to Hastings via Sevenoaks in a cavalcade of motors cars supplied by the AA — the first such occasion that soldiers have been transferred by this method.

July: Kent cricketers, Frank Woolley (185) and Arthur Fielder (112 not out) score 235 runs for the last wicket against Worcestershire. It is a record that may never be beaten.

A Scout Troop is formed in Sevenoaks by a master at Lady Boswell's School, William Hicks.

'St Nicholas horse boxes thrown out at last'

open and all the high pews cleared away... This was a great change but it was an excellent one. The Church stood clear and its fine proportions were apparent... At last the clustered pillars were freed from the old 'horse boxes' and their elegance shown up."

It was during this time that Thomas Curteis wrote to the archbishop suggesting that, in view of the increase in population Sevenoaks should have another church in the parish.

With funding provided by the great Sevenoaks benefactor William James Thompson, St Mary's Church, Kippington was consecrated on June 14, 1880.

Thompson, a governor of Sevenoaks School and founder of Sevenoaks Water Works Company, also provided the town with the Volunteer Drill Hall in Argyle Road. He died at Kippington Court in 1904 aged 87.

Sevenoaks was proud of its Drill Hall but even prouder of the Children's Hip Hospital which was built on two acres of land in Eardley Road and opened in 1901. It cost £1,300 and the money was raised by public subscription. Here, the scourge of tuberculosis, so common in the early years of the century, was fought with love, skill and patience by a team of dedicated nurses.

The hospital was founded by Emily Jackson, daughter of an architect. In 1872 she found a little girl, Ellen Merry, suffering from a tubercular hip and living in a state of squalor in a "Sevenoaks slum". Miss Jackson rented a room in a cottage to nurse the child and then enrolled at the Queen's Square Hospital to learn everything that the science of the 1870s could teach her for Ellen Merry. On her return she opened more beds, bearing all the costs herself and doing all the work. She was nurse, matron, accountant — "anything so long as it pulled in the big battle for succour". In 1874 she invited subscriptions to enable her to expand the work still further. By this time she had 11 beds and her cottage was the only hospital for tubercular children outside London. A larger building was acquired and called the Vine Hip Hospital.

Miss Jackson was joined by Miss Rose and by 1897 they had raised enough money to buy the site in Eardley Road.

At the beginning of the century the mail was delivered by horse-drawn post wagons which were stabled behind the Royal Crown Hotel. Pictured left is Postman Atkins who was responsible for many of the outlying areas.

Edward Stubbs (centre) the head gardener at Knole and his men were among those who mourned the death in 1908 of Lionel Sackville West, 2nd Baron Sackville and formerly Her Majesty's minister in Washington. The white-bearded old gentleman, who took up residence at Knole in 1889, had presided over great improvements, most of them organised by the mistress of Knole, his daughter Victoria (right). Lionel was one of the few people to have a telephone in his bedroom, hot running water in the bathroom and electricity. There were 24 servants in the house and a huge staff outside, including 20 in the gardens, to look after almost 8,000 acres of parkland. Lionel had five illegitimate children by his mistress of 19 years, a Spanish dancer called Pepita. Victoria, the eldest, was married to her first cousin, also Lionel who was the heir to the great house. The couple had one daughter, Vita, who was born in 1892.

Two employees of Sevenoaks Gas Company pause for a photograph while delivering with their handcart. The gas works were first established at the corner of Hartslands Road and Holly Bush Lane (now a laundry) in 1838 when a company based on £10 shares was set up for the making and distribution of gas. In 1862 the company, then known as the Sevenoaks, Riverhead and Seal Gaslight and Coke Co, moved to Otford Road, close to the newly-opened railway station at Bat and Ball, and gas was stored in three giant holders. Later, a line was laid out from the gasworks to the station along the side of Cramptons Road and two shire horses and two men employed to pull the coal in trucks. By the turn of the century the High Street was illuminated by gas lanterns on metal standards and gas was available in all but the humblest of homes.

In 1905 J. Salmon Ltd celebrated the 25th anniversary of trading in Sevenoaks with the knowledge that they had grown into one of the most successful companies in Kent. Each year they printed the local guide book, published and printed scores of children's books and pioneered the soon-to-be lucrative postcard business.

The firm was founded in 1880 when Joseph Salmon came from London to buy an established bookshop and steam printers that had been started in the High Street, Sevenoaks in 1815. The firm expanded briskly and enjoyed a successful partnership with Charles Essenhigh-Corke, whose landscapes of Knole and other nearby beauty spots were turned into postcards. In time they became a valuable and a most sought after commodity among postcard collectors.

It was in 1908 that Salmons introduced pictorial turnover calendars. They also became popular and, in time, thousands were exported all over the world.

A second business liaison started in 1910 with the well-known artist, A.R. Quinton who exhibited at the Royal Academy and travelled through the British Isles on his bicycle sketching and paiting. Quinton worked for Salmons until his death in 1934.

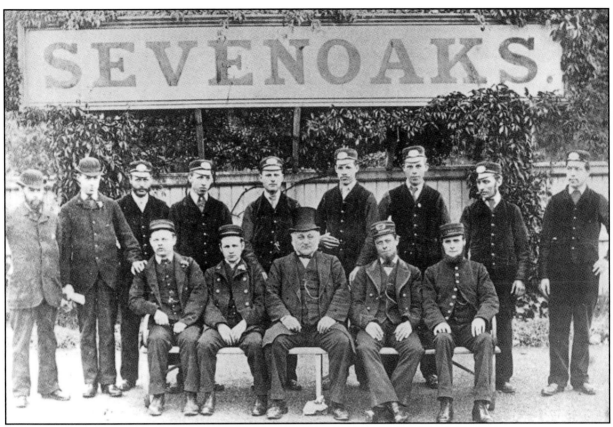

The station master, in top hat and frock coat, sits with his staff at Tubs Hill Station around the turn of the century. This was the height of the great railway age. The signalmen, pointsmen, switchmen and gatemen worked a 12-hour day and rarely had a Sunday off.

It was a privilege to be on duty and to look after the travelling public, most of whom walked to the station from their new homes on the slopes of Sevenoaks or took the horse-drawn bus which ran nine times a day. Some were driven to the station in their carriage by the coachman to join the army of trainee lawyers, book-keepers and city-bound girls who gathered there.

The South Eastern Railway had reached Sevenoaks (Tubs Hill) in March 1868, six years after the rival London, Chatham and Dover Railway had opened its station at Bat and Ball.

Amos Pett, basket salesman (on the left), is seen here with three cronies, G. Hooper, A. Bartholomew and C. Allwork outside his High Street shop (later Freeman Hardy and Willis). The men were almost certainly regular customers at the Holmesdale Tavern next door and were always seen on the Vine during the summer months; in fact Amos was responsible for levelling the ground before the turn of the century.

His grandfather, William Pett, who died in 1786, ran the shop on the same site. But he didn't make baskets for he was England's leading cricket bat maker and supplied the best willows to fine players such as John Frederick Sackville, Third Duke of Dorset and the father of organised cricket.

It is possible that Father William Pett, as he was known, supplied bats for the Vine's first recorded match in 1734 although this may have been some years before he entered into large-scale production.

A Pett bat, dated about 1755, which is in the town museum, was almost sold in the mid-1980s to raise funds for the Vine Club. It was saved for the town after a massive local controversy.

When Father William died his son Thomas ran the shop and then handed over to Amos.

Little is known about Hooper and Allwork but Amos Bartholomew (third left) lived at 157 High Street and had been employed as a rent collector. It is believed that his brother was a hairdresser in Bank Street.

Gas lamps and triumphal arches

1910-1914

THE presence on the Sevenoaks roads of reckless motorists, driving in excess of 10 mph and terrorising carriage horses and farm animals was bad enough. Now there were airships, balloons and dirigibles overhead and — even more outlandish — a new-fangled flying machine creating havoc in the Kemsing area. In letter after letter to the editor of the Chronicle, older residents complained about the lack of peace, the loss of character and how they yearned for a return to the "good old days".

Typical, was this letter from a Sennockian who declined to give his full name. "Sevenoaks 10 years, nay even five years ago, was a spot we could be proud of. A place of peace and pleasure 'far from the madding crowd'. Now, with its recreation ground and electric palace [cinema] we, the residents of past years, can only look in dismay at the terrible change which has taken place. Bands now play on two days of the week and last year, it will be remembered, even the Sunday peace was broken by the strains of 'sacred' music."

The points which raised his ire were the acquisition of 12 acres at Holly Bush Lane by Sevenoaks Urban Council for a recreation ground, the Vine bandstand — then in regular use — and worst of all, the opening of the Palace (or Electric Theatre) at Station Parade on January 6, 1911. To the majority of people, however, this was something of a red letter day. With a raked floor, velvet plush chairs and musical accompaniment, the Palace Theatre was soon attracting a full house, although the auditorium was stuffy and cramped. Early classic silent films included *The Law of the West* and *The Heroic Shepherd*. Small boys took turns to crank the projector incurring the wrath of the manager when they reversed the handle for sheer devilment. The cinema age, with all its fun and frequent breakdowns, had arrived.

So had the age of electricity, a subject that was debated at every meeting of the urban council for two years with the

From his garage at 166 High Street, George Humphrey ran a flourishing business as a coach builder and motor car engineer. He hired cars, carried out repairs and, in 1911, introduced the first motor bus which carried passengers, on solid tyres, between Sevenoaks and Oxted. By then his business had been established for more than 120 years.

October 21: Mr M.Clement's dirigible passes over Sevenoaks on its historic journey above the Channel. It is hoped the War Office will acquire the dirigible for the army.

Brewing of beer ceases at Golding's Brewery in Crampton's Road.

1911

March 17: Col W.F.Tipping leaves £2,000 in his will to build almshouses at Brasted with an additional £3,000 for the endowment of the houses.

June 23: Coronation of King George V. Gas illuminations in the town.

August 9: The great heatwave, which has lasted through May, June and July, shows no sign of letting up. Today the temperature reaches 98F — believed to be the hottest day ever known.

August 25th: 70 old folk are treated to tea and entertainment in the gardens of the Rose and Crown Hotel by No 1 Lodge R.A.O.B. (Royal Ancient Order of Buffalows).

November 11: Lord Amherst dedicates Otford's village green to the public. Lady Amherst plants a copper beech.

One Tree Hill, Underriver, and 30 acres of land are sold to the National Trust by Lord Derby for £1,000.

Sevenoaks Urban Council decides not to lower the prices of railway season tickets to London. "It will lower the tone of the town," says Cr Frank Robinson.

Lionel and Victoria return to Knole in triumph

majority view erring against those who advocated electric street lighting. The UDC elections in March 1911, in fact, were fought on the "electric issue" and the Chronicle described it as "a bad day for the lighters" when E.J. Payne, Geo White, Jabez Mann, G. Marshall and F. Swanzy were returned and Ibbett, Ritchie and Herbert Wood were defeated. So, to the dismay of many, gas lanterns remained in Sevenoaks High Street and were destined to do so for the next 50 years.

There were gas illuminations for George V's coronation celebrations on June 26 — an event which was observed in great style with a special service at St Nicholas, a marathon race, won by T.E. Record, and the handing out of coronation mugs to hundreds of local schoolchildren. In the afternoon 3,000 people marched through the town to a grand sports day in Knole Park and the evening dance in the Drill Hall, notable for the brief appearance of Lord and Lady Sackville, was an "event to be remembered".

A year earlier, in February 1910, Lionel and Victoria — having won their great battle for the title and the inheritance of Knole in the High Court — returned to Sevenoaks in triumph. Accompanied by their 17-year-old daughter Vita, the couple travelled by car to the foot of Tubs Hill where a pair-horse victoria awaited them. In this, the delighted couple travelled to the top of the hill and under a triumphal arch, erected from the offices of Potter and Harvey (now Phillips the autioneers) to the other side of the street.

At the Royal Crown a deputation of councillors received the couple in their carriage and led them to a reception inside the hotel. Suitably refreshed, Lionel and Victoria waved to the crowds outside and watched the horses being led away from the carriage and ropes attached to firemen in uniform. The procession, headed by the Town Band and the Temperance Silver Band, was followed by Sevenoaks, Seal and Combe Bank fire brigades and by Boy Scouts under Scoutmaster Hicks and Scoutmaster Paskin. They passed under another triumphal arch at Rockdale and yet another at the entrance to Knole Park. The whole route was lined with cheering inhabitants. Lord and Lady Sackville had come home to Knole.

The Chronicle reported the event in great detail with photographs of the historic return. The High Court case itself — in which Victoria's illegimate brother, Henri Sackville-West, had lost his sensational claim to Knole — lasted six days and was covered in full by every daily newspaper in Britain and America.

Two years later and the wireless telegraph was buzzing with another sensational story — the sinking of the *Titanic*, pride of the White Star Line, in the icy waters of the North Atlantic early on the morning of April 15, 1912. There were no reports of any Sevenoaks people on board but Col J.J. Astor, cousin to William Waldorf Astor of Hever, was among the 1,800 passengers and crew to perish. Apparently he declined to join the millionaires in one of the first lifeboats but instead helped his new bride and other women and children into other boats.

The Chronicle also reported the passing at her home in Crockham Hill of Octavia Hill, one of the three founders of the National Trust and a lady committed to the ideal that the green open spaces of Britain as well as historic buildings

The amazing scene in the London Road as Sennockians crane their necks to get a glimpse of the triumphant couple after the great High Court case. This is close to the junction with Lime Tree Walk.

1911

May: Superintendent Taylor retires after 12 years in charge of Sevenoaks police station.

Guy Rooker, son of the Rector of Sevenoaks, is taken for a motor car ride during recuperation from a wounded leg. The car collides at the foot of Polhill, Mr Rooker is thrown into a field and breaks the already injured leg.

October 20: John Hughes dies in a fire which destoys six hoppers' huts at Chartwell Farm, Westerham.

The King Edward Memorial Fund reaches £5,328 for the intended enlargement of the Cottage Hospital.

1912

Henry Swaffield dies.

The Palace Cinema opens at Station Parade, Tubs Hill.

Boots Cash Chemists store opens in the High Street.

Welcome home — a sea of boaters, bowlers, trilbies at the park gates as Lord and Lady Sackville pass under another triumphal arch and into Knole. With them is their daughter, Vita.

1912

Work starts on a new telephone trunk link between London and Tonbridge via Sevenoaks following the takeover of the National Telephone Company by the Post Office.

1913

Sevenoaks Electricity Company is formed.

Kippington Meadow is given to the town by the Rev Henry Percy Thompson.

The Queen Elizabeth Grammar School, Sevenoaks, is now known as Sevenoaks School. Headmaster since 1898 is George Heslop.

The Kent wicketkeeper, Fred Huish from Otford, claims the highest ever number of victims in a season — 102 (32 stumped and 70 caught).

Dr Gordon Ward, an authority on clinical haematology, joins Dr Arthur Carnarvon Brown as an assistant general practitioner.

Old brewery becomes electricity generating station

should be saved for everyone to enjoy. Miss Hill was buried in the village churchyard. Inside the church an inscription was unveiled in her honour: *"Noble in aim, wise in method, unswerving in faith and courage, she devoted her life to raising the bodily condition of her fellow citizens."*

Alongside tributes to Miss Hill were more letters opposing the "rapid spread of electric power". By then the "anti-lighters" were in the minority. Electricity was coming to Sevenoaks and the plan to set up a public generating station in the old Smith's Brewery buildings behind Suffolk Place went ahead with the minimum of fuss. It was to be a temporary measure; a larger plant was soon found at Sundridge and within months scores of Sevenoaks consumers were taking advantage of this most advanced form of lighting and heating.

By the end of 1913 the grim prospect of war in Europe was looming large. Correspondents to the Chronicle spoke of the great arms race which, they said, was threatening to run out of control. Most Sennockians seemed confused by the complexity of the political situation but, in a leader, the editor explained how territorial greed in Eastern Europe seemed to be the root of the problem.

In 1914, soon after the last horse-drawn bus had made its final journey through Sevenoaks, the news came of the assassination of Archduke Franz Ferdinand, the heir to the Austro-Hungarian throne, and his wife in the streets of Sarajevo. This latest crisis in European affairs was reported in the Chronicle alongside the news that the urban council had bought land in the Greatness area from the Filmer Estate and would soon begin to build a new housing estate.

This is almost certainly a photograph of the Sevenoaks Volunteers taken sometime after the Boer War. The Volunteers began life as the 33rd Sevenoaks Company of the Kent Regiment in 1859 when war with France was imminent and paid 10s for the privilege of joining. They fought with distinction in South Africa and were eventually put onto a regular military footing. They trained in Mr Bligh's hop-drying barn.

1914

Mr F. Swanzy, chairman of the council opens the new Holly Bush Lane pavilion.

Council houses are built in Greatness Lane — the first in Sevenoaks.

An electricity generating station is opened in Sundridge.

Sevenoaks Swimming Baths are presented to the town by Mr E. Kraftmeier of Ashgrove.

August 4: War is declared on Germany.

Intrepid pilot Jon Moissant, with his passenger Fileux (above), who became the first airmen to fly between Paris and London and win a silver cup from the Daily Mail in September, 1910. It took them just over three weeks!

The journey in a two-seater Bleriot monoplane was dogged by ill-luck throughout. They force-landed at Tilmanstone, came down with a bump in a turnip field at Sittingbourne, crashed into a brickworks at Upchurch and made further forced landings at Rainham, Chatham and Wrotham where they managed to buy petrol from a local garage.

Their worst landing was at Kemsing where they ran into the side of a hill near the Beechy Lees Estate. The propeller and part of the plane were damaged but Fileux bought whipping glue and repaired the airframe. As the airmen waited for a new propeller to be delivered from Paris, they stayed at St Clere and Mr Akehurst of the Rose and Crown pub provided a carriage and pair for their use. On their way to the landing ground at Crystal Palace they came down at Otford and Beckenham. National newspapers reported their adventures daily.

THE SEVEN OAKS.

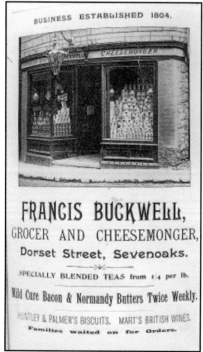

BUSINESS ESTABLISHED 1804.

CHEESEMONGER

FRANCIS BUCKWELL,
GROCER AND CHEESEMONGER,
Dorset Street, Sevenoaks.

SPECIALLY BLENDED TEAS from 1/4 per lb.

Mild Cure Bacon & Normandy Butters Twice Weekly.

HUNTLEY & PALMER'S BISCUITS.   MART'S BRITISH WINES.
Families waited on for Orders.

Francis Buckwell, grocer and cheesemonger, established in 1904.

Two striking features about this photograph of the Tonbridge Road by the White Hart, apart from the absence of any motor vehicles, are the seven healthy looking oaks and the tall wooden 'H' telephone poles which had only recently been erected.

It is believed that the tradition of growing seven oaks at this spot goes back about 200 years. The original seven oaks after which the town was named (if they existed at all) were in a circle on the common and nearer to the centre of the town.

The monster telegraph poles were introduced by the Post Office, after their takeover of the National Telephone Company, to replace the single poles which were frequently being blown over.

Established 1820.   Telephone No. 1y2.

W. FRANKS & SON,
Furnishing and ‐ ‐ ‐
Builders' Ironmongers,
90, HIGH STREET, SEVENOAKS.

90 W. FRANKS & SON 90

BROOMS AND BRUSHES.
CUTLERY AND TOOLS.

OILS AND OIL STOVES.

Wilfred Franks established his ironmonger's business in 1820 and it was passed down through four generations without changing the name.

1914

August 7: All Sevenoaks motor car owners are recommended to place their cars at the disposal of the Government. Chauffeurs are advised to accept National Service.

Cricket matches on the Vine are suspended until further notice. The ground is given over to troops for drill practice and — to the alarm of Vine members — football matches. The square is fenced for protection.

1915

Mr Robert Mond of Combe Bank, Sundridge, entertains 1,500 troops to lunch and presents each with a knife, fork and spoon set.

January 1: One hundred trees are blown down in Knole Park in a terrible blizzard.

March: Mrs K. Mansfield, wife of Dr Mansfield, is appointed Commandant of the VAD hospital at the Cornwall Hall.

April: Sevenoaks Swimming Club is formed.

Chlorine gas is introduced by the Germans during fighting near the town of Ypres

May 17: Hugh Whitcombe of Dudbourne House, Eardley Road, escapes from the torpedoed liner *Lusitania*. More than 1,000 lives are lost.

Sevenoaks strikes a blow for justice
1914-1918

SEVERAL million soldiers, forming the vanguard of many armies, were on the move throughout Europe on the morning of August 4, 1914, and they included the Yeomanry and the Territorials of Sevenoaks. *"The terrible European War"*, said the *Chronicle*, *"so long regarded as one-day inevitable by students of foreign politics, is upon us. Today the voice of local controversy is stilled and Sevenoaks has set out unhesitatingly and fearlessly to play her part in the determination of England to strike a blow for righteousness, honour and justice."*

From Sevenoaks and district it was estimated that 250 men — including sailors and naval reservists — had responded to the call to arms. On Wednesday morning (August 5) four sections of G Company, 4th Royal West Kent Regiment, fell in at the Drill Hall and marched to Tubs Hill Station led by the Town Band. The Chronicle wrote:

"The men marched between continuous lines of inhabitants who had gathered in their hundreds to honour the departure of their 'Terriers'. With Major John Laurie in command and accompanied by Lieut Frank Norman and Colour-Sergeant Wood, the men were in excellent spirits. The band managed to get onto the platform and played the National Anthem as the Orpington and Westerham contingents joined their Sevenoaks comrades on the train for the journey to Dover."

Among the other officers who sailed away during that historic first week were Major Lord Sackville of the West Kent Yeomanry, Guy Rooker, son of the rector of Sevenoaks, Donald Campbell (later Lord Colgrain) of Everlands and Mr R.P. Wilson of the Polhill family. As soon as they had left, scores of local young men offered themselves as recruits and were sent away for preliminary training. Others enrolled for field ambulance work and other duties. *"It is questionable"*, said the Chronicle, *"whether there is a man left in Sevenoaks who is not ready for the struggle ahead."*

As the war progressed, Lord Kitchener, Secretary of State for War, called publicly for more volunteers and Sevenoaks became a giant military camp. Tents were erected at Knole Park, Wildernesse,

On August 7 Lord Kitchener called publicly for another 100,000 volunteers and within days his face appeared on recruiting posters pointing imperiously at the viewer with the statement 'Your country needs you'.

Inhabitants gathered in their hundreds at Tubs Hill station to honour the departure of the Terriers.

1915

Corporal Cox of the North Middlesex Supply Column, son of Charles Cox of Cobden Road, is killed in France.

July: Vita, daughter of Lord and Lady Sackville, moves into Long Barn, Sevenoaks Weald, with her husband, Harold Nicolson. The 15th century house is claimed to be pioneer printer William Caxton's birthplace.

August 13: Three women escape from a fire at the Amherst Arms by means of knotted sheets.

1916

A local tribunal deals with 39 claims for exemption from military service.May 8:

British Summer Time is introduced. All clocks are advanced by one hour.

Solefields and Bligh's Meadow. The Cornwall Hall, Chipstead Place, The Congregational Hall and stables at Wildernesse were converted into receiving hospitals and an appeal was launched for bedding and linen. With the withdrawal of so many breadwinners from the town, the rector formed a fund to help wives and children in distress. Sevenoaks Rifle Club offered use of their range at Shoreham for anyone wishing to learn how to shoot. And there were letters to the Chronicle deploring the habit of panic buying among the mistresses of large households.

By October 1914 wounded Belgian soldiers, most of them fighting alongside the British Expeditionary Force, were pouring into Sevenoaks with news that the struggle was not going well for the Allies and that General French's stand at Mons had become a retreat. One hospital was at St John's Hall, Holly Bush Lane, and the first commandant was Vita Sackville-West who later relinquished her position to Aurea Lambarde of Bradbourne Hall and then to Lady Angela Campbell of Everlands. The medical officer was Dr Sterry.

Chipstead Mission Hall was also converted into a hospital and an appeal made for nurses to come forward. Mrs W.L. Anckorn of Three Corner Mead, Dunton Green, received a message at 9 am one morning to say she was needed at the mission hall urgently. She later told a *Sevenoaks Chronicle* reporter: "I rushed to Martin's in Dunton Green, bought a uniform, borrowed a governess cart and drove to Chipstead. There I helped to scrub the floors and put up beds. We were hardly ready when the first Belgian soldiers began to arrive. They had

New swimming baths — a platform for German guns?

walked from the station and were covered in blood, filthy, bedraggled and unshaven. We gave them soup and bundled them into beds after cleaning their wounds."

News of the war dominated the columns of the Chronicle. Tradesmen and businessmen trying bravely to cope with everyday life found their horses commandeered by military authorities. Many were willing to make the sacrifice but for farmers it was hard. The Kent branch of the NFU complained that the War Office was "collaring horses in a very free manner".

Meanwhile the local branches of the St John Ambulance Society, the British Red Cross and the Territorial Force Voluntary Aid were amalgamated, working together under the title Voluntary Aid Detachment. The dedication of VAD nurses was to prove invaluable.

There was one local controversy in 1914. Soon after presenting the excellent swimming baths in Eardley Road to the town, Edward Kraftmeier of Ashgrove and his family quietly left the area. Rumours abounded that he was a German spy and that included the fantastic suggestion that the floor of the baths had been specially reinforced to provide a platform for German guns which would bombard London.

Mr Kraftmeier, who called himself Edward Kay, may have had German nationality and certainly did not want to join those who were being rounded up and sent to concentration camps. He was, though, a true benefactor and his generous gift was enjoyed by thousands of people.

The wounded patients lying in their beds at St John's Hall were also privy to a little bit of Sevenoaks history. A young, hopeful musician, living in a Romany caravan at Biggin Hill, was invited to entertain them. During the evening he sang and played a song which had not yet been published. It was entitled *Keep The Home Fires Burning*. The musician, David Ivor Davies, who was 21, later took his mother's maiden name and called himself Ivor Novello!

In February 1915 the Chronicle began to publish a weekly "Roll of Honour of officers, NCOs and men who have answered the call to serve in the armed forces". It began with two whole columns and grew as the year progressed. Amendments were made to include those who had been killed or wounded and among the first to be

Chipstead Place, converted in 1914 into a hospital for wounded soldiers. A Belgian woman, desperate to find her husband who had been injured in the fighting at Mons, managed to pass through the German lines to the coast and was given a free passage to Dover by the captain of a Merchant Navy vessel. Without a word of English she found her way to Chipstead and was reunited with her husband. Chipstead Place was demolished after the war.

1917

January: A Military Road Race organised by Holmesdale Athletic Club is won by the 2/7 Devons.

George Richter, tailor and cutter, oldest member of the Oddfellows Society, dies at 87. His father fought at Waterloo.

February: Sevenoaks Urban Council invests £1,650 in the first War Loan.

The Royal Flying Corps testing park moves from Joyce Green to a new 80-acre airfield at Biggin Hill. A canvas hanger is established and a childrens' home commandeered for a Mess.

March 23: Royal Crown Hotel announces that all horse-drawn cabs and carriages have been withdrawn from public use. Taxis and first class motors are still available.

The Government of Ontario builds new wards onto its military hospital at Orpington.

Germans introduce a terrible weapon — chlorine gas

reported were the Hon C.T. Mills of Wildernesse (killed in action), Corporal W.E. Cox of Cobden Road (died under a lorry) and John Baldwin (fatally wounded while trench digging). The column was to be a grim, sombre and tragic feature of the next four years.

The report of the first battle of Ypres in April 1915 described the new terrible weapon introduced by the Germans — "chlorine gas, a swirling yellow vapour which attacked the throat and eyes."

By now nearly 500 men had passed through the Sevenoaks Recruiting Committee since its formation. *"Not enough,"* wrote the Chronicle. *"A man may have a dozen reasons for not doing his share in the khaki but no man with eyes and limbs intact and good health has a solitary legitimate excuse for not learning the rudiments of drill and the method of handling a rifle..."* A few weeks later a whole page advertisement was devoted to an appeal for the men of Sevenoaks to enlist.

As the war intensified so did the Chronicle's coverage. U-Boats in the Channel and local torpedo victims, Zeppelin attacks on north Kent towns, the part played by the Royal Flying Corps, the enthusiastic response by women to sign on for war work in trade, industry, agriculture and arnaments and the "Glorious" West Kents capture of Hill 60 near the town of Ypres.

Just after Christmas, 1915, local families waited anxious for news of the soldiers of the Royal West Kent Regiment and the Kent Fortress Engineers who took part in the successful evacuation of the Gallipoli Peninsula. Among them was Private

Dinner for the wounded soldiers in the Cornwall Hall VAD Hospital. The Commandant, Mrs Mansfield, who had a large and dedicated team of nurses, was awarded with the Royal Red Cross by the King.

Among the soldiers who returned home in 1919 were the former members of the Kent Cyclists Battalion, formed in 1908 as part of the then new Territorial Army to replace Volunteers. Their first commanding officer was Lieut-Col Charles Warner of Tonbridge.

When war broke out the home defence force included ten cyclist battalions whose main role was to patrol the coastline and watch for invaders.

Although these two-wheeled marksmen were capable of crossing virtually any terrain at eight miles an hour they never took their bicycles into action. Posted to India in 1916 to replace troops needed in Mesopatamia they saw service against rebellious tribes on the North West Frontier and in the war against Afghan invaders.

Wallace Manktelow, for several years a choirboy at St Mary's, Riverhead, who wrote regularly to the Rev G.F. Bell. "On Sunday we were shelled all day," he wrote. "It gets jumpy at times." On another occasion, describing the charge of the 54th Division across the Anfarta Valley, he said: "We had not got far when we heard the shrieking of shrapnell shells coming towards us. Crash! Crash! They exploded all around. Two poor chaps just in front of me went down. One was writhing and groaning. The air was full of bangs but I had no thought of stopping..." Wallace Manktelow was eventually hit by a sniper's bullet, taken to a dressing station and invalided home to Riverhead.

Captain Donald Campbell of Bowzells, Sevenoaks Weald, son of Lord Colgrain who was chairman of the London Clearing Banks, was also injured at Gallipolli. In the field hospital he met and fell in love with Margaret who helped to nurse his wounds. The couple intended to get married when the war was over but General Allenby ordered a new offensive so they decided to marry in Gallipoli. Charles Ponsonby (later MP for Sevenoaks) was best man and among the guests were his pals Jack Horncastle and Charlie French.

By 1916 the war had taken over more and more of the life of the people of Sevenoaks. Railway servives were curtailed, the Otford to Sevenoaks trains discontinued and the Bat and Ball station closed to passenger traffic. Every village organised money-raising events for the Red Cross and Agricultural Relief. In January, Sevenoaks UDC sanctioned the playing of military football matches at Hollybush Lane on Sunday afternoons — a decision which provoked a great deal of indignation.

It was also the year that the Sevenoaks Chronicle's printing staff were offered the opportunity of joining Mr J. Salmon's Sennocke Press because of "the present abnormal economic conditions." From that time the entire appearance of the newspaper changed, with much more news from Tonbridge and Tunbridge Wells. The paper had passed into the safe hands of the Kent and Sussex Courier

July: General Sir John French, former Commander of the British forces on the Western Front reviews the troops billeted in Knole Park.

September 14: Sugar rationing is introduced.

It is now known that the 5th Battalion of the King's Own Royal Lancs Regiment who were billetted in Sevenoaks from November 1914 to February 1915 were almost wiped out during the 2nd Ypres campaign. Sevenoaks was the last town they knew.

October 1: Air raid warnings are introduced as Gotha bombers fly over Kent.

December: The son of Mr and Mrs Alfred Wells of Crown Terrace, Shoreham has been lost on *HMS Vanguard*. Five other sons and a daughter are all serving in the army.

1918

January: Sevenoaks Urban Council resolves to establish a market site at Tubs Hill station if a rental can be obtained from the South Eastern and Chatham railway company. The Farmers' Union approves the proposed move.

Heartbroken headmaster loses his soldier son

of Tunbridge Wells where it was to remain for most of the century.

On May 14, 1916, the Chronicle reported that Captain George Heslop of the 16th Middlesex Regiment, son of the headmaster of Sevenoaks School, was missing believed killed. The "Old Man", as he was known, George Heslop senior, was devastated. The school was already going through troubled times with a much-depleted staff but the heartbroken father seemed to lose all interest in life and the school dwindled to a mere handful of boys. In fact by the end of the war there were fewer than 50 on the school roll.

More bad news came in early July, soon after the opening of the Battle of the Somme when 19,000 Britons were mown down attempting a massive infantry assault on the German lines. The thunderous noise on the first day of that Somme campaign could be clearly heard from upper Sevenoaks and for many years after the war older residents spoke of the intense barrage of gunfire which came from the East. On August 4, 1916 the Sevenoaks Roll of Honour bore the names of 28 local soldiers killed in action.

In December the Chronicle announced that the Hon Charles John Sackville-West (the future Lord Sackville) had been wounded and printed the first pictures of the men who had made the supreme sacrifice, a feature which was to continue week after week until the end of the war.

By now the Riverhead boy, Wallace Manktelow had recovered from his wounds and was in Egypt still writing his letters home. In October he told his mother: "I was reading Italian in the trench by moonlight; my thoughts would wander away and I was thinking a lot about you. I hope the war will end before another winter brings more misery to Europe. The world is very beautiful, one can hardly realise the insanity of man in turning God's beautiful creation into devastation."

On February 11, 1917 Wallace wrote to Geraldine Parkes of Riverhead. "We are on the road to Syria, 100 miles away. Can you picture our long march across sand... This morning we passed several wooden crosses which show us the last resting place of some of our English Tommies, fallen on the field of honour. At night I saw those magnificent stars. This heavenly roof. It is so superb, shining and grand. It is enough to make one think and see further than the blood stained battlefields of Europe..."

In April, 1917, Wallace's father received a letter from his son's brigade officer. "Your son was seriously wounded on the outskirts of Gaza at a place called

---

Chronicle January 18, 1918

Mr and Mrs Sears of Oak Cottage, Kippington heard that their only son Bernard has been promoted to Leading mechanic in the R.N.A.S. He was employed by Messrs Humphrey as a motor engineer.

Private Sheppard of Seal has been killed in action. He was in the Royal West Kents.

We are sorry to hear that Rifleman Charlie Baker, Queen's Westminster Rifles, son of Mr and Mrs Baker, 92 High Street is lying ill in hospital near Alexandria.

We hear that Sgt Herbert Terry of Bushes Road, Sevenoaks has been awarded the Dinstinguished Conduct

Medal. He was badly wounded in Ypres and had to have his leg amputated.

Private Frank Singleton of Lime Tree Walk of the "Snipers' Section of the East Surrey Regiment is home on leave. He has been wounded three times.

We are sorry to hear that nothing definite has been heard of Private Harry Cripps of St John's Private Cripps took part in the Big Push and has been posted as missing. His wife has been told by Harry's Commanding Officer that he may have made the supreme sacrifice.

Rifleman Harry Hords of the Queen's Westminster Rifles has written to his parents to say that a piece of shell passed through his jaw. He is progressing well in hospital.

1918

A plea is made by Kent Temperence Federation to reduce the number of licensed houses in the county. The ratio of licenses per 10,000 population, is 28.12 in Kent and 23.3 for England and Wales.

Fred Turner, bootmaker of Dunton Green has seven sons in the army. All are in France and four have been wounded.

Six sons of Mr and Mrs Howard of Springfield Cottage, Westerham, are serving.

February: Readers demand the establishment of a secondary school for girls in Sevenoaks

Wallace Manktelow — writing home.

to "save that long return trip to Tonbridge".
March: Sevenoaks Cattle Market Company is formed.

A kitchen opens at the Club Hall to provide civilians with cheap meals.

A site for a war memorial is chosen — on the spare land to the south of Bligh's Hotel in the High Street.

March 22: Mrs Mansfield, Commandant of Kent VAD, 76 Cornwall Hall Hospital, is decorated by the King with the Royal Red Cross.

Riverhead boy died on a green hill — in the Holy Land

The Green Hill... He lingered for a few hours but did not suffer pain as we gave him morphia. I saw him just before he died. I cannot write too highly of him. He was an example to his officers as well as to the men... and would hold Evening Services in his tent... He, like the Master he loved and served with his whole being, died on a green hill far away, without a City wall — if not at Jerusalem — in the Holy Land."

The Chronicle files of 1917, reflecting the total involvement of the entire population of Sevenoaks in the war and the sacrifices by so many, make depressing reading. Impoverished women, whose men were away at the front, were found guilty of stealing cleft wood from Knole Park, and fined 2s. 6d. "You all deserve to go to Maidstone Prison," said the chairman of the bench.

An even greater scandal was reported in March 1917 when George Marshall, chairman of Sevenoaks Food Production Committee, found a number of men at Holly Bush Lane engaged in playing bowls. "In view of the difficulties", he told the Chronicle, "in obtaining the necessary labour to turn the recreation ground into ploughed land, it seems a slur on the town that men able to bowl should not devote themselves to more beneficial work."

The bowlers were quick to reply. "Every one of the members playing bowls that day", said the secretary of the Bowling Club, "is doing his bit for the war in the way of exceptional effort..."

Scandal was followed by tragedy. On July 3, Lieutenant Bill Hicks of the Royal Garrison Artillery, a former master at Lady Boswell's and founder of the 1st Sevenoaks Scout Troop, succumbed to his wounds. Bill Hicks, whose father was butler at Knole, had led the troop for five years before the war began and was a hero among countless boys and girls. On his last leave from France he was spotted near the fountain at the junction of London Road and the High Street and borne shoulder high through the town.

With the war entering its fourth year there was an almost hopeless tone to the Chronicle editorials and certainly no indication that the slaughter would soon end. In the first issue it was announced that only a few soldiers had attended Robert Mond's annual lunch at Combe Bank — the rest had gone to swell the numbers in France.

Imagine Sevenoaks in the winter of 1918. Few men in the streets under the age of 30, except those dressed in khaki. No street lighting because of the air raids. A blackout in force and many shops boarded up. A shortage of foodstuffs, especially meat. No wireless and no Sunday newspapers. On most evenings of the week an anxious crowd would gather outside the post office in South Park to read official telegrams, written in long hand and posted in the window. The news was grim, the tension unbearable.

The Chronicle continued with its popular column *Our Boys* where good news was mixed with the tragic and hope became despair. Bob Rosser of Buckhurst Avenue (wounded), Lt Albert French of St John's Road (promoted to captain), Lance Corporal Ashby of Underriver (suffering from trench fever), Private Charles Bond of Holyoake Terrace (wounded), Private John White of High Street, Sevenoaks (twice wounded, then killed).

April: Mr Alfred Dyson Laurie is adopted by the farmers as their candidate for the new Sevenoaks Constituency. Thomas Bennett is the prospective Conservative and Mr Joseph Skinner, a local blacksmith is standing for the new Labour party. Mr H.W. Foster, MP for West Kent for 25 years will contest Bromley.

May: 141 Squadron, based at Biggin Hill, celebrate the station's first "kill" — a Gotha bomber which crashed at Frinstead.

With the passing of the daylight saving bill, clocks will go back for an hour between May and August.

November 15: Victory Day in Sevenoaks with unprecedented scenes of public revelry. A short service is held at mid-day at the fountain. On Wednesday there will be a thanksgiving service in the Market Place.

December: The Dowager Lady Hillingdon dies at Wildernesse.

1919

Sevenoaks raises £675 during Gratitude Week in January.

Football posts are removed from the Vine cricket ground.

'You knew a chum who could pull soil over your grave'

Young officers lasted only a few weeks at the Front and in the terrible fighting around Ypres in the summer and autumn of 1917 many experienced leaders also fell. Captain Thomas Colyer-Ferguson of Ightham Mote was just 21 when he died. Tom and his company (down to a sergeant and five men) captured an enemy trench but found themselves under heavy attack. The young officer managed to take an enemy machine gun and turn it on his assailants. He was eventually killed by a sniper and posthumously awarded the Victoria Cross.

Each Friday the Chronicle contained longer and longer reports but *"after Passchendaele there were no tunes of glory. This was the battle above all others in which raw, dumb courage was offered uncomplainingly and squandered. After Passchendaele patriotism was no longer quite enough.*

"If you were lucky you might receive a wound just bad enough to send you 'Down the Line to Base'. And thence, perhaps, to dear old Blighty. And if you copped it, you knew you had a chum who could pull the soil over your grave and write home to your mum because you would do the same for him."

Eventually in 1918 came the news of the final desperate attempt by Ludendorf to break the Allied lines, the French and American counter offensive and then Douglas Haig's stirring call that "every position must be held to the last man" as he ordered his final push. The tanks broke through the entire German front before Arras and Germany appealed for an armistice.

On November 11 the guns in Europe fell silent and the church bells tolled to proclaim peace. The Chronicle wrote: *"The Great War has come to a dramatic close and Sevenoaks, like other places, has made the most of the event to express, in a rational way, their gratitude at the stopping of the carnage...the cheeriest note of all came from the wounded soldiers who had felt the bitterness of war in their own experience."*

The first week of January 1919 was Gratitude Week and an advertisement in the Chronicle, announcing that the national target for £3m would be donated to the King's Fund, was paid for by Uridge's Stores.

Although national politics were far from people's minds the General Election, for the first time, saw women voting. In a straight fight T.J. Bennett (Coalition)

One man who saw the futility of that war was the poet Siegfried Sassoon, who was born near Paddock Wood and became a pupil at the at New Beacon School, Sevenoaks, just before the turn of the century. He was also a fine cricketer and played on many local grounds.

Sassoon had enlisted as a trooper in 1915 and soon became well-known for his bravery. Nicknamed "Mad-Jack" he was awarded the MC for bringing back a wounded lance-corporal under heavy fire and was later wounded himself.

Back in Kent he felt compelled to write a violent attack on the conduct of the war. "I believe the war is being deliberately prolonged by those who have the power to end it... I have seen and endured the sufferings of the troops and I can no longer be a party to prolong these sufferings for ends which I believe to be evil and unjust."

Sassoon should have been court-martialled. A private soldier making such protests would certainly have faced the firing squad but he was declared to be suffering from shell shock and, in the summer of 1917, attempts were made to prove him insane.

A huge dossier was collected and marked "not to be destroyed as it refers to a person of international fame". That dossier, along with other personal service records was eventually made available by the Public Record Office 80 years after the Great War, in 1997.

An open air thanksgiving service was held in Sevenoaks Market Place in November 1918.

1919

Demobbed soldiers are entertained at the Lime Tree Temperance Hotel.

Peace Day celebrations in Sevenoaks are a damp squib, most people "migrating" to Tonbridge.

September 26: Sevenoaks Carnival is revived with the Knole stage coach leading the procession.

Building work begins again on the council houses in the Greatness area. Work stopped during the war.

beat Labour's J.E. Skinner for the Sevenoaks seat. The turnout was less than 50 per cent of the electorate.

More important was the great desire by Sevenoaks to have a war trophy. The Chronicle wrote: *"Sevenoaks has done its share in the winning of the war not only on the field of battle but in the way in which it has backed up the fighting man by feeding the guns and providing aeroplanes. It is only right that we should have one of the spoils of conflict."*

A German field gun was delivered postehaste to the town and became a familiar sight on the lawn in front of the council offices in Argyle Road.

By now Sevenoaks was turning its attention towards the provision of a war memorial and several possible sites were suggested. The rector, the Rev John Rooker, wrote to the Chronicle suggesting "that a soldier in khaki should be erected on the Vine". His idea was adopted although "A.H.N" objected to the urban council's intention to provide a road and footpath from the top of St Botolph's to Dartford Road and wrongly prophesied that "an epidemic of iron railings, asphalt paths and primitive shrubs would appear on the waste ground that is left after the road has been built".

A memorial appeal was launched, a house-to-house collection instigated and the people of Sevenoaks responded with typical generosity.

Unveiling of the War Memorial
Roll of Honour

SUNDAY was a day of remembrance in Sevenoaks when the people assembled in their thousands on the Vine to pay their public tribute to the memory of 225 sons of Sevenoaks who laid down their lives that others might be spared and that this glorious land of ours might be preserved from the tyranny and oppression of a jealous and merciless foe.

All classes were there from the Lord of the Manor to the humblest cottager. Overnight the monument had been veiled with the Union Flag bearing the town coat of arms in place of the tarpaulin sheet which had enshrouded it for weeks.

A temporary platform had been erected and those around it included Lord Sackville, Lieut-Col J.D. Laurie, the Bishop of Rochester and all the clergy and ministers of the town, Mr T.J. Bennett, MP and Mr F. Robinson, chairman of the urban council.

In the enclosure were relatives of the 225 men who died and, at each corner of the mound, a Boy Scout took his stand.

Before Lord Sackville unveiled the memorial he said that an appeal had been launched and when that was accomplished the remaining funds were directed towards the enlargement of the Holmesdale Cottage Hospital as a central memorial for the district. A house-to-house collection in Sevenoaks by four ladies under Miss Cameron had realised £5,663.

After the unveiling, Cr Robinson read the names of the 225 men from Sevenoaks who had died — more than 15 per cent of those who saw service. Sevenoaks had paid heavily.

The following are the names of the fallen:

Royal Navy: Herbert E. Greenleaf, Archibald E. Langridge, Ernest E. Mitchell, Sydney Price, George W. Quinnell, Percy Sutton.

R.N.D: Gordon T. Brown, William Newell. **R.N.R**: Thomas S. Phelps. **R.N.V.R**: Geoffrey C. Bowles. **R.M.L.I**: Joseph H. Fulton.

Royal Artillery: George W. Akhurst, Edward Ames, Horace A. Aldridge, William R. Copper, Wilfred Dennes MC and Bar, Thomas A. Garrett, James B. Goodman, Richard M. Hammond, William G. Hicks, Robert Jappe, John Luckman, William Pettit, Herbert J. Richardson, Henry F. Stephens, DSO MC, Percy H. Townsend, Gordon B. Winch.

Royal West Kents: Ernest J. Accleton, Clement F. Aldridge, Percy T. Ashdown,

Alfred E. Baker, Lawrence A. Bowles, Leonard Bowles, George Broad, Harry Brown, William Bryant, William H. Chamberlain, George H. Champion, Walter Chatfield, George Coleman, Benjamin Copper, Silas G. Copper, Edward W. Cross, Frank Draper, James Elworthy, John Fermer, Thomas E. Francis, James R. Garland, Frederick J. Gibson, Frederick E. Gilks, George Granger, Charles W. Hale, Edward C. Harland, Jesse G. Harland, Alfred G. Heath, Frank Heath, Albert T. Hedgecock, Martin J. Hilder, Thomas Hills, Alfred Hope, Frank Hounslow, Herbert H. Jury, Jack Lewis, Ernest H. Marsh, Herbert Martin, Harry G. Nash, Oliver Older, Askew W. Palmer, Thomas Pattenden, James Pettit, Henry A. Poland, Victor Record, Ernest Richardson, Sydney A. Sargent, William W. Sims, James Skinner, John Slade, Alan S. Stevens, Henry F. Stevens, George B. Taylor, Frank Taylor, Arthur C. Terry, Henry Terry, Cecil C. Theobald, George F.W. Turner, Horatio J. Vioat, Arthur Warren, Alec D. White, Douglas U. White, Issac E. White, Edwin J. Wilkins, Thomas W. Wright.

9th Lancers: Jack Baldwin. **Royal Engineers**: Thomas E. Colegate, Robert B. Flint, DSO, Francis P. Lefroy, Herbert S. Turner.

Royal West Surreys: Lionel H. de B Crawshay, James Edwards, John T. Smith, Charles Winch, Frank Young. **Buffs**: Bernard G. Bowles, Sidney G. Cowell, William G. Cronk, Edward H. Gross, Albert Hayward, Thomas Sales.

Northumerland Fusiliers: Horace H. Checkley, Gordon S. Field, John S. Richardson, Frank Robinson. **Royal Warwick**: Frank Odell. **Royal Fusiliers**: Henry B. Burrows, Thomas R. Fishenden, Arthur W. Greagsbey, William G. Green, Charles A. Henry, Herbert

V. Morrison, Charles R. Payne, Obadiah Pollington, Geoffrey W. Tattersall, Sidney E. Thompson, George W. Westmore.

Norfolk: Percy E. Fuller, Leslie W. Mattholoi, Charles J. Self. **Lincoln**: Thomas F. Cale. **Suffolk**: Thomas F. Castleden, George W. Priest, Herbert Renshaw, Alfred G. Toms. **East Yorks**: Douglas B. Stamp.

Bedfords: George H. Pinchin, Arthur G. Simmons, Jack A. Wolf. **Lancs Fusiliers**: George S. Bassett, Reginald P. Gasson. Scottish Rifles: George Barnes. **East Lancs**: Albert W. Seal. **East Surreys**: Thomas G. Barnett, Alfred J. Martin, Herbert J. Pattison, Arthur Reeves, Syney F. Snashall. **Duke of Cumberland LI**: Walter Hodder, Harry Macarthy, Herbert Poole.

Duke of Wellington's Own: Frederick H. Vicat. Border: Donald J. Gordon, Edwin Norman. **Royal Sussex**: John T. Batchelor, William Griffin, Percy H. Hare, Albert Kingsland, Henry Ramsdale, John Stanley. **Worcesters**: George S. Kipps, Albert E. Quinnell. **Oxford and Bucks LI**: Sidney P. Pidwell, Basil C. Warde.

Essex: Peter S. Hayward, William W. Manktelow. **L.N. Lancs**: Edward R. West, Henry J. West. **Northampton**: Geoffrey G. Batty. **Royal Berks**: Leonard Brooker. **King's Own Yorkshire**: Charles D. Jones, Arthur H. Thompson. **Middlessex**: Bertram, Foster, George H. Heslop, Edward Marchant, William Miles, Frank E. Older, Herbert G. Skinner, Sidney Theobald.

K.R.R: George H. Bellingham, Ernest G. Chatfield, Samuel W. Powley, William J. Price, Edwin C. Reynolds, Richard Sutton. Wilts: Arthur E. Young. **Manchester**: George H.S. Moyce. **Seaforth Highlanders**: Frank A. French, Percy F. Hayward. R.B: John R. Berridge, Maurice Hammant, James O. Lott.

MCG: Geoffrey Harrison. **R.A.M.C**: Adrian M. Bartholomew. **A.S.C**: Henry Ashton, Frederick Dobson. A.V.C: Cyril Sotham. **E.C. Depot**: Herbert A. Sears. Tanks: Herbert T. Lethebe, James E. Millis. **RAF**: William S. Clark, Bernard W. Gordon, Nimrod King, Thomas Sillis George H. Walford (chaplain to forces), Basil P. Plumptre, M.A. M.C.

Lanc Hussars: James Terry. P.O Rifles: Frederick Cox, Arthur F. Weller. **C.S. Rifles**: George E. Westcombe. L.R.B: Raymond W. White. **Australian I.F**: Frederick H. Bourne, Francis G. Carnell, Frederick H. Clouting, George J. Drummond, Arnold Jarvis, George Marshall, George Richter.

Canadian: Clayton H. de Vine. **British Columbian**: Alan R. Bell. **Egyptian Camel Corps**: John N. Hill. **Unknown regiments**: Walter Davies, John Harland, Mark Humphreys, D. Smith, Reginald T. Sudds and John A. Tester.

This was a drawing made by Charles Essenhigh Corke in 1900 from descriptions of those who had seen the Sevenoaks Fair 50 years earlier. Colourful booths were also set up for the weekly Saturday market and pens stretched from the fountain towards the Vine.

1919

Henry Essenhigh Corke, aged 35, dies at his home, New Park Villa, Eardley Road, Sevenoaks from influenza. Born in Sevenoaks, he studied nature became a botanist and, in 1911 pioneered colour photography, winning gold medals at many international exhibitions.

The derelict Greatness Mansion, built many years ago by Peter Nouaille and then purchased by the Filmer family, is blown up by a film company so the ruins can be used for battle scenes.

Geoffrey Garrod, a qualified barrister, becomes headmaster of Sevenoaks School. His senior masters include "Scaly" Wright and "Jockey" White.

By 1919 the new Sevenoaks cattle market was well established on a site by the sand works opposite Tubs Hill Station, under the management of Kent and Sussex Farmers Ltd. The town had always been famous for its Saturday market in the High Street (not to be confused with the traders' Wednesday market on the same site) but when that closed in 1880 it seemed that a long tradition had really come to an end. The revival was masterminded by the Sevenoaks Farmers' Union who negotiated with the urban council and the South Eastern and Chatham Railway Company for the sandworks site at the junction of Hitchen Hatch Lane.

It is believed the original market was established as long ago as 780 and was still a going concern when its charter rights were recorded in the Doomsday Book of 1087. Later the market rights for the Hundred of Codsheath were vested in the Lord of the Manor of Knole.

Historians say the market site was close to the parish church and moved to the market square in the middle of the 13th century. Then, every Saturday, temporary pens stretched along the road from the fountain to the Vine alongside multi-coloured booths selling a variety of wares. That colourful scene was a feature of Sevenoaks for more than 500 years.

A fine photograph of Bligh's Hotel. One man who remembers the place well is Bill Kay (in his eighties in 1999) who lived there with his family when he was a boy of 16. His mother, Alice — an innkeeper — came from Camberwell and was invited by the then brewers, Messrs Hoare and Company, to transform the run-down, rather dilapidated hotel into a thriving business concern. She succeeded and by the time that Watneys took over Bligh's was both popular and profitable.

In 1919 the oast houses and barns of Bligh's Farm were so derelict and in need of repair that they were demolished and the land put up for sale by Cronks, the estate agents. A sizeable plot was bought by Dr Gordon Ward, who had now resumed his partnership with

Dr Carnarvon Brown after almost five years working in dressing stations in France where he operated on the wounded in makeshift tents.

Dr Ward built a large flat-roofed, red-bricked house on the corner of the High Street and Pembroke Road and called it Oastfield Court. It was notable for its fine domed ceiling and the view of the North Downs from the roof.

In 1920 Dr Ward was elected to the urban council but resigned after three years and instead devoted his life to his practice, to philately, archaeology and to the Holmesdale Cottage Hospital where he served on the management committee.

By the early 1930s Dr Ward was finding his house too expensive to run and so he built a new and less grand Oastfield Court in the garden and sold the original house to a property developer who turned it into the shops and flats which stand on the site today. Dr Ward enjoyed a keen interest in local history and later published the **Sevenoaks Essays.**

Dr Gordon Ward He erected the first X-ray apparatus to be used in Sevenoaks which was housed in a large wooden shed next door to his home in Pembroke Road.

1920

George Bennett, aged 20, is appointed Sevenoaks Librarian.

The Sevenoaks War Memorial is unveiled on the Vine.

1921

Roland Hodge of Chipstead Place, a Tyne shipbuilder until his retirement, is knighted.

War memorials are unveiled at Chevening, Sundridge and Ightham.

It is reported that almost 300 former pupils of Lady Boswell's School served in the Great War and 24 gave their lives.

Otford beat Orpington in the final of a new knock-out competition for a cup donated by Mr Smith of Shoreham.

The Rev W.E. Gilliatt is inducted rector of Sevenoaks.

Sevenoaks Services Club is opened on Bligh's Meadow by General Lord Horne, Commander of the 1st Army in France.

Lady Louisa Lascelles, wife of Baron Hillingdon, dies at the Wildernesse Estate. Her father, Henry, the 3rd Earl of Harewood had fought at Waterloo.

When pacifism flourished
1920-1929

WITH the War Memorial in place overlooking the Vine and Knole Park, with the treaties all signed and with pacifism flourishing, Sevenoaks settled down to enjoy the 1920s with a renewed sense of comradeship and belonging.

This desire to achieve a better social life and greater equality was raised time and again in letters to the editor of the Chronicle. Women now had the franchise, class distinctions were slowly beginning to fade and servants were better paid.

Controversy was never far away. In 1921, the matron of the Holmesdale Cottage Hospital, Miss Baynes, was instructed by her executive committee to evacuate all patients and equipment and install them in the Fig Street Isolation Hospital, while workmen from Tye's Builders got on with the hospital extension.

This she did but imagine how horrified the builders must have been when a woman, with her clothes on fire, was seen running towards the now-empty hospital, screaming for help. There was no help. The woman, Margaret Quinnell from Greatness Lane died, Miss Baynes was sacked, Charles Plumptre Johnson, chairman of the executive committee resigned and Lord Sackville held an inquiry at Knole into the whole sorry incident, apologising to all the hospital subscribers. And there were many of those.

It's not difficult to imagine what Sevenoaks was like in the early 1920s. It was the age of the emergence of voluntary bodies when the active and intelligent middle class saw in club and group activity the machinery by which they could achieve a better social life. Many new families, attracted by the development of the Sevenoaks Park Estate, were now living in the town and enjoying this new age of togetherness.

The Drill Hall in Argyle Road was a meeting place for those who served in the forces and when they were asked to leave because the hall was required for other purposes, the servicemen were given temporary use of the Vine

Holmesdale Cottage Hospital was built in 1873. Sir Joseph Lister, who introduced the principles of antiseptic surgery was the honorary consultant surgeon here for 13 years, until 1905.

Left to right: Roger Wethered, Lord Sackville, George Peacock, D. Peploe and Bernard Darwin who played in the opening golf match at Knole Park.

pavilion. Come May and the start of the cricket season the men were evicted in such an "underhand way" that scores of vitriolic letters appeared in the Chronicle. Dr Gordon Ward, then a councillor and never slow to speak his mind, was a particular target.

There was a happy ending. A new Services Club on Bligh's Meadow was opened later in the year and the former soldiers and sailors, with a smattering of airmen, were able to mix in a more relaxed atmosphere and, no doubt, relive their own individual roles in the Kaiser's dramatic downfall.

In contrast to the domestic dramas of the previous year, 1922 was a year of mourning for Sevenoaks. Lady Collett of St Clere, Kemsing died and so did Sir John Kirk of Wavetree, Sevenoaks who had lived in Sevenoaks since 1886 and served with the volunteer medical corps in the Crimean War before making a journey to Syria and up the Nile.

His most famous exploit began in 1858 when he accompanied Dr Livingstone on his Zambesi expedition for five years and was nearly drowned when his canoe was upset in the Kebraska rapids. John Kirk was one of the true founders of the Protectorate of Nyasaland.

Members of Sevenoaks Urban Council, who prided themselves on their ability to act quickly for the good of the community published, on October 13 1922, a large drawing of a proposed new by pass road from Polhill to Riverhill. It was the first hint of a highway which was to be brought into

Sevenoaks Players make their debut with *HMS Pinafore*

use a mere 50 years later.

The state of the roads at the time was poor. In September Laslett Dane of Bat and Ball asked the council if the route of the annual carnival procession could be extended to include St John's Hill. This was refused because of "the uninhabited road between Tubs Hill Station and St John's Hill and the problems which cars would face in having to descend the hill in bottom gear"!

In 1923 Sevenoaks welcomed two new organisations which still play a major role in the sporting and social life of Sevenoaks. An amateur dramatic society, called Sevenoaks Players, was formed in January with Lord Sackville as President and a rugby club was introduced in the autumn. The 11.5 acres, long known as Knole Paddock, had been purchased for Knole by Earl Plymouth about a century earlier. Now they were released to the town and formed part of the sports fields for rugby, soccer and cricket.

It was in February 1923 that Sevenoaks Players eagerly-awaited first production of Gilbert and Sullivan's *HMS Pinafore* took place in the Club Hall. The leading lights were Norman Warwick, Wilfred Taylor and Captain Michael Mitchell. It was their idea to form a Sevenoaks operatic and dramatic society and they enlisted the help of George Calder, a brilliant amateur actor, who had already delighted Sevenoaks audiences.

Pinafore was an outstanding success. Notable performances were given by Geoffrey Garrod, then headmaster of Sevenoaks School, Stuart Hills, T.W. Morgan, Harry Mitchell and Hilary Standen, not yet in her teens, who took the part of the midshipmate.

In 1925 Geoffrey Garrod resigned as headmaster of Sevenoaks School after six years to become Principal of a large academic institution in Belfast.

Support for the Players came from Sir Thomas Bennett, Sevenoaks' long-standing Member of Parliament but in December this Conservative stalwart was thrown out of office in the most surprising election result the town had ever known — for the victor, Major Ronald Bennett of Brasted Hall, was a Liberal!

Cr Tommy Skinner's controversial, rather odd notion that the Old Market House should be converted into public lavatories found support at last and in 1923 the council entered into a 42-year lease with Lord Sackville. Skinner's Palace, as it became affectionately known, was opened with little ceremony.

Poor Tommy lost his seat in the

Rain on Christmas Day 1927 turned into snow just after dark. The snow turned into a blizzard. The blizzard raged all night — and the next morning roads were hopelessly blocked, trains snowbound, vehicles buried and villages marooned. This was a blizzard to rival the greatest of the nineteenth century. It was followed in early January by a thaw which was then accompanied by heavy rain and the inevitable floods. Picture shows the Rye bus abandoned on Polhill.

1925

Miss Isted, headmistress of Cobden Road School since 1889, retires.

Mr James Higgs-Walker is appointed headmaster of Sevenoaks School.

There is a triple wedding at St John's Church — the brides being Mabel, Violet and Elsie Pickering.

With the death of the Fourth Earl, the Amherst family sell their stately home at Riverhead, Montreal, named in honour of Jeffrey Amherst's famous victory in Canada. It is purchased by Mr J.J. Runge of Kippington Court.

Four bootblacks have been given pitches in the town but no action has been taken over the appointment of an official town crier.

urban elections the following year to popular newcomer Fred Jarvis. Some months later he committed suicide.

There was more sensational news in 1924. *"Vine Cricket Club to be disbanded,"* said a Chronicle headline. It was suspected that alcohol was being sold in the club after matches and it was not registered to do so. When the council attempted to discipline its thirsty tenants, the club responded by threatening to disband because of these "harassing and reactionary rules". The council climbed down. Vine members carried on drinking.

Just as serious was the fact that Sevenoaks children were using the Hollybush Lane swings on a Sunday. Strong protests came from the Baptist and Congregational churches. The Sabbath breakers were severely reprimanded.

Another desperate situation was developing in the Wildernesse area over the sale of land by Lord Hillingdon and the break-up of the estate. It meant the famous golf club, first laid out as a nine-hole course in 1890, would have to close. Wildernesse House (now Dorton House) was turned into a country club and plans released to build hundreds of luxury homes in the park and on the golf course. In the event houses were only built in what is now Parkfield, Wildernesse Avenue and Woodland Rise.

Wildernesse golfers, shattered by these events, instructed their secretary to write to Lord Sackville asking if a new course could be laid out in Knole Park and telling him they would have no trouble raising £1,000 — the estimated

The foundation stone of the Swanzy Block at Sevenoaks School is laid in memory of Francis Swanzy who left £5,000 to Sevenoaks School in his will. The Kent Education Comittee have given an additional £10,000 towards the school's new buildings.

1926

The village pond in Otford, given by Lord Amherst, is enclosed by a high iron fence to the indignation of residents.

Mr and Mrs Fred Pearce of Linslade, Pembroke Road, celebrate their golden wedding. Mr Pearce, who came to Sevenoaks in 1864 at the age of nine, owns the fish shop next to Webbs Alley.

Frank Green is the new secretary of the Sevenoaks and District Football League.

The Church of St Thomas of Canterbury in South Park is opened by the Bishop of Southwark.

Sevenoaks Urban Council begins a new housing programme on part of the Wildernesse land. It will be known as the Hillingdon estate.

1927

With her first long poem *The Land*, Vita Sackville West has won the Hawthornden Prize of £100 for what is said to be "the best literary production of 1926".

Work on building council homes continues on the Hillingdon estate, part of the Wildernesse land.

Bradbourne House and 122 acres is offered for sale.

The fourth Lord Amherst, who had been a leading light in many aspects of Sevenoaks life, dies aged 71 in his town house at Wilton Crescent, London.

Anger over plan to build a road through Knole valley

construction fee for 18 holes. At first His Lordship said No but later changed his mind and said he was prepared to arrange a lease for 21 years. Thus followed years of negotiation with Lord Sackville, considerable anguish and eventually great joy. James Braid, a professional at Walton Heath and a great name in the golfing world designed the course alongside Mr J.A. Abercromby. The constructors were Franks Harris Brothers of Guildford who laid out six short holes, six two-shot holes and six longer holes. The clubhouse was built by A. Tye for £3,900, the secretary was H. Reece, head greenkeeper, H. Lovejoy from Sunningdale and the first professional, George Peacock from North Berwick, renowned as a brilliant teacher.

The opening day, in 1924, was a historic one for Sevenoaks and the *Times* correspondent wrote: "Lord Sackville drove off the first ball with an arrow-like straightness worthy of a sylvan course". His grandson, Nigel Nicolson, then aged seven, was also present and he later wrote: "My grandfather practiced for days beforehand and we all feared he would do an airshot. In fact it was a decent drive". A few weeks later it was reported that "golf at Wildernesse lives on" with the take-over of the 18-hole course by the country club. Two courses, almost side by side. In golfing terms, Sevenoaks was the envy of Kent.

In March 1925 the foundation stone for new buildings at Sevenoaks School was laid, which eventually enabled the school to double its number of pupils to 225. The ceremony was carried out by the wife of Francis Swanzy, whose gift had made the new buildings possible.

During the summer the Club Hall on the Vine provided temporary accommodation for Sevenoaks cinemagoers while the old High Street cinema in part of the former Smith's Brewery buildings was demolished for a more modern threatre. The red letter day came in July with the showing of *Zeebrugge*, commemorating the famous St George's Day raid on the German submarine base.

A "philistine" council proposal to solve the town's traffic problems by building a road from the hole-in-the-wall, through the valley of Knole Park to the top of Riverhill broke on June 25, 1926 and was followed by the most vehement objections by almost every resident. Col Fisher, chairman of the committee which suggested the road, resigned but it did little to stem the flow of letters. Sevenoaks seethed with anger.

Indignation was also directed at the council over a plan to restrict the number of bus services coming into the town. Redcar Motor Services was the most popular but they were competing with

Doctors on call

The following doctors were in practice in Sevenoaks in 1929:

J.F. Alexander, 6 Suffolk Place.
A. Carnarvon Brown, Dartford Road.
F.M. Burnett, 34 High Street.
A.N. Crawford, Pembroke Road.
R.J. Dick, Morven, St John's Hill.
E.W. Fish, Buckhurst Lodge.
J.M. Harrison, 1 Tubs Hill.
W.B. Kirkpatrick, The Drive.
P.A. Mansfield, Suffolk Lodge.
Richard Roberts, Pembroke Road.
E. Leonard Taylor, Vine House.
Gordon Ward, Oastfield Court.
W.G. Scott-Brown, Riverhead.
N.G. Imlach, St John's Road.
G.E. Twynam, 18 Pembroke Road.

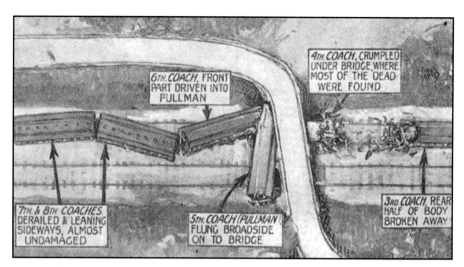

6TH. COACH, FRONT PART DRIVEN INTO PULLMAN

4TH. COACH, CRUMPLED UNDER BRIDGE, WHERE MOST OF THE DEAD WERE FOUND

7TH. & 8TH. COACHES DERAILED & LEANING SIDEWAYS, ALMOST UNDAMAGED

5TH. COACH (PULLMAN) FLUNG BROADSIDE ON TO BRIDGE

3RD. COACH, REAR HALF OF BODY BROKEN AWAY

1927

West Kent Motor Services is registered as a company with an authorised capital of £3,000 and offices at 9 London Road, Sevenoaks.

James Outram dies aged 79. He started his leather goods business in Sevenoaks more than 50 years ago.

July: A Royal Dutch airliner crashes at St Julian's with nine passengers aboard. One dies.

September: Nine charabanc drivers are fined by Sevenoaks magistrates for driving at more than 12 mph. The bench says "we're determined to stop this speeding". They are each fined £2.

An urban council proposal to fell all the horse chestnut trees in St Botolph's Road is defeated after a wave of public indignation. Apparently the roots, projecting in the pavement, are considered dangerous.

1928

In the postponed Smith Charity Cup final Dunton Green beats the Black Eagle, Westerham by a record 8-0. The prolific Stan Wimsett scores four goals.

Westerham, Shoreham and Otford are badly flooded as snow from the great Christmas blizzard melts.

Greatness Mill, erected in 1745, is damaged by fire.

The Owls Motor Club holds its first annual dinner.

St Nicholas' parish hall in Lime Tree Walk is opened by the Bishop of Rochester.

A sweeping proposal to rebuild the village of Dunton Green is rejected.

A new appeal to raise £2,500 for the extension of Sevenoaks Hospital is approved.

scores of smaller operators, creating traffic chaos near the Market Place.

The headlines that appeared in the *Sevenoaks Chronicle* of August 26, 1927 were quite sensational. *Terrible train disaster at Sevenoaks. Twelve dead and many injured. Like a battlefield. Heroic work by hundreds of helpers. Full story of the disaster.*

And disaster it certainly was. The 5 pm commuter train from Cannon Street to Folkestone via Ashford, crowded with passengers, had slammed into the central pillar of the Shoreham Lane bridge at Riverhead with such an impact that the brickwork disintegrated. The engine and two carriages passed through and came to rest on the other side. The third coach became embedded in the bridge and the first class Pullman car was thrown across the track.

It was like a battlefield. Bodies lay everywhere, some on the track and others entangled with the twisted wreckage. Passengers, who had managed to extract themselves from the carnage, were walking in a dazed manner along the track towards Sevenoaks station. Others had stayed behind to help the injured. The River Cray engine, on its side half buried in the embankment, was emitting great clouds of steam. The driver, Bill Buss, and his fireman were still alive.

The people of Riverhead had heard the crash and were rushing to the scene — some to just stand and stare, others to help. Within minutes sheets, blankets, flasks, hot tea and brandy were being passed down the embankment from the bridge while the emergency services gave what assistance they could to those who were still unconscious. The dead were placed in a long row and the early evening newspapers, which were to be delivered to the wholesalers, were used to cover their faces. It was a grim sight.

It was more than four and a half hours before the last of the dead was found and the badly injured taken to hospital. The final toll was 13 killed, 21 seriously injured with a further 40 suffering from slight injury or shock. As the emergency services left and "spectators" returned home the salvage gangs employed by the South Eastern and Chatham Railway began to clear the wreckage. It was imperative that this vital commuter line reopened quickly.

The inquiry, conducted many months later by an officer in the Royal Engineers, concluded that the rolling motion which driver Buss had experienced on his approach to the bridge was caused by the subsidence of ballast which

1928

Sevenoaks Chamber of Trade
· is reformed after a lapse
of 14 years.

The 1st Sevenoaks (Hick's
Own) Scouts Troop, under the
leadership of Skipper Garnett,
moves to new headquarters off
Oak Hill Road, Kippington.

1929

The route of the Southern
Heights railway, via
Farnborough, Downe, Biggin
Hill, Westerham Hill and
Tatsfield, is fixed.

Sevenoaks Urban Council
borrows £4,950 to buy Knole
Paddock.

Talkies are introduced to
Sevenoaks at the Tubs Hill
cinema. The first film is *The
Broadway Melody* starring
Anita Page and Bessie Love.

A runaway horse falls into a
trench near Tubs Hill causing a
jam involving 160 cars.

supported the wooden sleepers.

The huge elevated bank on which the railway line runs between Dunton Green and Riverhead was built from waste taken out of Polhill tunnel by the original miners in the last century. 1927 had been a wet summer and part of the bank and ballast had given way. Sir John Pringle in his report said: "It seemed clear that this excessive rolling was caused by irregular depressions of the road (rail) at various points, apparently owing to the sleepers not being properly packed and to defective drainage... If the location of the irregular depressions in the road (rail) should coincide with the rolling periods of engines, a dangerous and unstable condition would arise."

The inquiry also decided that the 'River' class of locomotive should be withdrawn from fast traffic and used as tender engines for slow-moving freight traffic. The process of track laying was also reviewed and new practices recommended.

This was then the worst accident for the South Eastern and Chatham company but the new safety features which emerged eventually made rail travel much safer.

Following the inquiry and inquest the recriminations continued for months and well into 1928, a year which provided a more parochial "disaster". At least that is how Dr Gordon Ward of Pembroke Road described the proposal to turn

The crash scene at Riverhead. Coaches were hanging on at crazy angles and one entirely filled the archway of the bridge. Cushions, newspapers and huge pieces of woodwork were strewn across the line.

Frank Robinson, proprietor of the Royal Oak, four times council chairman and the man who led the campaign to turn Knole Paddock into playing fields, dies aged 62. He was also chairman of Sevenoaks Cinemas Ltd which owned both the Tubs Hill and High Street cinemas.

Lloyds Bank is enlarged by the purchase of Salmon's printing and stationery shop.

Knocker and Foskett, a firm of solicitors, moves to the White House, believed to be more than 200 years old.

Zeebrugge hero becomes MP for Sevenoaks

Bligh's Meadow into a car park and bus station. He took out a private summons and was delighted to see Sevenoaks magistrates order the council not to proceed, awarding costs in favour of the good doctor.

The Bligh's Meadow saga rumbled on and on. So did the plan for a bypass, now amended so it would not have to pass across Sir Edward Meyerstein's land at Dunton Green. The great bus battle, principally between Autocar and Redcar, resulted in such a price war that it was possible at one time to travel between Sevenoaks and Tonbridge for one penny. The inevitable happened. First there was a merger, then a takeover by Maidstone and District Motor Services and finally, the prices went up.

It was in 1928 that the urban council voted to divide the town into four wards for election purposes. It was rather premature for the division did not occur until well after the second world war. Other notable events in that period included the opening of Donnington Hall, Dunton Green, the re-opening of the New Picture Theatre on St John's Hill, the inauguration of the Kent Cob golf competition at Knole Park and the adoption of Sir Edward Hilton Young as prospective Tory candidate for Sevenoaks. Sir Edward, who lost an arm at Zeebrugge, took the seat with ease in the 1929 general election which saw Ramsay MacDonald forming Britain's second Labour Government.

Despite the tragedies and local controversies, Sevenoaks enjoyed the 20s with a sense of well-being. The General Strike of 1926 which paralysed so many parts of the country hardly affected the town and even the strikers were extremely well-behaved. One great talking point late in the decade was the sight in the skies over Sevenoaks of the R101, the world's biggest airship, on her maiden voyage across Kent. Another was the Wall Street crash of October 24, 1929, the economic depression which followed and the immediate effect it had on the City of London where so many local residents worked.

The third decade of the 20th century ended with a succession of happier stories. A new

The advertisement shows the charming collection of new styles available at Youngs in the Spring of 1927.

Lionel Sackville, the third Lord Sackville, died at Knole in January 1928, aged 61 and he was buried in the family vault at Withyham Church. The coffin was borne from the doorway of Knole by a horse-drawn estate wagon which moved at walking pace through the park to the main gates in Sevenoaks. Edward Stubbs, head gardener, led the procession which included Sackville's daughter Vita, her husband Harold Nicolson and Major General Charles Sackville-West who inherited both Knole and the peerage. By the time of Lionel's death his marriage to Victoria had broken down, the couple were on the coldest of terms and Victoria's life was one of extraordinary eccentricity. She owned several homes but lived mainly in Brighton. Vita, who grew up at Knole and loved the house and park, had hoped to inherit but the title passed through the male line to her father's younger brother.

bowling green was opened at Hollybush Lane by Mrs E.B. Jago, Diana Sackville-West, daughter of Lord Sackville was married to Lord Romilly in the private chapel at Knole, Sevenoaks School's Rugby lst XV crowned an unbeaten season with a record 75-0 win against Reigate and the Sevenoaks Players produced *Yeoman of the Guard* in the Stone Court at Knole in aid of the Sevenoaks and Holmesdale Hospital.

There was also a new estate being laid out of 122 acres in the area between the A25 (Riverhead to Bat and Ball) and the Charing Cross railway line from Tubs Hill. Bradbourne Hall, built by William Bosville in the early 18th century, had been put up for sale by Major William Gore Lambarde on May 11, 1927 — the contents having been sold at auction the previous year.

The house and land was purchased by Hugh Goff on behalf of the New Ideal Homesteads Company who demolished the great mansion and gave the chain of artificial lakes, which had been created by Henry Bosville almost 200 years earlier, to Sevenoaks Urban Council. It was a wonderful gesture, appreciated especially by those who were to live in the bungalows surrounding this new public park.

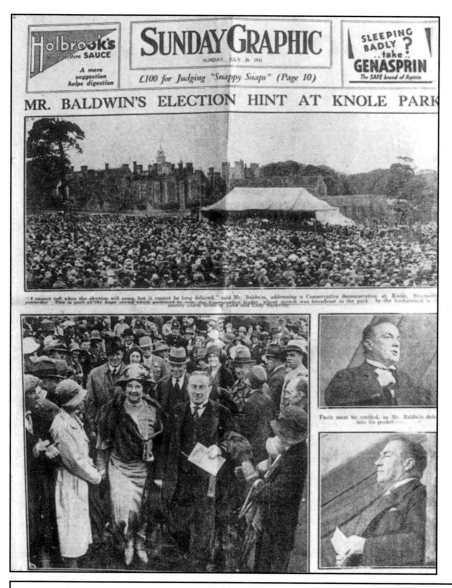

SUNDAY GRAPHIC
SUNDAY, JULY 26, 1931

£100 for Judging "Snappy Snaps" (Page 10)

MR. BALDWIN'S ELECTION HINT AT KNOLE PARK

Conservative leader Stanley Baldwin launched his General Election campaign in 1931 with a massive 'demonstration' in Knole Park by courtesy of Lord Sackville. Hundreds of Model T Fords and other black cars were parked in the valley and the former Premier was given a rousing reception. In his speech, which was broadcast over a loudspeaker, he urged Ramsay Macdonald to 'go to the country' immediately. The election came in October with a landslide win for the Coalition Government, formed to deal with the growing financial crisis. Mr Macdonald remained as titular Prime Minister.

When Mr James Higgs-Walker, headmaster of Sevenoaks School expressed his regret at the lack of a school song for the school's Quincentenary celebrations his distinguished director of music, John Longmire, quickly went to work.

With evocative words supplied by Old Sennockian Peter Warwick, he produced a song that was destined to be sung regularly by the scholars and certainly as long as Higgs-Walker remained headmaster.

Thousands of old boys will know the words and the tune. Here is the first verse and the refrain:

*Some there are who never hear the voices of the trees,
To whom the words they utter are but rustlings of the breeze;
But we from the Seven Oaks have learned this old time song,
Trust time to end their lack of faith and prove them in the wrong.*

*Green Oaks, Seven-oaks, strong and broad of girth,
Spreading out your mighty limbs over all the earth;
Binding us with living bonds, ties that none can sever,
Ties that bind a Kentish Man. Seven-oaks for ever.*

Talkies, turmoil and tyranny
1930-1938

ENTERTAINMENT in Sevenoaks was never to be the same again after 1930. This was the year when the silent cinema gave way for ever to the "talkies" — described at the time as "the eighth wonder of the world". Tubs Hill Cinema had set the trend on December 30, 1929, by showing *The Broadway Melody* with Charles King, Anita Page and Bessie Love. On that first night the 400-seat auditorium at The Palace was full with people standing in the aisles and what they saw was a "100 per cent singing, dancing, talking dramatic sensation".

Later in the year the High Street cinema was to enter the "talkie age" with Ronald Colman in *Condemned*, a story of the penal settlement of Devil's Island. And down at St John's Hill, the New Picture Theatre came a commendable third in December when Maurice Chevalier starred in *The Innocents of Paris*.

Life in Sevenoaks was not entirely confined to celluloid figures. There was live entertainment at the Club Hall, talks, lantern slides and debates at the Cornwall Hall, weekend golf at Wildernesse and Knole, rugby and cricket at Knole Paddock; in fact cricket was played in the summer in every Sevenoaks village and most of the hamlets.

The population was now more than 10,000 with 136 registered as unemployed, a figure that was considered quite shocking but, in fact, remarkably low compared to other towns. This was the start of the depression when many families in the Medway area were living on little more than bread and dripping and 'hand-me-down' clothes. In one inspired moment the Chronicle suggested that those out of work should all be employed on building the then-imminent Sevenoaks bypass. Good idea — but they would have to wait for nearly 40 years!

The *Sevenoaks Chronicle* received many letters about the unemployment situation and the decision to widen Seal Hollow Road — a controversy which ended with the resignation of Mr H.S. Munns, chairman of the planning committee. The Chronicle was busy at the time with plans for its golden jubilee and the content of a special supplement which actually came out — not on the 50th anniversary of the launching of the paper — but the 49th. First again with the news!

Local schools were in the news in 1932. On June 24, 800 guests were invited to Quincentenary celebrations of Sevenoaks School

1930

August: Tony Branson returns to his home in Sevenoaks from a record breaking non-stop motor cycle ride from Lands End to John O'Groats on a Matchless Silver Arrow.

For sale:
Brick-built freehold house near main-line station. 10 rooms with bathroom. Could be converted into shop. £1,500. Apply Messrs Cronk.

Proceeds from *The Wives of Henry VIII*, which took place in the gardens and Stone Court at Knole, will go to the jubilee fund for Waifs and Strays. Among those making a special appearance is the American actress, Cornelia Otis Skinner.

Sevenoaks Town Planning Association is formed.

Piggins stables at Bat and Ball are no longer big enough for the growing fleet of West Kent buses so a move has been made to the aerodrome at Sundridge where a hangar is used to garage the buses.

— too many for the Assembly Hall so speeches were made in a marquee with even more boys listening outside. Guest of honour was Dr Temple, the Archbishop of York, who was once Higgs-Walker's headmaster at Repton. In the same year West Heath school opened at Ashgrove, a mansion built in 1759 on land belonging to the Sackvilles.

The Bligh's Meadow saga (have we heard that before?) was still dragging on. This substantial open space in the middle of a busy town had been a valuable recreational area — used on occasions by Lord Sanger for his travelling circus, by the army for a camp during the Great War and for a variety of other events. Now, at last, it was acquired by the urban council to be converted into a car park with an omnibus station and ticket office in one corner. At the same time the parking of cars was banned from the lower High Street.

By now Dr Gordon Ward was embroiled in a new controversy concerning the administration of the Holmesdale Cottage Hospital. Unhappy because of the resignation from the hospital board of Edward Meyerstein, Mr R.B. Polhill-Drabble and Mr D.H. Peploe, who felt it was wrong to proceed with the proposed extension costing £27,000 when only £20,000 was available, and dissatisfied with the way the hospital was being run he wrote a letter to all subscribers and received immediately a reply from Mr H. Woodall, chairman of the board, who said that Dr Ward was wicked and evil. A public meeting endorsed the extension plans and also the building of a nurses' hostel.

By January 1932 the unemployment problem was really serious. With the depression beginning to bite, 414 were registered at the town Labour Exchange and there was little hope of any of them finding a job. An occupational centre

The Sevenoaks and Holmesdale Cottage Hospital after the extension as rebuilt in the early 1920s. A new proposed wing on the west side was causing all kinds of trouble in the early 1930s.

1931

Because of the general economic climate, Sevenoaks RDC officers have agreed to a substantial cut in their salaries.

Sir Edward Hilton Young has been returned unopposed as Conservative MP for Sevenoaks in the recent General Election.

An application by the Kent County Council for a new central school in Seal Hollow Road has been refused by Sevenoaks Urban Council. The county will appeal.

A newborn baby is discovered among the refuse from London which is being transported each night by train and taken to the Newington Vestry depot on the Otford Road. Kent Ratepayers Association will seek statutory powers to prevent London dumping garbage in Sevenoaks.

Chipstead laundry, once the village school, is demolished.

Chipstead Place, built in 1693 and formerly the home of the Polhill family, is sold for demolition. The house has been unoccupied since the Great War.

Suffolk Place, offered for sale by auction as a freehold business block, fetches £9,500. Jane Edwards, the 19th century diarist, once lived in one of these terraced homes.

James Kirkwood-Browne, better known as Kirky, editor of the **Sevenoaks Chronicle** *from the mid-1920s until 1959.*

was provided at the Lime Tree Hotel where the unfortunate men could gather for light refreshments and useful handicrafts such as woodwork and boot repairing. The well-off provided as much work as they could find.

Yet Sevenoaks' charitable efforts were to spread over a far wider field when the town learned of the distress facing thousands of mining families in Durham. Following a public meeting Sevenoaks adopted the villages of Quebec, Cornsay, Hamsteels and Binchester. They sent food parcels and blankets, offered practical help and paid for the conversion of an abandoned Drill Hall into a community centre.

Another matter of great concern to all caring people in Sevenoaks was the appalling number of road accidents, particularly at weekends when there was a great exodus from London to the coast. The St John Ambulance Brigade raised sufficient funds to set up dressing stations on both Polhill and Riverhill and they were manned constantly each weekend throughout the year.

One organisation which was to ally itself closely to St John Ambulance Brigade was the newly formed Sevenoaks Rotary Club. Head postmaster, Mr A.H. Trinder was credited with the spade work required for setting up the club and with help from Fred Woodhams he invited local businessmen to hear Rotarian Harold Young outline the aims and objects of Rotary. An inaugural meeting was held at the White House and the interim officers elected were president Barty Foskett, vice president Fred Woodhams, secretary Mr A.H. Trinder, treasurer Mr N. Pick and associate editor James Kirkwood-Browne.

The latter, a Scotsman, was editor of the *Sevenoaks Chronicle*, a post to which he had succeeded following the retirement of his father. Two of his reporters were Gordon Anckorn from Dunton Green, the son of an eminent Fleet Street journalist and poet, and Victor Froud from Riverhead. Both had been educated at Sevenoaks School, Gordon leaving in some haste after an incident with a bottle of ink and Vic with great distinction, particularly for his prowess on the playing field. These two great characters were to give stalwart service to the newspaper and to Sevenoaks for the next 40 years.

By 1933 the town was ringing the changes, not to everyone's satisfaction. Southern Railway's announcement that high tension cables were being placed along railway embankments, a 600-volt current introduced to a third rail and that electric traction would soon reach both Tubs Hill and Bat and Ball was considered a tragedy by the Rev Thomas Harrison, chairman of the town planning committee. "It will be a threat to the hospital at St Johns," he said. "I suggest we find a new site instead of paying £30,000 on an extension."

Just as controversial was the decision to demolish the Royal Crown Hotel in London Road, the social centre, once the pride of Sevenoaks, where gentlemen in tails and ladies in full sweeping dresses once stepped out of their carriages, walked through the pillared entrance and up to the ballroom where the great clinking chandeliers symbolised a town of substance and wealth. Now it was virtually derelict, sold some years

This photograph of a staff party at the Royal Crown Hotel was taken in 1929. Secure in their employment they would not have know that within three years plans were afoot to demolish this great landmark and replace it with a super cinema.

earlier to make way for another cinema — the town's fourth.

The demolition men moved in and Sevenoaks Urban Council licenced Cohen and Raper to build the Majestic Cinema. And majestic it was. Large, decorative arched windows, a vitreous enamel floor in the foyer, a circle with its own lounge and an auditorium for 1,250 with green, gold and scarlet flecking. The first night audience on August 26, 1936 saw *When Nights Were Bold.* The golden age of the silver screen had truly arrived.

Or had it? The competition forced the Tubs Hill cinema to close on December 19 but, briefly, it became a repertory theatre. Rep soon died so Angus Herbert, a member of the Owls Motorcycle Club, renowned as an Isle of Man TT competitor, opened a motorcycle store on the site. Noises Off!

By now the great hospital controversy had exploded into a scandal that was interesting the national newspapers. The wealthy, generous Edward Meyerstein of Morants Court wrote to the Chronicle offering to donate £10,000 to the Sevenoaks and Holmesdale Hospital on condition that Dr Gordon Ward, himself and the other resignees, automatically serve on the committee. The offer was rejected and Sevenoaks was enraged. Correspondent after correspondent to the newspaper blamed the board for allowing a principle to get in the way of a £10,000 gift. Imagine the outcry when Mr Meyerstein presented a cheque to the Middlesex Hospital for £30,000. Two full columns of readers' letters on the theme of "I told you so" were published in the Chronicle. The tumult raged for months.

The Great Hospital Scandal was directly linked to the establishment in Sevenoaks of a new local newspaper — the *Sevenoaks News.* This welcome bit

The bicentenary of the match played at Sevenoaks in 1734 between the Gentlemen of Kent and the Gentlemen of Sussex was celebrated on Saturday July 21, 1934 with a costume match on the Vine. On this occasion Lord Sackville's X1 challenged Viscount Gage's X1 and won comfortably by 64 runs. The match attracted much publicity and there was a huge crowd. Later an agreement was drawn up in which the Vine must pay two peppercorns per annum — one for the ground and the other for the pavilion — to the local authority who in turn must pay, when asked by Lord Sackville, one cricket ball within the wicket gate of Knole on July 21, each year.

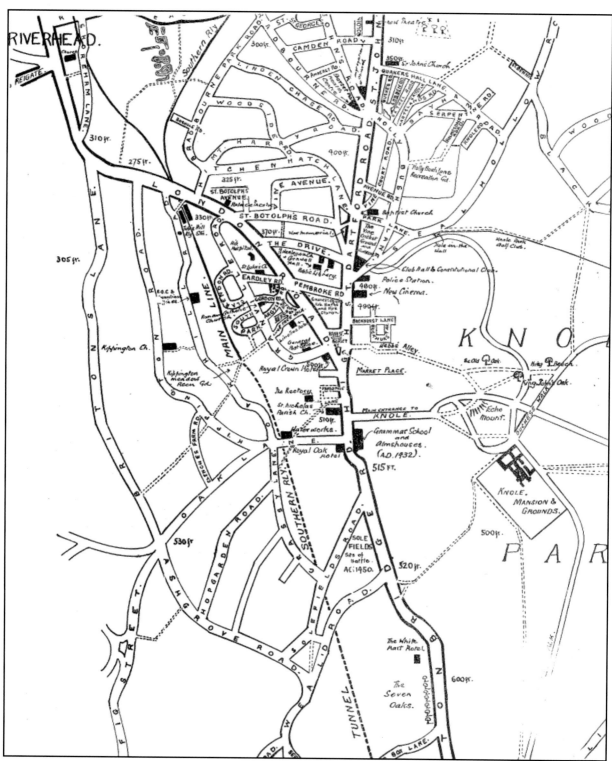

Although the modern Sevenoaks was taking shape when this map was published in 1931 there was yet no sign of the Solefields, Hillingdon or Bradbourne estates, although the lakes of the latter are clearly shown. Cinemas are represented by the Palace Theatre (Tubs Hill), the New Theatre (St John's) and the New Cinema in the High Street. Hotels include the Royal Crown, the Royal Oak and the Lime Tree. Notice the site of the Waterworks in Oak Lane, the Club Hall (destined to be destroyed by a bomb in the war) and the three famous trees in Knole Park.

1932

Sevenoaks Gas Company merges with the South Surburban Company bringing the benefits of profit sharing to its employees.

May 13: Dunton Green's swimming baths open at Longford Mill.

Dunton Green parish council sells its fire station, because it has no firemen.

50 cattle and a herd of sheep are slaughtered at Court Farm, Brasted, following an outbreak of foot and mouth disease.

Bungalows in Bosville Road, Sevenoaks, are advertised for £575 with no legal costs.

Henry Pett, basketmaker, dies. In 1880 his father Amos had supervised the levelling of the Vine cricket ground.

The 14-year partnership between Messrs Welch, Parsons and Ibbetts has been dissolved. A company will now practice under the name Parsons, Welch and Cowell, estate agents.

1933

Sevenoaks unemployment figures have risen to 450.

Chipstead, Dunton Green and Riverhead form a Three Villages Carnival Committee. Edna Dixon of Riverhead is the first carnival queen.

Cobden Road Girls' School wins the English Folk Dance and Song Society's championship at Maidstone. The team is Nita Crowhurst, Irene Beecher, Doris Turner, Marjorie Marriott, Gladys Chapman, Irene Richards, Nellie Box, Nellie Gibbard, Muriel Stephens, Gladys Marshall, Violet Mills and Myrtle Haine.

100 people attend Sevenoaks Rotary Club's Charter Night at Bligh's Hotel. Barty Foskett is the first president.

of local enterprise, which took the town by great surprise, was masterminded by the Sevenoaks manager of the Kent Messenger, Donald Hooper, who was friendly with Mr Meyerstein but, at one stage refused to print a certain contentious letter about the hospital.

Hooper and his chief reporter Cyril Harris found themselves in trouble with their peers at Maidstone and, rather than transfer to another Kent office, they resigned and began to plan the *Sevenoaks News*. They acquired the former Lime Tree Hotel in Lime Tree Walk and the newspaper was produced on a second hand semi-flatbed press, which had originated in Little Rock, Arkansas. With a great sense of timing it was launched on Jubilee Day 1936 and was soon a very popular rival to the well-established *Sevenoaks Chronicle* and *Kent Messenger*.

One story which enjoyed some prominence in the *Sevenoaks News* was the visit to Sevenoaks in 1937 of Queen Mary to open the Vitasan Clinic in South Park. The royal visit was the culmination of a great dream for Beatrice Wilson, one of the country's first and most respected physiotherapists who had always promised to give the town its first physiotherapist centre. Miss Wilson (later Mrs Lockhart) was also the leading light behind the formation of Sevenoaks Soroptimists Club, a ladies' luncheon club. Her founder colleagues included Miss Ramsay, headmistress of Walthamstow Hall, Ethel Breething, a pianist and Dr Abelson, general practitioner.

Just to show that he had not entirely abandoned Sevenoaks, Mr Meyerstein gave Carrick Grange in Dartford Road as a fully-equipped nursing home. The

---

Sevenoaks Chronicle October 1938

THE GREAT-GRANDFATHER OF OUR MODERN AMBULANCE

SAD and forlorn, battered and beaten by the wind and rain, his coat chipped and jagged, his features paling with age, stands, at Dunton Green, the grandfather of our modern ambulance.

There, by the side of a scrap heap in Milton Road, stands the old "Pest cart", used over 50 years ago to convey residents of Sevenoaks and district, smitten with fever.

The Pest House, now the Sevenoaks Isolation Hospital, stood in Fig Lane and was leased by the Local Board from the churchwardens in 1874 and passed to the urban council when that was formed in 1894. The old Pest House closed in 1902 when the council built a new hospital near the junction of Fig Street and Oak Lane.

This relic of the past, which has suddenly come into the limelight was purchased recently by Mr S. Nash of Dunton Green, after it had rested for many years at Ide Hill.

It was "discovered" by Mr W. Holdaway, antique dealer, of 149 High Street, Sevenoaks, who has suggested its transfer to Sevenoaks.

The cry went up — 'we must save Whitley Forest'

Edward Meyerstein

1933

Lady Stanhope opens the new Nurses' Hostel at the newly-named Sevenoaks and Holmesdale Hospital.

The light opera *Karleen*, written by the late Mrs J.A. Findlay of Sevenoaks, opens in the Club Hall.

April 21: Bertha Daws becomes the first woman chairman of Sevenoaks Urban Council.

1934

Sevenoaks approves the names of Swaffield, Swanzy, Wickenden and Coombe Avenue for new roads in the Bat and Ball area.

millionaire benefactor, greatly distressed by the fire which destroyed the Crystal Palace in November 1936, suggested that a convalescent home, serving all the great hospitals, be built on the site. He wrote to *The Times*: "Since it was built for the Great Exhibition in 1851, it has stood as a link with the Victorian era and the whole world knew the Crystal Palace. Should His Majesty (Edward VIII) give his approval I am willing to be responsible for the sum of £100,000."

While Mr Meyerstein was petitioning for a new Crystal Palace, all kinds of ambitious building plans for the Sevenoaks of the future were coming to fruition. Or so the public were led to believe. The first was the acquisition of the terrace of shops in the narrow part of the High Street (opposite Bank Street) by the Kent County Council for widening purposes. This meant the family firm of Wyntie, drapers and outfitters, were forced to close. Other proprietors wisely preferred to wait for the proposed scheme to progress.

Few objected to the High Street widening plans but a statement by Cr Fred Jarvis in the council officers that a syndicate was being formed to purchase the Knole Estate for building purposes was taken a little more seriously. The agent, Captain E.B.Glasier, quickly declared that "Knole was not on the market".

But Whitley Forest — that great area of woodland between Riverhead and Ide Hill was — and Sevenoaks Urban Council received a warning letter from Major G.E. Streatfeild to say that the whole of the forest and adjoining lands were about to be bought for building development. Metropolitan London had already swallowed Bromley and Orpington and was encroaching nearer and nearer towards the North Downs. The council was urged to buy the land themselves just as local authorities had done in Epping and elsewhere. The cry went up: "Save Whitley Forest."

By 1937 Sevenoaks, like the rest of the country, was preoccupied by news of the death of George V, the abdication of Edward VII, and preparations for the coronation, in June, of George VI. The Chamber of Trade announced its proposals for the illumination of the High Street, Lord

The Congregational Church Boys Brigade in 1933. Bert Rosser (2nd from right back row), Jack Morley (3rd from left 2nd row up) and Les Richards (second row up extreme left) are among the budding musicians.

1934

An application from Marley Tile to build a factory at Riverhead is rejected by Sevenoaks rural district council. Owen Aisher, chairman of the company, will go to appeal.

June 1: The Marley Tile factory appeal is adjourned but rural district council relent and give permission — with conditions.

June 22: Lord and Lady Sackville entertain the King and Queen of Siam at Knole.

The Capital Cinema opens in the High Street.

R.C.S. Dick, son of Dr James Dick of Sevenoaks, becomes captain of Scotland Rugby XI.

A new assembly hall opens at Sevenoaks School and is named in honour of its donor, Mr Charles Plumtree Johnson.

Sevenoaks' 60-year-old cottage hospital is demolished to make way for a controversial new wing.

Excavations begin on a new site for Sevenoaks Waterworks in Crampton's Road.

A pilot and his three passengers are killed as a light aeroplane crashes in Shoreham.

1935

A Sevenoaks Sunday Club for young people is opened in the Club Hall.

June 7: Unionist candidate, Col Charles Ponsonby, becomes MP for Sevenoaks in today's General Election.

The Carlton cinema on St John's Hill opens with 350 seats — 70 in the balcony.

An appeal for £1,250 to build a new pavilion on the Vine is abandoned as the club fails to reach its target.

Charles Lindbergh, the American who made history in 1927 by completing the first non-stop solo flight between New York and Paris in his monoplane, The Spirit of St Louis, lived for a number of years at Long Barn, Sevenoaks Weald with his wife Anne and son Jon. He came to England soon after his baby son was kidnapped and murdered to escape the attention of the ever-present American press. Charles Lindbergh later said that his years at the Weald were among the happiest and most peaceful of his life.

Sackville posed for the *Chronicle* in the robe his great grandfather had worn for the coronation of George III and disclosed the news that the Westminster Abbey thrones for the new King and Queen were to be modelled on two early Jacobean chairs at Knole.

The main feature of Coronation day was a match on the Vine against Frank Woolley's XI and a carnival in the evening followed by fireworks at Knole Paddock.

Those who gathered in the Market Place on the spring evening of May 12 to talk about their new diffident shy King, known to his family and friends as Bertie, were fully aware of the turmoil in Europe and the growing disquiet. The first faint shadows of war were beginning to appear — an air raid precaution lecture in which it was stated that only seven minutes warning would be given and gas would be a feature of any conflict.

Nazi aggression completely influenced the way of life in Sevenoaks in 1938. The council's outdoor staff were trained in decontamination against mustard gas, volunteer village fire brigades were absorbed in the rural district council's fire protection scheme — a forerunner to the AFS — Colonel John Dunlop, Assistant Adjutant-General to the Territorial Army told Sevenoaks Rotary Club to support the TA, and Chipstead caves were earmarked as an air raid shelter.

On September 30, Prime Minister Neville Chamberlain returned to England from an historic meeting with Adolf Hitler and declared: "I believe it is peace in our time." Soon after he finished speaking two decorators putting the finishing touches to the flat above the new shop, Timothy Whites and Taylors in the High Street, wrote across the wall: "There nearly was a war." They then papered over the message unaware of the irony of the moment.

Despite the Prime Minister's confidence the airmen at Biggin Hill were "on complete readiness for war". Two squadrons, 78 and 32 with Gloster Gauntlets were on standby and, in Sevenoaks, anti-gas drill classes were being well attended.

1936

Commander P.A. Long RN of Holly Bush House, Sevenoaks, dies in the explosion at Woolwich Arsenal. (It was revealed after the war that the five men who died were testing an explosive more powerful than TNT called RDX. Research into this new explosive had taken 16 years).

Fort Halstead is purchased by the War Office for rocket research.

Shoreham paper mill and its 80-foot chimney stack is demolished. The mill, empty for 12 years, had previously made paper for 150 years.

The Rose and Crown Hotel in the High Street is pulled down. Always known as the "market pub" it used to be full of buyers and sellers doing deals on market day.

1937

The Sevenoaks Territorial Army Unit (Section 314 AA Coy, Royal Engineers) is disbanded.
The Drill Hall is put up for sale.

Edward Meyerstein sends a cheque for £4,000 to clear the overdraft on Sevenoaks and Holmesdale Cottage Hospital.

The reconstructed cricket pavilion on the Vine is opened by Lord Sackville.

Bradbourne Hall, former home of the Bosvilles and later Lambarde families, is demolished.

W.P. Banks' tender of £6,536 to build new council offices for the urban district council is accepted.

Percy Wilson opens a preparatory day school for boys at 64 Granville Road to be known as Winchester House.

Goodbye to the market pub! The Rose and Crown in Sevenoaks High Street was demolished in 1936 and the licence transferred to the Black Eagle, Badger's Mount.

For some years Young's department store in the London Road was among the most popular in Sevenoaks. In 1938 this successful business opened another shop in the High Street on the site of the old Rose and Crown.

A box for 'talkies' in every home

FIFTY years hence Sevenoaks will be on one of the outer rings of London but not sufficiently a part of the Metropolis to surrender its individuality. On one side a long avenue of houses and shops will run through Riverhead and Dunton Green towards Bromley; on the other side there will be an unbroken line to Tonbridge and Tunbridge Wells.

This article appeared in the jubilee edition of the Sevenoaks Chronicle in May 1930, prophesying what Sevenoaks would be like 50 years hence (in 1980). It has been heavily edited.

Happily, the process by which manorial land is wrenched from the possession of its owners and by which smiling fields, woods and forests are given over to the speculative builder is so slow that there will still be a vast and pleasant country stretching beyond the town. It will still be possible to pick primroses in Whitley Forest, to look from Ide Hill to the unspoiled Weald and to find a fox in the spinneys.

The design of the homes of New Sevenoaks will be on cubist lines. In place of the garage there will be accommodation for the family plane while, inside, there will be labour-saving devices. All the modern houses of tomorrow will have their hot water system direct from the main. It will be heated in a central building in the industrial centre of the town.In every house, in place of the overmantel of Victorian memory, there will be a large oblong frame in which there will be a screen to transform every home into a Talkie and Television Palace. In the morning at breakfast, instead of reading about a famous personage, you will see the actual ceremony of welcome, hear what is said and listen to the cheers of the crowd.

In the afternoon there will be no need to clamber for a seat or stand in the crowd at Twickenham or Aintree. Only the enthusiasts will do that, missing the opportunity of just turning a switch from either of these places to another in a different part of the country.

Every house will be lit by electric light. The latest homes will be wireless, the current being picked up from a beam or sent across the Hertzian wave from the great new station at Sundridge. Homes will be heated by this current, all the cooking will be done by it and, in the kitchen, will be set in motion various devices for washing the dishes and clothes, for polishing the boots and for a hundred other uses...

G.P. KING   K.A. LATTER   C.J. CABLE   C. RICHARDS   J.P. MAY   T.W.E. PUGH   J.J. HOLGATE   H. WRIGHT   W.L. JERWOOD

C. GOWER   Dr P.A. MANSFIELD   A.V CRAZE   J. PASKIN   N. GADSDON   D.D. HOOPER   F.A STRANGE   E.B. YOUNG
G.T. BRADBURY

A. BEVERIDGE   F.D. IBBETT   E.B. JAGO   A.H. TRINDER   B. FOSKETT   F. WOODHAMS   N. PICK   J. GILLESPIE   J.K. BROWNE
T.W. MORGAN

Charter members of Sevenoaks Rotary Club pose for a photograph soon after the formation of the club in 1932. The first president was Barty Foskett, senior partner in the firm of solicitors, who had moved from the White House into the Red House.

For the professional men and those who ran their own businesses in the town, it was a great privilege to be "invited" to join Rotary because there was only one representative of each vocation. An exception to this rule applied only to ministers of the various denominations and editors of newspapers. For example, James Kirkwood-Browne of the Sevenoaks Chronicle and Donald Hooper of the Kent Messenger were both founder members. Alongside the Sevenoaks Preservation Society (formed in 1952) Rotary soon provided the most influential voice in the town. They were entertained each Friday lunchtime at their regular meeting place in Bligh's Hotel by top-class speakers whose subjects reflected the great topics of the day. Their opinions were frequently sought and given and many of the members sat on other bodies in the town.

The offices of the Sevenoaks Chronicle decked out for the silver jubilee celebrations of 1935. On the left is Old Post Office Yard leading to Terry's Forge.

Sevenoaks at war again
1939-1945

1939

London Passenger Transport Board has acquired the West Kent Motor Services company.

Martin Hawkes, son of the Rev E.A. Hawkes, vicar of St John's, is recovering in hospital after being mauled by a lion. Mr Hawkes is a lion tamer with Rosaire's Circus.

An eagle belonging to Captain C.W.R. Knight of Bessels Green, the well-known explorer-naturalist, kills sheep at Manor Park, Sundridge, after escaping.

Dunton Green parish council opposes the plan to evacuate children from other areas to the village in the event of war. They hope that Knockholt, Halstead, Shoreham and Chevening will support their protest against the scheme.

A start will be made in the autumn on a new school for boys in Seal Hollow Road.

3,000 people visit Sevenoaks Rotary Club's Craftsmanship Exhibition at Bligh's Hotel.

Sevenoaks Soroptomist Club celebrates its first birthday with a party at Riverhead.

May 4th: A landslide of 1,000 tons in the mouth of the Riverhill tunnel blocks the main railway line.

1940

Following the death of Lord Hawke, Sevenoaks Urban Council acquires Kippington Grange to accommodate Shooters Hill School, evacuated from London.

August: F.J.Castle (129) and K.J.Smart (120) score 220 for the first wicket — a record opening partnership for the club on the Vine. This is beaten the following week with 253 by M.J.Cassey and C.C. Russell Vick. The game is interrupted five times by air attacks. Players take cover in the basement of Stormont Engineering Company.

THE months leading up to the outbreak of the second world war were hectic and confusing for the people of Sevenoaks. Air raid precautions were discussed and exercises held. Shelters were built, decontamination centres opened and refuge rooms gas proofed in many homes. Everyone was convinced that poisonous gasses used in the trenches in 1917 were likely to be a feature of this modern conflict so an order was made to issue gas masks to everyone.

In March the Prime Minister's appeasement policy brought strong support from Colonel Charles Ponsonby MP and Sevenoaks Unionists who met at Bligh's Hotel. They passed a resolution expressing their gratitude for the efforts Mr Chamberlain was making to obtain peace and expressed their sympathy with his present disappointments.

By July Col Ponsonby was telling Sundridge Conservatives that England had to meet force with force. "It was a great shock when the good work at Munich came to an end," he said. "Germany has become a giant steam roller. We have got to stop that steamroller."

July was a month of growing tension. Blackouts were tested, air raid sirens sounded at frequent intervals, road beacons were covered with sacks, motorists drove with side lights only and traffic lights were deflected away from the sky. Mr A.G.Anderson, in charge of the Air Raid Precaution, warned the public that stiff penalties faced those who did not comply with the regulations.

The blackout claimed its first victim on July 14 when motorcyclist Frederick Dow, aged 24, from Grove Park collided with a car at the bottom of Polhill and was killed. At the inquest the car driver said he was hugging the kerb because of the blackout and did not see the bike.

As Sevenoaks teetered on the brink of war, German nationals living in the area were told they would be handed over to the military courts and interned if war broke out, Francis Soyer of Granville Road appealed to the women of Sevenoaks to make the Evacuation Plan a success should it be put into force and John Holgate, newly-installed president of Sevenoaks Rotary Club, informed his members that "international goodwill with peace must be our final goal".

Eight days before Mr Chamberlain's historic speech from Downing Street, Sevenoaks went ahead with its annual Three Villages Carnival in aid of the Sevenoaks and Holmesdale Hospital. The Sevenoaks News wrote: *"The Three Villages handed that man, A.H., the complete cold shoulder. There were more people in uniform lining the route than in previous years and the line of the*

January 25: ARP sub controller, Mr A.G. Anderson walks out of Sevenoaks Urban Council meeting during a debate over confidentiality reports saying: "I am fed up after what I have done for this town. I am resigning".

January 30: Clerk Mr G.T. Bradbury receives letter from Mr Anderson apologising for losing his temper. His resignation, though, still stands.

April: Mr F.G. Humphrey is the new chairman of Sevenoaks Urban Council. "My immediate object," he says, "is to prevent the German Swastika flying over Sevenoaks."

April 25: The First World War field gun on the lawn outside the council offices is to be sold for scrap iron. "It belongs to the Territorials," say Sir John Laurie. "The Terriers would be delighted if we turn it on Hitler," replies Mr F.S. Soyer.

May 16: Fifty aliens, mainly German and Austrian, are rounded up in dawn swoop on homes in the Sevenoaks area.

Seal, the submarine minelayer, adopted by Seal village, is lost in waters between Denmark and Sweden. It is believed the crew of 55 are in the hands of the Germans as PoWs.

Details of the emergency evacuation plan are released. Sevenoaks will look after 700 children from Bexleyheath and Gillingham.

June 6: All signposts in the district have been taken down in view of the impending invasion. This includes the Union flag outside the council offices.

Caves at Chevening are now ready as air raid shelters.

July 4: Bradbourne College boarders and some day pupils are being evacuated to Avening in Gloucestershire. Oaks Bank School pupils will go to Ottery St Mary, Devon.

Crisis carnival as the threat of war looms

procession was shorter for lorries had been requisitioned. It was crisis carnival all right but it was just as happy an event as ever.

The Carnival Queen was Betty Clark of Garden Cottage, West Heath and her attendants were Rose Ball, Jessie Box, Faith Simmons and Florence Sears. They would not have known that they were facing the final week of peace and the next carnival was to be many years away. But life in Sevenoaks was as normal as the situation allowed. Southern Railway advertised excursions to Margate for 5/3d return, Rex Bentall sold navy raincoats for one guinea and Harold Daws, son of William Daws, builders merchants, married Barbara Rawlinson. In the last cricket match on the Vine before the outbreak of war, Sevenoaks Wednesday scored 227-3 against Swanley with the irrepressible Arthur Hammond unbeaten on 97.

September 2 was a busier Saturday than usual. There was a queue of people at Marley Tiles in Riverhead buying, for £18, their portable air raid shelters. Men were strengthening their blackout arrangements and, at New Beacon School, Major Cazalet spent the day interviewing those who wanted to join his new anti-aircraft battery, the 16th Light. *Sevenoaks Chronicle* reporter Victor Froud was among those who had already signed on. The next morning at 11.15 came the voice of Neville Chamberlain on the wireless. "...I have to tell you now that no such undertaking has been received and that consequently this

The evacuated children of Caldecot School arrive at Sevenoaks Station. Like hundreds of others they were placed in the sheep pens and waited to be "chosen".

1940

July 4: Bradbourne College boarders and some day pupils are being evacuated to Avening in Gloucestershire. Oaks Bank School pupils will go to Ottery St Mary, Devon.

August 29: A YMCA centre opens in premises between the Westminster Bank and the Majestic Cinema. The building is owned by Mrs Constant of The Old House.

September 19: The Dowager Lady Hillingdon, of Wildernesse House, dies in London. She was married to Lord Hillingdon in 1886 and widowed in 1919. Her youngest son now has the title.

September 26: Eileen Countess Stanhope dies aged 51. Her funeral will be held at St Botolph's, Chevening, the Rector, the Rev A.H. Head officiating.

October 24: Because of the bombing of the Lime Tree Hotel, the *Sevenoaks News* moves to temporary offices at 49 High Street in premises occupied by Percy Potter, architect and surveyor.

October 31: Agnes Taylor of Bessels Green, who is fined £3 for permitting a light to be shown at night, knits "for the troops" through her hearing at Sevenoaks. Major C.E. Pym, chairman, is not amused.

December: Through the helping hand of Sir Edward Meyerstein, the Vitasan Clinic, South Park, will put on the road the first physiotherapy mobile unit to be produced in England.

December 19: A new youth movement is formed in the town. 250 people attended a meeting at Bligh's to launch The Acorn Club.

December: Holly and evergreen from the Toys Hill National Trust ground now decorate a new assembly hall occupied by Free French troops at a military centre in England.

country is at war with Germany."

Nerves were soon put to the most strenuous test. Air raid sirens wailed, giving a clear message raiders were on their way across Kent. As people made their way calmly to the the shelters this 30-minute-old war claimed its first victim. Robert Frederick Leigh, a butcher, aged 25 of Turnbulls Cottages, Goathurst Common, hurrying home after the alert, got into a speed wobble on his motorbike and fell off. He abandoned his machine near the drive to Everlands, Bayley's Hill and walked home feeling very dazed. Dr Roffey of Bessels Green was called and diagnosed a fracture of the skull. Robert Leigh was transferred to the Sevenoaks and Holmesdale Hospital where he died on Monday morning.

By the evening of Sunday September 3, Sevenoaks had received most of their quota of London evacuees. The operation was smooth for the organisers but painful and humiliating for the children who were placed in the sheep pens at Sevenoaks Market where they waited until being transferred to local homes. Some waited longer than others. They all wore warm coats, labelled with name and address and school number. It was a hot weekend.

The final batch of children arrived on Tuesday taking the total to 7,000. They settled down to a strange life in a country town with their "posh families" unaware that it would be many months before the real action began.

The largest group of all came from Shooters Hill School. The boys, aged between 11 and 17, were billeted in homes in upper Sevenoaks and Kippington Grange was requisitioned by the urban council as a temporary school. During the five years they stayed in Sevenoaks the Shooters Hill boys made many lasting friends and took an active part in the social life of the town. A few even joined the Home Guard and it was a great tragedy in 1941 when Gordon Hibbert, aged 17, was found accidentally shot dead on Home Guard duty at Underriver. One of the pupils was William Wyatt who became a well-known artist.

There was much tension in Sevenoaks during the "phony war". Women said goodbye to their conscripted men, Mr Anderson organised his wardens to be vigilant in their evening blackout checks, sandbagging of all public buildings continued apace and ARP exercises were carried out at frequent intervals. One small boy who volunteered to be a bomb victim found himself abandoned on a stretcher outside Sevenoaks Hospital. He decided he didn't want to be a "casualty" after all and went home for lunch!

January 1940 saw the introduction of rationing and one of the most severe winters that Sevenoaks had ever experienced. Places like Tatsfield and Knockholt were cut off by great drifts of snow, Biggin Hill pilots were grounded and all references to the weather was censored. The *Sevenoaks Chronicle* complied. They didn't want Hitler to know that Seal Hollow Road was impassable!

The phony war ended abruptly in April with the news that Denmark and Norway had fallen and the German blitzkrieg was rolling into the Low Countries. Within days Holland, Belgium and Luxembourg were crushed and France braced herself for a Nazi attack. The Minister for War, Anthony Eden, gave his clarion call for men "not presently engaged in military service, between the

Scouts and Guides head the Empire Day Youth Sunday parade in 1943.

ages of 17 and 65, to come forward and offer their services".

Almost as he was speaking volunteers from all over the country were signing on and some were still enrolling at midnight. Eden's private secretary and the man assigned to oversee the smooth establishment of this new citizen's army was Colonel Charles Ponsonby, MP for Sevenoaks,

Sevenoaks soon had its own efficient looking LDV (Local Defence Volunteers) who were badly equipped but well briefed on the assumption that they would soon be attacking invading German parachutists and providing military protection at all points of importance.

By the end of May the Sevenoaks battalion of the new army was complete and ready for business under the command of Colonel G. Shaw. "On the sounding of the General Alarm", wrote the editor of the *Sevenoaks News*, "these men will rally to their appointed places, armed and resolved to apprehend every German who sets foot in this area until the Ironsides Mobile Columns arrive. They Shall Not Pass."

Such confidence was not shared by the scores of Sevenoaks families with husbands and sons in the British Expeditionary Force. These men were now trapped in a diminishing pocket of land centred on Dunkirk and the Government ordered their immediate evacuation.

As plans for *Operation Dynamo* went ahead it suddenly became clear that the Royal Navy destroyers and other vessels, earmarked by Vice Admiral Bertram Russell as sufficient to lift the troops off the beaches, would, in fact, not be enough. Group Captain Victor Goddard, who lived at Meadowgate, Brasted Chart, was ordered to fly from France with a message from General

Invasion imminent but 'Sevenoaks will stand firm'

1941

Sixty boys have joined the Sevenoaks Squadron of the ATC (No 1023). Speaker at the inaugural meeting, Squadron Leader Gordon, says flying is going to get more and more important in the future. "When you get to my age you will fly in an aeroplane as you ride in a bus today."

Guy's Hospital opens a special annexe at the Wildernesse Country Club with 120 beds.

May 22: A saloon bar brawl in the Chequers Inn, wild west style, results in 12 Canadians appearing in court. Two are sent to prison, the rest bound over to keep the peace.

July: Pilot officer Walter King, younger brother of George P. King, the photographer, dies on active service. He is 22.

Lady Sackville opens a prisoner of war centre at 87 High Street from where parcels can be sent to Germany and Poland.

November: Morrison steel air raid tables are now ready for distribution in the Sevenoaks area. They are free for those whose incomes do not exceed £350 per annum.

Gort, Commander-in-Chief of the British Expeditionary Force. He actually interrupted a meeting of the Chiefs of Staffs with an impassioned request for more ships.

Ramsay responded positively to Goddard's plea and a unique manoeuvre, unprecedented in naval history, swung dramatically into action — the little ships were summoned. Motor launches, pleasure boats, lifeboats, yachts, trawlers, drifters, tugs and paddle steamers sailed from Kent through wrecks and minefields to help snatch some 338,000 troops from the beaches. The people in Sevenoaks, like those in the rest of the country, waited nervously for the first reports.

The good news came first, the tragic took a little longer. Lt Trevor Rouse, 23, of Pendennis, Sevenoaks, was killed off Dunkirk when his vessel was sunk. Trevor, who had been with the BEF since September, was accompanied by a puppy he had bought in France. The puppy was with him to the end. Flight Sergeant Hugh Alston of 19 Vine Avenue was reported missing, believed killed and so was Second Lt Peter Pugh of Stidulphe Mead, Seal, son of Major Pugh, the veterinary surgeon. Weeks later came the news that Peter was recovering from his injuries in a German prisoner of war camp.

In the first issue after the evacuation, the *Chronicle* said: *"For the first time in our island history the enemy holds the Channel ports and the whole European coastline from Norway to Boulogne. His plan now is to conquer Great Britain and seize our Empire. His troops may be borne by air, in troop carriers and then by parachute or by sea on some misty night in fleets of small fast transport vessels, landing at points with motorcycles and armoured cars and tanks. We now stand in his way."*

The paper was right. The LDV (Home Guard) had already surrounded Sevenoaks with their weapon pits and road blocks. Steel shutters had been placed in the windows of School House which was planned to be the strong point for anyone attacking from the south. All signposts had been taken down.

Some with time to write letters to the newspaper felt the preparations were inadequate. One correspondent wrote: "Sevenoaks must wake up. The white tower of St George's, Weald, the grey tower of St Nicholas' and the chalk pit at Polhill form landmarks from the air. They must be camouflaged — NOW."

With the invasion imminent there was little to smile about but some light relief came with the news that a bundle of leaflets containing a message from Hitler, entitled *A Last Appeal for Reason*, had been dropped on Sevenoaks and

---

Group Captain C.F. Gordon, better known as Skipper, took over as scoutmaster of the 1st Sevenoaks Hicks Own during the war. To the boys he was a hero and they were proud of him. During the First World War, in France, he lost a leg as a result of a detonation of a grenade by an experienced recruit. He managed to get a transfer to the Royal Flying Corps and became a one-legged flyer taking his flimsy biplane into the thick of action. So great were his heroics that his was honoured by five countries.

Roy Greenwood, formerly of Dartford Road remembers him well. "He went camping, ran a market garden business and was always full of energy despite his peg leg. Born into a famous family he became a man of deep humility which sparkled with naturalness and humour."

Below: The Club Hall attached to the Constitutional Club on the Vine, held 500 people and was the largest venue available in Sevenoaks for live entertainment. In 1940 it was hit by a high explosive bomb and destroyed.

were for sale at the police station in aid of war charities.

With the proximity of Biggin Hill and the "dummy" airfield at Lullingstone, Sevenoaks had a ringside seat for the Battle of Britain which began officially in July 1940 and ended on October 31. Day after day Spitfires and Hurricanes would suddenly appear from the direction of the North Downs on their way to intercept the German bombers flying in V formation and usually escorted from the rear and above by Messerschmitts 109s and 110s. The greater part of the battle coincided with the summer holiday so children, when not in the shelters, saw much of the action. For those around at the time these dramatic 15 weeks of aerial combats were to be the most memorable days of their life.

The first big raid on Biggin Hill occurred at lunchtime on Sunday August 18 when nine Dornier bombers flew low over the airfield and were met by the Hurricanes of 32 Squadron. The sirens in Sevenoaks had wailed their warning. More than 500 high explosives fell at Biggin Hill and hundreds of craters pockmarked the airfield. Two were killed. The storm had broken.

That evening five separate formations converged on Kent and the sirens wailed sending Sevenoaks underground once again. The public shelters at Russell and Bromley, Warren's Opticians, Young's High Street store, Buckhurst Lodge and Stanhay's Garage in the Dartford Road were packed as stick after stick of incendiary bombs rained down.

Day after day it continued. The scrambles, the sightings, the interceptions and the vapour trails but life continued as normally as possible — so normally that cricket was played on most Saturday afternoons. On August 31 the Vine entertained Richmond Public Schools and local solicitor Clive Russell-Vick, later to be a partner at Knocker and Foskett, scored a magnificent century. Five times the game was interrrupted by air raids while players and spectators took cover in the basement of the Sennocke Engineering Company opposite. Five times the game continued as if nothing had happened.

A week later scores of people saw a German Dornier and a Spitfire MkI locked in deadly combat over the Sevenoaks side of the North Downs when suddenly they collided. The bomber dived head first into the River Darent by the Sundridge Electricity

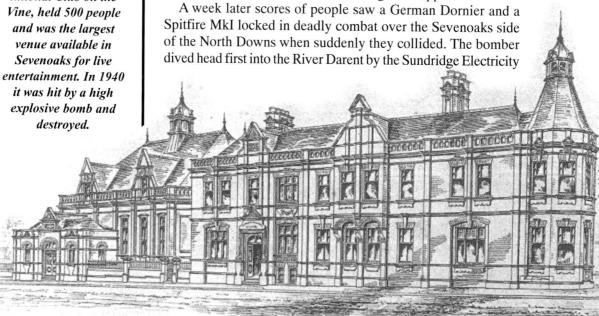

Wally Hall gymnasium — hit by a landmine.

Mrs Dorothy Packman opens a new school at Fairways, Seal, which is known as St Hilary's. There are just two boys and two girls but she hopes to expand.

Mr H.Larnder of Weald Road, Sevenoaks, is one of the four experts working under Robert Watson-Watt on the development of Radio Direction Finding (later known as radar).

A British Restaurant opens in the Cornwall Hall. A one shilling lunch consists of roast beef, beans, brussel sprouts and mashed potatoes followed by jam tart and tea.

Sir John Laurie becomes Sevenoaks Rotary Club's first honorary member.

Bertha Daws, wife of William and mother of Harold and Frank Daws dies. She was Sevenoaks Urban Council's first woman chairman.

Company. One German baled out and was arrested in Westerham. His three colleagues perished.

The Spitfire pilot, Pat Hughes, an Australian of 234 Squadron crashed at Dark's Farm, Dry Hill Lane, Bessels Green and was killed. The young fighter ace, married for one month, had already accounted for 15 enemy aircraft and was one of the real heroes of the Battle of Britain.

On that day the greatest attacking force yet seen flew across Kent on its way to London — a staggering total of 348 bombers and 617 fighters along a 20 mile front. The men on the observer posts could hardly believe their eyes.

Shirley Salmon, aged 10, a boarder at Walthamstow Hall was sleeping in the school reception room with four other girls when a landmine fell on the gymnasium next door. "I remember standing up", she said, "and the wire netted window frame flew past me and landed on the girl furthest away. I ran into the hall to find Nurse standing with stained glass from the dome in the ceiling sprinkling down on her. I must have fainted because the next I remember is being down in an air raid shelter with all the domestic staff and no other girls. Taxis then took us to a community centre in Sevenoaks."

Although the Wally Hall boarders survived they did not return to the school. They were evacuated to Pontisford House on the west side of Shrewsbury.

The bombing continued, so did the drama and so did the death toll. By September 15, Sevenoaks had endured about a dozen raids in which several people had died and many more injured. During this time one famous

Family escapes as Buckhurst Lane blazes

Pat Hughes who died in his Spitfire at Dark's Farm, Bessels Green.

1942

Sheila Hider of Crampton's Road wins Sevenoaks beauty contest. The judges are three Australian sergeant pilots.

A German lady is found in Knole Park looking for her lover whom she last met three years ago. She is sent to prison for two months.

All women in the Sevenoaks area between the ages of 20 and 45 are now required for fire watching duties.

A Red Cross gift shop opens in Bank Street.

Sunday's concert at the Majestic, arranged by Richard Hearne in aid of the prisoner of war fund, has sold out. Stars like Cyril Fletcher and Jessie Matthews will appear.

No they won't! The concert is cancelled because of objections by the Lord's Day Observance Society. 1,444 people are disappointed and the West End stars are livid.

Cyril Harris, aged 32, the reporter who helped to launch the *Sevenoaks News* is missing, believed dead. He was called up by the Navy some months ago.

Sevenoaks landmark disappeared. The Club Hall on the Vine (now the Vine gardens) received a direct hit and was destroyed. Since the end of the 1914-18 war the Club Hall, attached to the Constitutional Club, was the largest meeting place in Sevenoaks, holding just over 500 people. It was here that Sevenoaks Players gave their three annual performances and it was in great demand by dozens of other organisations.

Members of the Sevenoaks Auxiliary Fire Service who attended were now at full stretch; hundreds of incendiaries were falling in the district and, at one time, those looking at Sevenoaks from the top of Star Hill, Knockholt, saw what looked like one continuous fire from Sevenoaks Ridge to the Shoreham Valley. One of the worst incidents occurred right in the centre of Sevenoaks when Rose House and Skinner's cottages in Buckhurst Lane, Youngs depository and a number of shops in the High Street blazed away all night. Before the all-clear had sounded John Ogley, his wife Florence and small boys, Roy and Bob, were advised to leave their flat above Timothy Whites and find shelter. The Buckhurst Lane entrance to the High Street was impassable so they walked down Webbs Alley into Knole Park and back through the main gates to the Coachmakers pub where they were given a warm welcome. The Buckhurst Lane bomb site remained a scar on the town for many years until it was eventually converted into a car park and later a bus station.

Friday September 27 was a day to be remembered especially by those who came out of their shops, offices and shelters to see a Junkers (Ju88A-1) in trouble after a bombing raid on London. It was 3.30 in the afternoon and the German bomber, racing back to France, had been singled out by the fighters from Biggin Hill. There was no escape. The blazing Junkers nose-dived towards the High Street, miraculously missed the houses and crashed close to Knole Park between Knole Paddock and Holly Bush Lane. Four of the crew were killed and Fw Zinmeister captured. Scores of boys were at the scene before the wardens, police or auxiliary fire service.

Earlier on the same day a Hurricane, flown by Flight Lt L.H. Schwind was also shot down during combat and crashed onto the Wildernesse golf course near Godden Green. The pilot died and the Hurricane was a write-off. Many years later Ken Anscombe of the Halstead War Museum unearthed the aircraft after an eight-year search for the exact site. He found the shattered remains of the Rolls-Royce Merlin engine, rocket gear and hydraulic pump. He also discovered that Lionel Schwind, 27, flying with 213 Squadron from Exeter, was buried at Crowborough. In 1980 local trader Bill Terry arranged for the erection of a memorial plaque at the site of the crash.

Knole escaped lightly although incendiaries fell with worrying frequency. On one occasion a parachute mine floated down on to the outer wicket gate, blowing it off its hinges and shattering windows right around the house and even in the High Street. Each incident was reported in full by the *Chronicle*, *News* and *Sevenoaks Telegraph* (*Kent Messenger*) but because of wartime restrictions on reporting no locations and no names could be given.

BOMB CRASHES INTO WEST KENT NEWSPAPER PREMISES

FOURTEEN PEOPLE HAVE MIRACULOUS ESCAPE FROM INJURY

WOMEN AND CHILDREN FROM FLATS IN UPPER PART OF BUILDING LEAVE CALMLY BY BACK STAIRCASE

[BY C.R.H., FORMERLY A MEMBER OF THE EDITORIAL STAFF]

FOUR FAMILIES, IN ALL FOURTEEN PEOPLE, INCLUDING SIX CHILDREN, HAD A MIRACULOUS ESCAPE FROM SERIOUS INJURY WHEN A HIGH EXPLOSIVE BOMB CRASHED INTO THE PRINTING WORKS AND OFFICES OF A NEWSPAPER IN A WEST KENT TOWN ON FRIDAY NIGHT.

None of the occupants was injured, but several were treated for shock at a first aid post near by. Two dogs which ... ... were hurt and had to be destroyed.

... ... at one time a hotel.

SEVENOAKS A.R.P. OFFICER APPOINTED

MR. W. P. TYRRELL OF NEW ...

SALARY ALLO ...

KEMSING RESIDENT REGISTER AS CONSCIENTIOUS OBJEC ...

At the South Eastern Tribunal conscientious objectors, held ... ... bury County Court on ... ... week, Ernest Maxwell ... a company secretary Kemsing, applied ... military serv ...

1943

Sevenoaks collects £547,000 for Wings for Victory Week. The huge indicator on the fountain announces the result.

Carrier pigeons are released from the Vine carrying messages of goodwill to Girl Guides all over the world.

Mrs Maude Davis, chairman of Sevenoaks Urban Council, opens a National Savings Centre in the High Street.

Rex Harrison and Margaret Lockwood have completed their filming in Knole Park for *The Man in Grey.*

An appeal is launched for £3,000 to complete the building of St Luke's Church, Kippington.

Captain Charles Emerson, son of Sir Herbert and Lady Emerson of Knole Paddock, is killed in action.

Another British Restaurant opens on St John's Hill at the junction with Camden Road.

An Inner Wheel Club is formed in Sevenoaks with Mrs B. Foskett as president.

Gift stamps to affix to 500lb bombs are available at Turner's Nursery. The bombs will be dropped over enemy territory.

The Majestic is taken over by Odeon Theatres Ltd from Messrs Cohen and Rafer who still own the Plaza and will shortly be buying the Carlton Cinema on St John's Hill.

It was not difficult for readers of the *Sevenoaks News* to detect the whereabouts of the high explosive which hit the town on the night of October 11. *Bomb Crashes Into West Kent Newspaper Premises,* ran the headline. *Fourteen People Have Miraculous Escape From Injury.* This was the biggest story in the then history of the paper. The bomb struck the Lime Tree printing works while Donald Hooper, the editor and his wife, Edith, were in their office. "We heard the whistle just after 10 pm," said Mr Hooper. "I crouched on the ground and Edith attempted to take cover in the knee hole of a desk. The bomb tore through the building with a rending crash and exploded in the entrance porch. We were plunged into darkness and ankle deep in plaster. The desk had collapsed across my wife's legs."

The families who occupied the flats above the printing works, including the Abbotts and the Shorters were in their rooms when the building collapsed around them. They donned clothes and were lifted through windows and carried down ladders by members of the fire and ambulance brigades who had quickly arrived.

The story of the night was reported the next week by Cyril Harris and the newspaper was printed by the Tonbridge Free Press.

There were more raids in Sevenoaks on October 17 and 24 and, on November 1, Riverhead's popular policeman, Pc T.J. Farrell was killed when bombs fell on the village. Farrell, aged 34, had been in Riverhead since 1934 and was married with two daughters. His funeral service took place at St Mary's a few days later, his coffin having a guard of honour of 100 members of Kent County Constabulary special constables. The villagers organised a collection and presented Pc Farrell's two daughters, Maureen, four, and Ann, two, with £94 of War Savings Certificates.

As the war progressed the scarcity of food and restrictions caused by rationing bit deeply into the average family's way of life. Many Sevenoaks people received food parcels from the Dominions and others were self-sufficient thanks to their skills in the garden or allotment.

But tragedy was never far away. In 1941 came the news that Sergeant pilot Maurice Woodhams, son of Fred Woodhams, a founder member of Sevenoaks Rotary Club and a well-known town builder, had been killed. Weeks later Second Lt Francis Daws, second son of William Daws, was reported missing in Crete. In fact the 28-year-old, like scores of local boys, was a prisoner of war.

The war years carried drearily on and as more men marched away to join units overseas so the women took over their jobs. The bravery of land girls, who worked on the farms while dog fights were raging overhead, was admired by correspondents to the Chronicle. One letter, however, caused a particular stir. This was an "open" letter from American broadcaster Quintin Reynolds to Col Charles Lindbergh, formerly of Long Barn, Sevenoaks Weald, who had become America's most influential isolationist. He wrote:

"I spend many great weekends near Sevenoaks just a mile or so away from Long Barn where you found peace and ease of mind. People still remember the

The Sevenoaks Battalion of the Kent Home Guard was the finest in the county. Under the command of Colonel G. Shaw the part-time soldiers twice won the award for the most efficient battalion in Kent and frequently displayed their skills in manoeuvres, with machine guns and with the use of explosives. Here they march towards the Vine after a Drumhead Service at St Nicholas Church. Captain C.M. Oliver was in charge of this parade and he congratulated his men for their "military picture of smartness". By the time of the farewell parade in December 1944, 6,000 men had passed through the Sevenoaks Battalion.

October: The commandos who secretly landed on the toe of Italy in the darkness before the main British Army came ashore were led by Lt John Nixon, son of Sir John and Lady Nixon, of Vinesgate, Brasted Chart.

The first three repatriated PoWs from Germany to arrive in Sevenoaks are Pte Dennis Edmeades of Bethel Road, Lance Corporal Sidney Bishop of Swaffield Road and Staff Sgt Harold Harlow of Lennard Road, Dunton Green.

Among the Sevenoaks lads selected as a Bevin Boy to work down the mines is Fred Rickett of St James Road. He says his height (over six feet) will be a bit of a disadvantage at the coal face!

1944

February: A National Cinema Club for boys and girls opens at the Odeon. 150 are welcomed by Vic Crawley, manager. Mary Green receives a birthday card from the club president, J. Arthur Rank.

Second-Lt David Arnott of Tanners, Brasted, is killed in action.

Fred Ibbett dies aged 80. He started his estate agents' business in 1900 at Station Approach.

Driver George Whiteman, RASC, of 18 Beech Road drives one of the first cars to enter Paris with General le Clere's liberating force. He is cheered throughout the city.

Squadron Leader Ken Campbell, shot down in his Spitfire in 1941, is among the pilots in Stalag Luft III to help plan The Great Escape. Fortunately injuries prevent him taking part and so he isn't among those murdered by the Gestapo.

silent Colonel and his lovely lady with the shining eyes, and your former neighbours often talk about you.

"Your charming red-walled 15th century house still remains as it was when you lived in it...but otherwise things are not quite the same in Sevenoaks Weald.

"Remember the youngster who used to deliver your newspaper every morning? He's in the East now, with his regiment. And those kids who served you when you went into town to shop — they're not around any longer either. They were 14-year-old boys then; now they're men before their time who are fighting for their country in the skies above your old home.

"Your rose garden, too, has changed Colonel. Roses are lovely but potatoes and beans seem much more beautiful to us here in England now..

"It was very quiet when you lived at Long Barn. Remember how Kent looked in the early morning, Colonel? It looked as if it had been washed by the mist of the night and then dried by the soft blanket of dawn.

"It is no longer so quiet in Kent. All day and all night you hear the singing of the Spitfires and the hum of the Hurricane. They are being flown by boys who were eight and ten-year-olds when you made your famous flight on May 10, 1927. Many are flying now because of you. You were their idol. Your magnificent flight when you fought and overcame the dark forces of nature lit a torch in their breasts. They wanted wings. Now they've got them. They fly over Long Barn on their way to France, on their way to Germany, fighting much darker forces than you fought...

"A few months ago you came out strongly in favour of negotiated peace. Do you know what this means in the Hitler dictionary? I'll tell you, Colonel. If in the dead of night a marauder breaks into your house and kills your child and then with great forbearance tells you that you may continue to live in your house — that is a negotiated peace, Hitler-style.

"That isn't the kind of peace you would wish your former neighbours in Sevenoaks, is it Colonel?"

The years 1942 and 1943 passed slowly and continued to knock down the divisions between class and sex. Sevenoaks' extraordinary reputation for collecting large sums of money for the "special" weeks was confirmed time and time again. £480,000 for the warship *HMS Gallant*, £580,000 for Wings for Victory and £533,000 for Salute the Soldier. In 1942 Sir John Laurie of Rockdale, the son of Alfred St George McAdam Laurie, became Lord Mayor of London, Sevenoaks' second such representative after William Sennocke in 1418. Hundreds of local people saw the traditional ceremony at the Guildhall.

On November 18, 1943, the three-year reprieve from heavy bombing ended with a raid that left six people injured and an infant of 17 months dead on his mother's lap. Five of those hurt lived in one bungalow.

As the concept of an allied invasion took shape, the woodlands around Sevenoaks were commandeered. Thousands of military vehicles appeared under the trees at Knole and in the area between Riverhead and Riverhill; in fact a network of roads was hastily built in Whitley Forest and in the chestnut woods near Bayley's Hill. Not one of the soldiers billeted in that area knew about *Operation Overlord.*

They soon did. On the morning of June 6, 1944, they found themselves part of the vast armada of ships carrying 185,000 men and 20,000 vehicles to the

1944

September 17: A dim-out replaces the blackout in Sevenoaks. The blackout remains in East Kent.

Lt Stanley Argyle, aged 20, son of the rector of St Nicholas' Church, dies in action in France.

The YMCA mobile canteen, under the direction of Glen Dunlop, visits 270 balloon sites during the 80 days of the V1 campaign.

December: The 20th Sevenoaks Battalion of the Kent Home Guard stands down after farewell parade on the Vine. In four years more than 6,000 men passed through the Battalion under the command of Col Shaw.

David Pugh, Eardley Road veterinary surgeon, chairman of Sevenoaks Gas and Sevenoaks Water Company, dies at home in Bayley's Hill.

1945

February 23: Frederick Johnson, a gardener, dies as a V2 rocket falls at Ash Platt, Seal. Three people are injured.

March 11: A rocket falls in Madan Road, Westerham and kills George Blake. 300 homes are damaged.

Author-journalist John Pudney of Bank House, Chipstead, is adopted as Labour candidate for Sevenoaks. Aged 36 he has written 15 books.

Sevenoaks Urban Council marks its jubilee year with a reception in the council chamber. The councillors are Drysdale (chairman), Phillips, Laurie, Craze, Baker, Valon, Soyer, Jarvis, Humphrey, Ellman, Berwick and Mrs M.E.Davis. Mr G.T.Bradbury (clerk) celebrates 25 years with the council.

May 10: Local units of the Civil Defence Services stand down.

Two ATS girls died when a flying bomb struck Beechmont in Gracious Lane on July 12, 1944, at 8.37 am.

coast of Normandy. The daily bulletins recording the successful landings were followed by the tragedies — Lt Henry Young of Zermatt, Hitchen Hatch Lane, Sub-Lt Ian Foskett, son of Barty Foskett, Pte Alan Morgan of Beech Road and Richard Long of Brasted Chart were among the local men killed in action.

A week later the *Chronicle* had more bad news for the beleaguered people of Sevenoaks. First, the district was under attack from Hitler's pilotless planes, the V1 and secondly, details of a new town between Sevenoaks and Sundridge had reached the ears of a stunned urban council. The application from Nash Development Co (of Sevenoaks) involved the building of 4,710 houses on 400 acres of land with 200 acres of open space. The new town would provide 20,000 inhabitants with shops, churches, schools and all modern facilities. And it would almost certainly scupper plans for the proposed Sevenoaks bypass.

As a Civic Society, under the chairmanship of W.H. Astell, was formed to fight the proposal, so arrangements were made for 500 children to be evacuated to Sidmouth to avoid the menace of the "doodlebug". Mrs M.E. Davis of South Park went with them.

Those who stayed behind missed the extraordinary sight of Hitler's much-vaunted vengeance weapon as it droned across the Sevenoaks skies, sounding very much like a badly-tuned motor bike. Propelled by a pulse jet engine it clattered along just above roof-top height and it claimed the lives of many Sevenoaks people.

Thomas White, aged 23 of Bushes Road, died on his way to work with his wife. Both were buried under mountains of debris. Vera Martin of Bowers Road, Shoreham, was one of eight who died after a flying bomb exploded under a railway bridge at Newington, near Sittingbourne and the train on which they were travelling plunged into the void.

Six fell within a mile of Sevenoaks town centre. Beechmont, the long

This is all that remained of numbers 42 and 44 Wickenden Road after the rocket struck. Nine people died and 13 were badly injured.

1945

May 31: A victory party is held for 100 children from the Wickenden Estate.

John Salmon, one of the earliest printers of coloured view cards in England dies aged 77. Founder of the printing and publishing firm which bears his name and of the Caxton and Holmesdale Press, he was associated with Sevenoaks for 55 years.

Col Charles Ponsonby (Conservative) is returned as MP for Sevenoaks but his majority is just 3,900 over Labour's John Pudney.

August: With the news of the Japanese surrender the great ordeal finally ends. Sevenoaks enjoys a two-day holiday.

1946

A "welcome home" dinner is held at Blighs for returning POWs. Lieut Peter Pugh speaks on behalf of the men.

rambling home built by the Lambarde family, was completely destroyed in July when a flying bomb landed square on the house. It had been requisitioned by the army and was used as a billet for the ATS girls who maintained the vehicles in Knole Park. Two died and 44 were injured; it could have been worse for minutes earlier the house had been full of girls preparing for a day's work.

A flying bomb crashed into the garden of South Park Lodge, the residence of Sir David Chadwick. Fifteen people were injured, the old Iron Church of Kippington was destroyed and windows in the town centre smashed. A few days later one landed in the lower Holly Bush recreation ground near Knole Road and 14 people were hurt by flying glass. On the evening of that day one exploded in the grounds of West Heath where crippled people were being cared for by the Shaftesbury Society. They were quickly evacuated to Doncaster.

Other flying bombs fell in Windmill Road, Weald and Knole Park, damaging the golf club but it was the rural area which took the brunt. 137 fell in or near the Sevenoaks villages with loss of life at Otford and Ightham. The worst incident of all was at Crockham Hill where 22 children and eight nurses died when Weald House, requisitioned as a short-stay nursery, received a direct hit. The building collapsed on top of the sleeping children who were identified by labels tied to their ankles. It was the most appalling tragedy.

Appalling, too, were the deadly, silent rockets (V2) which were launched in Holland and travelled at 3,500 mph via the stratosphere. The doodlebug gave a chance but now there was none. On March 3, 1945, when the war was nearly won, Sevenoaks received the rocket which sent morale plummeting as swiftly

Bright lights came on again in Sevenoaks as the town celebrated the news that the European War had finally ended. 200 people assembled outside George King's photographic shop to hear the King's speech, the Holmesdale Tavern was brightly illuminated and an impromptu victory party was held in Cyril Lee's optician's shop in the High Street. Sevenoaks School was floodlit and the Majestic used its neon lighting to great effect. Mrs Moody, landlady of the Bat and Ball, pushed her piano onto the crossroads and drew a large crowd who danced throughout the night. Effigies of Hitler were everywhere and gramophone music blared out from hundreds of homes. Standing on the highest point observers could see a spectacular ring of bonfires. The Sevenoaks News wrote: "Throughout this spontaneous joyful reaction was the realisation that the Japanese still have to be conquered. Above all we remember those who will not return."

as the tragedy which unfolded before hundreds of pairs of disbelieving eyes.

At 4.49 am a rocket launched from Walcheren Island ended its brief four-minute flight at Wickenden Road. The missile, travelling at four times the speed of sound impacted on nos 42 and 44, a pair of semi-detached houses which were blown to pieces. Around them three other houses collapsed and every home for a mile around suffered some damage. The explosion woke up Sevenoaks.

Nine people died in the debris of those shattered homes, including an entire family, Leonard and Gladys Webb and their two children, David, aged two and Deirdre, five months, at no 44. Next door at no 42, Earl Bereford Moyce and his wife Edith were killed. At no 38, Jim Tomlin, a foreman, lost his wife Hilda and six-year-old daughter Rosemary. His son, also Jim, survived. At no 49 on the other side of the road Frances Kidd died. Thirteen people were detained in hospital.

Within minutes scores of people had arrived and searchlights were employed to illuminate the grisly scene. The rescuers worked all night and into the next day. Many families were still trapped in their bedrooms but they were freed and taken to hospital still in their nightclothes. The rescue party was replaced by 200 men who covered roofs of damaged houses with tarpaulins and replaced all the shattered windows. Work on clearing the debris continued for another two weeks.

Two months later the war was over.

1946

Seven trees, presented by Dyson Laurie, are planted on the Vine Waste (outside the Vine Tavern). Four are planted by servicemen. They are: Gunner Charles Cox RA, Leading Seaman Cyril Baker RN, Sgt Bill Thrower RAF and Rosina Wilkie WRNS.

Kemsing WI, the third oldest in England, celebrates its 30th birthday.

March: Roy Arthur Vinson, aged 40, managing director of Patullo and Vinson, autioneers, has committed suicide by hanging.

Winston Churchill speaks of an "iron curtain" descending across the continent. "Russia", he says, "might even be preparing to spread Communist tyranny across the whole free world".

Miss E.L. Ramsay retires after 25 years as head of Walthamstow Hall. Her place is taken by Miss E.A. Blackburn.

June: 1,000 Sevenoaks children attend the Odeon Cinema for a special V-Day 1st anniversary treat.

Sevenoaks branch of the Women's Section of the British Legion wins the Queen's Shield for the largest sale of disabled men's goods.

60 children from Cobden Road School enjoy an outing to Dymchurch. Many have never been to the seaside.

August: Herbert George Wells, novelist and pioneer of science fiction, died today in London. He wrote his great book *The Time Machine* while he was a lodger in Eardley Road, Sevenoaks.

October: 14 homes in the "model" estate, Hillingdon Rise have been completed and the first occupants appointed. They are Mr and Mrs Shaw and their children at No55.

No words are required here. The picture tells the story. VE Day 1945 at the Majestic Cinema.

75

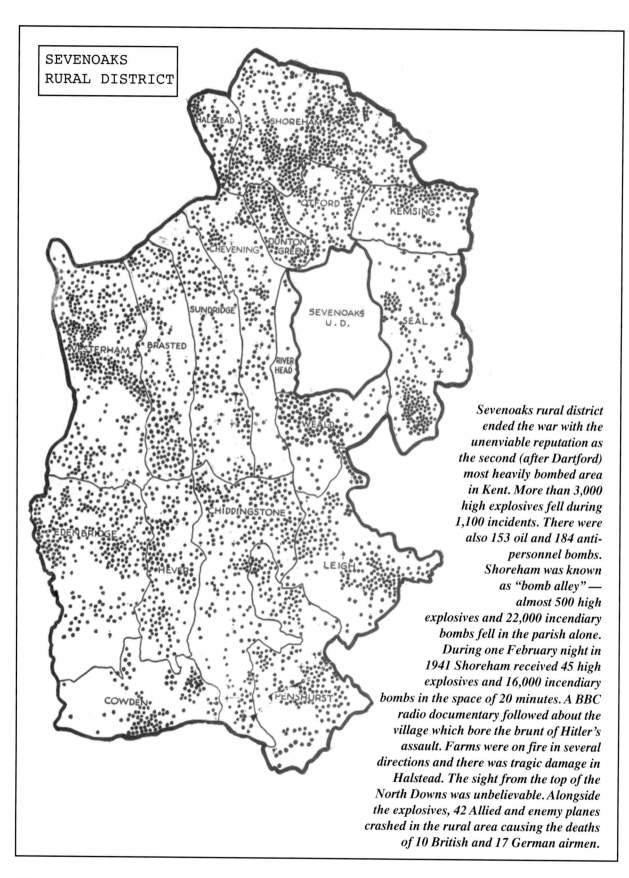

HALSTEAD
SHOREHAM
OTFORD
KEMSING
CHEVENING
DUNTON GREEN
SUNDRIDGE
SEVENOAKS U.D.
SEAL
WESTERHAM
BRASTED
RIVER HEAD
WEALD
CHIDDINGSTONE
EDENBRIDGE
HEVER
LEIGH
COWDEN
PENSHURST

Sevenoaks rural district ended the war with the unenviable reputation as the second (after Dartford) most heavily bombed area in Kent. More than 3,000 high explosives fell during 1,100 incidents. There were also 153 oil and 184 anti-personnel bombs. Shoreham was known as "bomb alley" — almost 500 high explosives and 22,000 incendiary bombs fell in the parish alone. During one February night in 1941 Shoreham received 45 high explosives and 16,000 incendiary bombs in the space of 20 minutes. A BBC radio documentary followed about the village which bore the brunt of Hitler's assault. Farms were on fire in several directions and there was tragic damage in Halstead. The sight from the top of the North Downs was unbelievable. Alongside the explosives, 42 Allied and enemy planes crashed in the rural area causing the deaths of 10 British and 17 German airmen.

1947

February: Sevenoaks is experiencing one of the coldest winters of the century. With hardship caused by rationing, power cuts, strikes and deep snow it is hurting people everywhere.

The roof of the nave of St Nicholas Church is badly damaged by fire.

1948

May: Sevenoaks School takes over Park Grange and a £90,000 legacy from the Johnson Trust.

June: Vine Baptist Church celebrates its 200th anniversary.

Fred Husband, uncrowned King of the tramps, passes through Sevenoaks on his way to visit the King of the Tinkers at Kerry, Southern Ireland. Fred, who has now tramped 142,000 miles, is dismayed by the Act which abolishes workhouses in July.

1949

Dr Hewlett Johnson the "Red Dean" tells a hushed audience at King's Hall that Britain must co-operate with Russia to avoid an atom war.

May: Clive Knocker retires after 40 years as magistrates' clerk. His father and uncle were clerks before him.

July: Stanford Young, the inspiration behind the success of S.Young and Son dies at his home in Bayley's Hill aged 85. The company employs 144 people.

December: Mr W. Breen of White Cottage, The Rise, demands that Southern Railway provide seats for first-class ticket holders. "I pay £57 a year", he says "and have to stand all the way to London."

Heads are appointed for the town's two new schools They are Fred Streeter (Wildernesse) and Elsie Lunden (Hatton).

The satellite town that never was
1946-1959

THE war was over but, in Sevenoaks, many battles remained to be fought. The biggest was against the Nash development project for a new satellite town west of Sevenoaks which Major Charles Pym said was "impossible to think about" until the Greater London plan was finalised. "Can you imagine the implications of such a scheme?" he asked the rural council. "A new railway station will be required, much wider roads and a fleet of buses morning and afternoon as if going up Bond Street. It's unthinkable."

Fortunately, Professor Sir Patrick Abercrombie agreed. He recommended the retention of the great green girdle around London. "We must limit the extent of surburban sprawl," he said. "Let's give to those who want to walk a series of footpaths which will enable people to go 10 miles across country."

The Abercrombie Plan said this about Sevenoaks: "The town is surrounded by some of the finest country in Kent with its well-known parks of Knole and Wildernesse, its forest of Whitley, the steep declivity falling away to the Weald on the south and the Holmesdale Valley and the Downs beyond. Any growth of the town must be controlled to prevent the destruction of its present character and little or no outward expansion is proposed. Under no circumstances should industry be introduced..."

The plan also laid down that the population of Sevenoaks should be a maximum of 17,500. The population was then 13,750 and limited development was needed, the vociferous Civic Society stressing that housing needs must be met by infilling rather than by outward expansion.

And so it was. Work began on building homes at Montreal Park destined to be the last luxury residential estate in Sevenoaks. The famous obelisk, erected in 1764 to commemorate the successful return to Riverhead of the three Amherst soldier brothers, remained as a memorial to the great family.

The Kent Education Committee acquired Hatton House on the Bradbourne Estate for a new secondary school for girls, the urban council began its housing programme at Quaker's Hall Lane, Kent County Council bought Kippington House from the Thompson family for conversion to a home for old people and an ambitious plan for 400 council homes and a school on 47 acres of Blackhall Farm were outlined to a worried public meeting. Sevenoaks was outraged; 400 council homes on the edge of Knole. The plan was thwarted. These may have been the austerity years and the country was heavily in debt but Sevenoaks forged ahead with its building programme, acquiring four large houses and gardens near Weald Road — Shenden, Hurst Lea, Clare Bank and Solefields (Solefields School).

To confirm that the era of country-house living was really fading, the Sackville

The new boys' secondary school under construction on Wildernesse Farm, Sevenoaks, is "Picasso-like and a blot on the landscape", Cr E.P. Hoad tells the urban council.

January 19: Seaman John Lynton Read of Jubilee Rise, Seal, is one of the 60 seamen who dies in the HMS Truculent disaster in the Thames.

February: John Rodgers is adopted as prospective parliamentary candidate for the Conservative party. Mr Rodgers pays tribute to Col Ponsonby, MP for 16 years, who "had little to say in the House but did sterling work in the Foreign Office as an Eden aide".

Dr Percival Mansfield dies after serving the town for 45 years. He was once the medical officer at the Cornwall Hall hospital and a founder member of Sevenoaks Rotary Club.

April 26: St John's United and Sevenoaks Football Club amalgamate to form Sevenoaks United F.C.

Lord Sackville gives Knole to the National Trust

family handed Knole over to the National Trust in 1946 with an endowment towards its maintenance. Lord Sackville had known for some years that rising taxes and, particularly, the thought of death duties could be the death knell for the great house. His negotiations were successful; the family retained possession of the park, many of the contents of the house and were granted a 200-year lease on various private apartments. Almost at the same time an anonymous group of Churchill admirers bought Chartwell, handed it to the National Trust on condition that Winston be given a lifetime tenure of the property. The gift came in the nick of time for Churchill who, with his election defeat of 1945 weighing heavily, had contemplated selling Chartwell and moving away.

He may well have moved to Sevenoaks. Kippington Court, where the great benefactor W.L.Thompson lived until his death in 1904, had been given to Churchill as a gift by the then owner Charles Hopkins. The great man now had no need for the house and in a memorable ceremony, on October 17, 1946, handed it over to a grateful Royal British Legion for use as a convalescent home. "My friend, Charles Hopkins gave this beautiful house to me and my wife because he wished to celebrate our victory in the war," Churchill told the assembled civic throng. "He was good enough to hold the private opinion that perhaps I had something to do with it!"

As post-war Sevenoaks took shape Sennockians continued to show their great concern for others. The Rotary Club led the way with its Dordrecht appeal. Several boxes of blankets and clothing were collected and despatched to the little town in South Holland which had suffered years of Nazi occupation and

persecution. Rotarians and councillors, led by Harry Fuggle and Stanley Berwick, president and chairman respectively, were guests of the Burgomaster and many gifts were exchanged.

The speech made by Hugh Micklem, chairman of Sevenoaks Hospital management committee on July 5, 1948, came in response to the most sweeping reform yet made by the Government. "We are handing this wonderful hospital over to the state," he said, "and they are lucky to have it. I would like to thank all the subscribers, all those who bought tickets and the tens of thousands of well-wishers who have contributed towards the upkeep of this fine institution."

Although the National Health Service had come into being on that day, offering free medical treatment for the entire population with free prescriptions, free dental care, free glasses and even free wigs, not everyone was made happy by the state takeover and predicted that "by selling our heritage things can only get worse". Some weeks before the Act was implemented medical consultants and specialists in

War heroes all. Winston Churchill meets the men and then officially presents Kippington Court to the Royal British Legion.

This Vine team of 1947 was, according to Ken Smart, Vine historian, the finest side with whom he played. Left to right they are: Back row: A. Begent (umpire), Jack Francis, John Sagar, Percy Acres (scorer), Pat Russell, Maurice Begent, Bill Fairservice (groundsman). Middle: Geoffrey Durtnell, H.T. Page (chairman), D.C.G. Raikes (captain), Norman Golds, Ken Smart. Bottom: D.A. Noble, Ralph Axten, C.R. Gibbons, R. Clough. The scorer, Percy Acres was a former army band sergeant who rendered oustanding service as the 1st XI scorer for 20 years. The groundsman, Bill Fairservice was the former Kent opening bowler who was 65 when he was given a five-year contract in 1946. The star of the team was Maurice Begent who Ken says was the best batsman ever to have played for the Vine. He turned down an offer to play for Kent, enjoyed four highly successful seasons in Sevenoaks and retired at the age of 26. The captain, Gordon Raikes led the club for 13 years and was succeeded by Norman Golds, a powerful and prolific run-getter.

the London area voted to boycott it on the basis that doctors would become paid servants in an administration run by civil servants. Some Sevenoaks doctors wanted to opt out.

A rallying call to co-operate was made on June 25 by the chairman of the Kent branch of the British Medical Association, Mr John Simons. "We are individually and jointly as a body going through times fit to break our hearts. Our profession has always thrived, not on what it got but what it gives. The state has now decided that it will buy our services. We are firm in our resolve that this must work, much as we hate it, because the sufferer would be an innocent person."

Doctor after doctor predicted bitter years and a poor outlook for the profession. "We must never lose our souls, never become a cog in the wheels of the state," said one. "How we live and behave in the ensuing years is going to mean happiness or misery

April 26: The roof of Caffyns Garage collapses in a surprise fall of snow. The manager, Mr W.G. Barton, who lives next door did not hear a sound, nor did his neighbours.

April 27: St John's United and Sevenoaks Football Club amalgamate to form Sevenoaks United F.C.

Anthony Mildmay, the great steeplechase jockey who lives in Shoreham is drowned in the sea. Mildmay was affectionately known as the "last of the Corinthians".

Stanley Berwick stands down after three years as chairman of Sevenoaks Urban Council. Mabel Jerwood takes his place and welcomes a new member, Dorothy Parrott.

June: Godfrey Russell-Vick of Wildernesse Chase, chairman of the general council of the bar, is knighted.

Sevenoaks School acquires the Manor House in Sevenoaks High Street.

Sir John Laurie, a councillor for 31 years and former Lord Mayor of London, offers Rockdale to the urban council. It is planned to build an assembly hall on the site to commemorate the forthcoming Festival of Britain.

July: Clifford Dolton, partner in the Sevenoaks antique business Martin and Dolton for 50 years, dies.

1951

Weald village wants the proposed Sevenoaks by-pass to go east of the town and link up with Seal Hollow Road.

It is proposed to build two more new schools on the 18 acre Blackhall Lane site.

A new school for Lady Boswell's is suggested on the school field site in Buckhurst Avenue.

'The fullest professional attention always,' say doctors

for many people. Let's keep our standards high," said another.

A few days later Sevenoaks doctors met to discuss the implications of the new scheme, issued a joint statement explaining how patients should register and ensured the whole population that they would receive the fullest professional attention always. That statement was signed by the following: E.C. Archer, M.I. Abelson, J. Arnott, M. Hay Bolton, A. Carnarvon Brown, K.C. Brown, D.M. Campbell, J.N. Daniel, T.H. Daniel, A.P. Gaston, James Harrison, J.C. Lloyd, D. MacArthur, A. Roffey, R.E.B. Spencer, F.G. Tucker, K.W.S. Ward, T.A. Weston, R.A. Walker, D.E. Yarrow.

This was also the year that the Western Allies carried out a round-the-clock airlift to beat the Russian blockade of Berlin. Among the airmen carrying supplies to the starving people was Flying Officer W.B. Cairns of Ashcroft, Vine Court Road. In all he made 90 flights to Berlin (representing a load of 720 tons). He logged 1,500 flying hours and played his part in keeping the city alive.

In 1950 came the first of many changes in the old order. John Rodgers was selected as prospective parliamentary candidate for the Conservative party, replacing the hard-working but uninspiring Col Charles Ponsonby. Rodgers' campaign was memorable for the speech made by his most famous constituent. Who can possibly forget that historic moment when the unmistakable figure of Churchill with cigar and V-sign appeared at the window of the Constitutional Club and spoke to 2,000 people gathered outside the police station and Caffyns Garage? He said: "I have spent the happiest days of my life in your constituency and I was bound to come over today to support John Rodgers, even though it's a Saturday and I've already done a week's work!"

Sir John Laurie retired, moved to St Botolph's Road and offered Rockdale to the urban council. Two years later Sevenoaks School appointed Old Sennockian Kim Taylor, 32, as headmaster and welcomed a new rector, the Rev Eric McLellan from Liverpool. Appropriate tributes were made to the Rev F.W. Argyle and to "Jimmy" Higgs-Walker whose influence on the school he loved was already legendary. He believed in discipline and the house system and his love of sport was undiminished. Corporal punishment was handed out to any boy who broke the rules and that included talking to a girl in public. On one occasion a pupil was given an extra stroke for having the impertinence to suggest that an attractive young lady he met in the High Street was his mother. It turned out that she was!

By now the plan for the great Nash satellite town between Sevenoaks and Sundridge had been killed by Abercrombie but in January 1953 came another bombshell. A disbelieving town was told by the Chronicle that Knole Estates wanted several acres of the park to be omitted from the Green Belt and allocated for residential development. Cecil Norman, headmaster of New Beacon and chairman of the newly-formed Preservation Society, called a public meeting and a succession of speakers made their feelings quite clear. A public inquiry followed. The Green Belt was inviolable.

It is estimated that 2,000 people gathered outside Sevenoaks Constitutional Club to hear Winston Churchill support his Conservative candidate, John Rodgers, who was fighting his first General Election. Introduced by Hugh Micklem, chairman of the association, Mr Churchill said that this was his 18th election campaign and a turning point in history. Rodgers won Sevenoaks with ease but Labour remained in office with a majority which Churchill said was untenable. A year later, in 1951, Churchill was forming his first peacetime government.

1951

The urban council officially adopts the Territorial Army. Cr A.C. Barnard says: "The tradition of the defence forces of Britain is built upon the foundation of local ties and local pride."

May: Hugh Micklem, last year's chairman of Sevenoaks Rural Council and president of Sevenoaks Conservative Association dies. He was 73.

Sevenoaks Rotary Club is sponsoring a boys probation home at Hollywood Manor, West Kingsdown. Cr Fred Woodhams did much of the spade work and a chapel in the home will be dedicated in his memory.

July: Rockdale becomes an Old People's Home. An appeal for £1,000 for equipment is launched.

Sgt Roy Greenwood of Dartford Road has conquered the Himalayan mountain of Trisul (23,000 ft) with two Sherpa porters. He manages a handstand on the summit!

Dyson Laurie, brother of Sir John, dies aged 69. He was secretary of the Sevenoaks branch of the National Farmers Union for 37 years.

Must the Seven Oaks die? 'Yes' says the council

Another controversy erupted early in 1954 when Sevenoaks Urban Council decided the seven oaks on the Tonbridge Road were so badly decayed they would have to be removed. This "outrageous death sentence" caught the imagination of the world's press and a Canadian tree surgeon offered to save the oaks by removing the decay and filling them with concrete. His offer was kindly rejected and the announcement of judgement day was accompanied by scores of letters to the *Chronicle*. "Surely", wrote Mrs Muir of Shenden House, "every means should be explored before cutting down the trees. Why, they haven't even consulted forestry experts." Vita Sackville-West (Mrs Nicolson) agreed. So did the Kent branch of the Men of the Trees. So did *The Times*, who briefly ignored the fact that rationing had ended after 14 years, to write a leader entitled Must the Seven Oaks die?

But die they did. On September 28, 1954, Peter Smith, timber merchant of Chipstead, wielded the axe that sent the 127-year-olds crashing to the earth. "They looked in good condition," he declared after the felling. They were. The council had been wrongly advised.

Any criticism was short-lived. The council had already unveiled its ambitious scheme to redevelop the centre of Sevenoaks, affecting 134 properties on 3.5 acres of land between Bank Street and Bligh's Meadow to the west of the High Street and the whole of the east between Old Post Office Yard and the Granada Cinema. The areas of greatest interest were the widening of the High Street, a pedestrianised precinct and a relief road.

Among the councillors there was just one dissenting voice. Cr E.H.P. Hoad, whose reputation for disagreeing with his officers and colleagues was growing weekly, said: "By adopting this plan the council is creating a Frankenstein monster for years to come. I implore you not to send it to the Kent County Council. They will love it. They will rub their hands and gloat over it for three years and then they will double their staff to cope with it."

No-one agreed. The plan was approved and the "monster" was born.

As Anthony Eden's former private secretary, Col Charles Ponsonby must have been relieved by his decision to retire from politics. Things were going badly wrong in the Suez Canal and his former boss, now Prime Minister, was sending British forces to the Eastern Mediterranean — against the advice of the United Nations. As John Rodgers was telling a public meeting in Sevenoaks that UNO had "no teeth" and Eden's action was "a momentous step in saving the free world from sloppy idealism and ultimate destruction", Sevenoaks Labour Party

April 26, 1950, and Caffyns Garage collapses under the weight of snow. The damage ran to thousands of pounds.

Watch them fall — and hundreds did. The mighty oaks on the Tonbridge Road are felled. A few months later, in March 1955, Miss E.S. Viner, chairman of the urban council, and Vita Sackville-West (Mrs Nicolson) planted seven new oak saplings from Knole. More than 3,000 people watched the ceremony.

Escape to Sevenoaks from the bloodbath of Hungary

were drafting a resolution urging the immediate withdrawal from Egypt before it escalated into another world war.

Correspondents to the Chronicle seemed more concerned by the increase in petrol prices by a massive 1s 5d per gallon. So were the garage proprietors and Messrs Bert Davies of Bluebird Garage, St John's Hill, Bob Bates of Seal, D. Maitland of Caffyns and A.J. Boakes, proprietor of Bluebird Taxis, had plenty to say about Nasser and his seizure of the Suez Canal.

The Sevenoaks Refugee Committee — keeping a wary eye on the situation in Egypt — were disturbed by the Hungarian Revolution and the fact that thousands of refugees, trying to escape from brutal Soviet repression, needed help. In early December 1956, 64 men, women and children, wrapped in blankets and a cup of tea in their hands, were sitting in The Chantry, Sevenoaks High Street, telling stories of atrocities and how they escaped to freedom from the Red Army tanks. Sevenoaks had become one of the first towns in Britain to give shelter from the Hungarian bloodbath.

With the world situation deteriorating almost every day came serious debates about the likelihood of an H-Bomb hitting London (or even Fort Halstead) and radioactive fall-out drifting over the North Downs. The council decided to ask the 4th Battalion of the Royal West Kents for permission to dig slit trenches in the War Department land opposite the Drill Hall in Argyle Road. Civil Defence officer, Col W.R. Brazier said it would provide great protection against the "typhoon wave of an H-Bomb".

"Absolute piffle," said Cr Hoad. "Does anyone really think a little hole in the ground would guard against the hydrogen bomb. Absolute piffle!"

The slit trenches were never built but the nuclear arguments and fears continued. In May 1953 the Chronicle revealed that Britain's first atom bomb was made at the Ministry of Supply Establishment, Fort Halstead, under the directorship of William Penny, conveyed to Australia in a frigate and successfuly exploded in the Monte Bello islands. Several young Sevenoaks men helped to make the component parts but only a few knew the real function of their work. Those who did go to Australia watched the initial flash and saw the heavy pall of smoke rise into the air. It had a ragged shape unlike the mushroom form of the American explosions. A number of Fort Halstead employees were transferred to Aldermaston and later found themselves bound for the South Pacific where more nuclear tests were carried out. Among them were Bob Combley of Mill Street, Westerham, and Don Cook of Sevenoaks who both attended the Christmas Island trials of 1957. "I had no idea at the time what we were doing to babies' bones," said Bob. "For us it was an exciting period; we were part of the team trying to beat the Russians and of course it was all highly secret."

The campaigning spirit of the *Sevenoaks News* came to the fore in 1957 when the newspaper urged the council to tidy up the Buckhurst lane bomb site where rotting rubbish was now alongside the rubble still left from the destruction of Skinner's Cottages in 1940. "It's a scar on the landscape", said the newspaper,

1951

Millbank Wood in Whitley Forest will be developed as a military training area at a cost of £100,000. It is proposed to erect 80 buildings there. The Civic Society want the CPRE to help them fight the project.

Rose and Company at Bessels Green is one of only a dozen works in Britain making typewriter ribbons. They have a staff of 20.

Residents of Prospect Road, Sevenoaks, sign a petition asking the council to close the Government slaughter-house in their road. "Its stench percolates our homes," they say.

John Rodgers increases his majority to 9,845 after a straight fight with Mr J.N. Powrie in the General Election.

November: The new Wildernesse School is opened by Lady de Lisle. Headmaster Mr Fred Streeter has 12 masters and there are 274 on the school roll.

December: With just 118 members left from the peak of 1,100 two years ago and less than £30 in the bank Sevenoaks Civic Society dissolves.

December 12: The London to Paris express makes an unscheduled stop at Sevenoaks to pick up Winston Churchill on his way to a summit meeting. He is met by the stationmaster Mr H. Catt.

1952

Antiques dealer Charles John Harrison of 77 London Road, Sevenoaks, dies aged 73. The brother-in-law of William Friese-Greene, the father of cinematography, Mr Harrison had a ringside seat to history. He remembered that exciting moment when Friese-Greene showed his flickering pictures of railway trains thrown onto a screen by his first primitive machine.

84

1952

A Sevenoaks Preservation Society is formed.

Alice Norman, who came to Sevenoaks with her husband John in 1882 to open The Beacon school, dies aged 99. In 1900 the school moved to Cross Keys and became the New Beacon.

In the first zebra crossing case ever known, a motorcyclist is acquitted of careless driving after Mr A.W. Vallis pointed out the stripes did not extend all the way to the studs.

March: Dominic O'Sullivan is ordained as deacon by the Bishop of Southwark in a Catholic ecclesiastical occasion unique in the history of Sevenoaks. The Rev O'Sullivan plays cricket and hockey.

A stampede of drinkers leaves Sevenoaks at 9.50 pm to catch a bus to Knockholt where licensing hours extend to 10.30 pm.

R. Baden Powell of Tunbridge Wells is appointed Sevenoaks' new police chief inspector.

May: Walter Smith Ltd wants another 19 acres for gravel extraction. There is already one artificial lake and an inquiry is told another will completely destroy the amenities of Chipstead.

Mr and Mrs Thomas Anderson and their daughter Alfreda survive the disastrous flood at Lynmouth, Devon, but endure a night of terror.

September: A rugby clubhouse opens on Knole Paddock.

November: An experimental electric light demonstration in Sevenoaks is described as hideous. The council will try to improve the look of the new lamp standards.

Thanks to the efforts of firemen from four districts, shops in London Road, Sevenoaks and Dorset Street were saved from serious damage when fire broke out in February 1956. The roofs were completely gutted.

Cecil Brown, master baker, whose shop was in the London Road and bakery in Brewery Lane. He was also a great billiard player and secretary of the Cornwall Hall Men's Club. Every Friday night during the 1950s a handful of members would gather at the bakery and help put jam in the jam puffs.

Teddy Boy problem — 'it's like the Elephant and Castle'

"and puts any East End slum in the shade." The issue was taken up by Cr Peggy Fenner who urged KCC (owners of the two acre site) to act quickly. They did. The headlines next week read: "At last: county action on Buckhurst dump." In time it became a car park.

A few weeks later (October 10, 1957) Sevenoaks was being compared with another dubious London location. "Strolling through Sevenoaks on a Saturday night", said the *Chronicle*, "is just like strolling through the Elephant and Castle. Gangs of garishly dressed Teddy Boys and their heavily made-up girl friends hang around street corners or parade up and down the road in guffawing groups. One girl we approached — tight-trousered and crepe shod — said: 'Why shouldn't we have fun while we're young. What business of yours is it anyway?'"

The *Chronicle* continued: "A few years ago the sight of an Edwardian suit in Sevenoaks High Street was a comparitive rarity. Now it is shockingly commonplace." Chairman of Sevenoaks and Holmesdale Youth Club, Stanley Berwick agreed: "The town has a youth problem of major proportions on its hands."

Perhaps it was this concern that prompted the urban council to ban the film *Rock Around the Clock* from being shown at The Granada. They had heard how teenagers in other towns had been jiving in the aisles, clapping and chanting to Bill Haley's music. Cinema seats had been torn up. Sevenoaks didn't want this sort of anti-social behaviour. Only one member (Berwick) voted in favour

The white-whiskered, kindly Bert Budgen ran his bazaar or emporium opposite Six Bells Lane for almost 50 years and sold everything from household supplies to fireworks. He was by training a skilful furniture repairer.

It was Dr Anthony Carnarvon Brown (seated centre) who conceived the idea of starting a health clinic on the junction of St John's and Bradbourne Roads, Sevenoaks. Run entirely by a voluntary committee for the first 10 years or so, it became so popular that hundreds of Sevenoaks mothers and babies attended on a regular basis. In the war years particularly orange juice, cod liver oil and dried milk guarded against a score of climatic ills. Pictured with Anthony Carnarvon Brown is his son Kenyon (in the background with glasses), Sevenoaks councillors, mums and their children.

Healthy babies at Sevenoaks clinic. In September 1949 it was voted one of the best clinics in the country and executive officers from the Ministry of Food made a special journey to congratulate Dr Carnarvon Brown and his team.

1953

The Wildernesses Estate is sold. For many years it had been owned by Mr G.E. Fawcett who rented it to the Wildernesse Club.

1954

January: Major Charles Pym retires from the Sevenoaks bench after 40 years as a JP.

Wildernesse Estate is sold to the Royal London Society for the Blind.

Leonard Clive Taylor, a former pupil, has been chosen from 80 applicants to succeed James Higgs-Walker as headmaster of Sevenoaks School. The school has 360 boys (135 boarders).

Carrick Grange, a 31-room mansion, is sold to Mr L.A.G. Hawkes for £10,000. It has five acres, a cottage and many outbuildings.

February: Sevenoaks Services Club is authorised by the Minister of Works to demolish its 1921 building and rebuild.

Gerald Micklem is elected president of the new Wildernesse Club which aims to buy 179 acres including most of the existing golf course and build a clubhouse with facilities for tennis and other activities.

April: Three "Spiv" photographers are to be removed from the High Street.

May: Mr G.T. Bradbury, urban council clerk for 34 years, retires. Mr A.C.Thwaites takes his place.

The Rev F.W. Argyle retires after 17 years at St Nicholas'. He is 74.

June: £18,500 is required to save St Nicholas' Church from the ravages of dry rot.

Whit Monday: Prime Minister, Winston Churchill attends Westerham Gala

Two Sevenoaks headmasters whose careers ran parallel during the war and into the 50s. Left "Jimmy" Higgs-Walker, the key figure in the revival of Sevenoaks School who reigned supreme between 1925 and 1955 and right J.R. Taylor. Hundreds of Sennockians who had the good fortune to attend Lady Boswell's School when "Jerry" was headmaster will remember a bustling, human dynamo who had that ability to generate tremendous enthusiasm and introduce teaching methods that were way ahead of their time. He burst onto the scene from Hosey School, Westerham, in 1943. He introduced Esperanto and his law enforcer was a small baseball bat!

of the film being shown.

Local newspapers, remembering the Riverhead rail crash with a series of 30th anniversary reminiscences from those who witnessed the grisly scenes, were soon aware of the irony of the moment. On December 4, 1957 came the news of another terrible crash — this time at Lewisham in thick fog.

Two trains crashed under the St John's bridge. One of them reared up, smashing the supports. The trains were packed with West End and City workers and 92 people were killed.

Fortune favoured Sevenoaks. The Cannon Street to Ramsgate steam express was not due to stop at Tubs Hill so few local people were killed. Hundreds of commuters, though, were close to the scene at the time and many were caught up in the delays which followed. Among those who died were John Berkeley who had only recently moved from Seal Hollow Road and Mr R.N. Morley, chairman of Sevenoaks Conservative Association.

Several people, including Dorset Street hairdresser Joe Russell, walked home. Four friends, Roy Cleveley, Jack Francis, John

Stanley Berwick, builder, national Toc H treasurer, football fanatic and four times council chairman.

Film-makers. Members of Sevenoaks Preservation Society outside Payne's Stores (now the Sun Do Chinese Restaurant during the making of their film, showing the best of Sevenoaks and how the town must be preserved.

Breething and Ken Styles made their way in thick fog along the line to New Cross where Roy telephoned to assure his wife they were all safe.

By 1959 the big issues returned to haunt the urban council. The 1951 town development plan had died a natural death and the urban council had engaged Max Lock and partners to prepare a new scheme. "History is repeating itself," said the *Sevenoaks News*. "Only a while ago the Buckhurst Lane plan was circulated and dismissed. Now we have new proposals which are simply breathtaking."

They were. A market site in the Shambles, a crescent shopping parade in the central triangle of Old Brewery Yard (which was described by Lock as the rehabilitation of the town's obsolete core), pedestrian shopping behind the High Street, the widening of the High Street between Buckhurst Lane and Locks Yard and a big assembly hall opposite the market house. On the edge of Knole Park, a substantial housing project. Breathtaking!

Correspondents didn't agree with this description. John Buckwell was upset by the proposal to demolish his centuries-old shop and drive a new road through the archway into the Shambles and Gordon Catling, describing Sevenoaks as a "supremely higgledy-piggledy town with quaint exciting passageways", said: "But of course this is the progressive age. Clear the decks. Sweep away everything that is mellowed by time. Subtopia must come. Multiple shops, glaring neon signs, cut prices. Big business is around the corner, leering at you as it destroys everything you held beautiful..."

1955

Wildernesse Club's new clubhouse is completed.

December: 22 Rural councillors are threatened with imprisonment by a High Court judge for failing to implement a scheme to prevent pollution of the River Eden.

1956

January: Col Charles Ponsonby, Sevenoaks MP from 1935-1950, is created a Baronet for political services.

The rabbit population continues to be wiped out by a disease called myxomatosis, including, now, tame rabbits. The first report of the disease in the UK was on a farm in Bough Beech.

The landlord of The Chequers, Ightham, Mr George Grimaldi, claims to be a direct descendant of a Prince of Monaco and in line for the throne.

February: Six local men who worked for the Special Boat Section of the Royal Marines during the war are guests at The Odeon to see the new film *The Cockleshell Heroes*. Among the men are Ernest Miles of Lennard Road, Dunton Green, A. Taylor of Wickenden Road and S. Coombs of Swaffield Road.

Cheyne Hospital in Eardley Road may become the long-awaited Sevenoaks Maternity Hospital.

April: 46,625 Kent children are vaccinated against Polio.

Parris' bakery in the High Street has been sold to Tip Top of Orpington.

John Rodgers votes in favour of capital pubishment. There are 100 murderers at large in London, he says.

Peter Clifton of Westerham and 18-year-old Kathleen Pond of Dunton Green elope to Gretna Green.

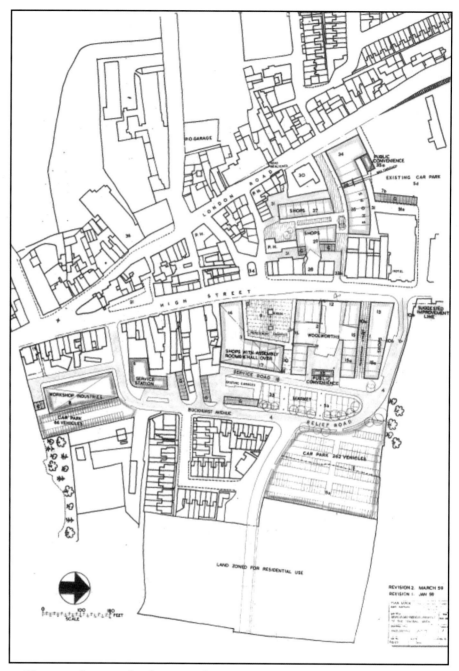

The second town redevelopment plan, devised by Max Lock and Partners and revealed to a sceptical Sevenoaks in the autumn of 1959.

The final gift, given to the beleaguered municipality of Dordrecht, Holland by the people of Sevenoaks — £370, has been spent in laying out and equipping about an acre of one of the city's parks as a children's playground. Burgomaster Bleeker said they will never forget the warm sympathy shown to them by Sevenoaks. "Out of gratitude", he said, "and to remind the population continually of the help given, we shall call this place the Sevenoaks Playground. Here our youngsters can enjoy health and happiness without the dangers."

1956

May: Five masked bandits escape with £1,700 by coshing the manager of Clenches Farm Dairies and his assistant as they deposit money at Lloyds Bank.

July: Restoration work is under way at St Nicholas. Gifts totalling £11,500 have already been received.

August: Cricketing history is made at Knole when Lord Sackville accepts, from the council, the nominal rent for the Vine cricket ground — a cricket ball.

Effie Ramsay, headmistress of Walthamstow Hall for 35 years dies.

October: Andrew Peacock celebrates 25 years as a golf professional at Wildernesse. He receives a cheque for £700.

There were no such things as chicanes and road bumps in the 1950s. Dangerous bends were a hazard and one of the "worst" was Botany Bay Bridge on the A25 which twisted twice and claimed quite a few unsuspecting victims. The decision was made in September 1959 to rebuild the bridge at a cost of £50,000. Five years later a huge crowd gathered after midnight in a floodlit Bradbourne Vale Road to see one of the great joists of the new bridge put in place. As the contractors began the meticulous task of lowering the huge beam, someone realised that the 12.35 am last train had not passed by and the "juice" rail was still alive. Two special mobile cranes lifted the joist and the train passed by harmlessly.

The controversy, of course, went on and on and by May was joined by another — the conversion of the High Street from gas lamps to fluorescent electric lighting set on 25-foot steel standards. Letters, complaints and petitions poured in and even the highly respected Sir John Dunlop was moved to write to the newspapers. "It is a tragic decision," he wrote. "The lighting scheme is over-grand, over-costly, unsuited to Sevenoaks and has been accepted by a non-technical council on the advice of so-called specialists. It means that £35,000 will have to be borrowed and another 4d put on the rates. Really, are we in a free England or a totalitarian state?"

So vociferous were the street lamp critics that the council called in the government-sponsored Royal Fine Arts Commission to add a comment or two on good taste and beauty. The assessment was equally scathing. "Too big, too

January: Sevenoaks Conservative (formerly Constitutional) Club closes after 68 years. The club was built on the junction of Dartford Road and Seal Hollow Road in 1889.

An indoor cricket school is to be built on land near Knole Paddock, Sevenoaks.

March: Fred Huish, the former Kent and England wicket-keeper, is buried in Otford churchyard. He was 87.

May: Dorothy Parrott is elected chairman of Sevenoaks Urban Council.

June: A new diesel-electric train service comes into operation. The journey from Sevenoaks to Cannon Street is cut to 29 minutes.

A young man, born in Linden Chase, is making a name for himself as a calypso-singing star. His name is Lance Percival.

The Rev Edward Hawkes retires after 37 years as vicar of St John's Church, Sevenoaks.

Alec Young retires from his executive position with S Young and Sons, so ending a tradition of unbroken family service that has lasted since the store opened in 1780.

October 6: The Russian sattelite, Sputnik I, is seen over Sevenoaks at 5.17am.

Terrified people living near the railway line complain about the new diesel trains which, they say, sound like the approach of doodlebugs.

Lord Dunsany of Dunstall Priory, Shoreham, poet, dramatist and sportsman, dies aged 79.

November: Sevenoaks' branch of the Royal British Legion wants the two-minute silence to return to November 11 instead of the nearest Sunday.

Former members of the Ist Sevenoaks (Hicks Own) Scout Troop will recognise some of the stalwarts pictured here. They include Skipper Gordon, Bob Morgan, Skipper Styles, Bunny Kimble, Fred Prior, Ray Kent, John Guest, Peter and George Whale, George Simmons and Frank Carter. In 1959 the troop was presented with new colours by Lord Sackville in Knole Park and among those present at the ceremony was Group Captain H.A. Murton (rtd) who had reformed the group in 1916 and became the scoutmaster. The scoutmaster in 1959 was Edward Styles.

conspicuous, badly sited and completely disturbing the view of the Downs. We recommend you take them down."

As smaller poles were erected older Sennockians recalled how Sevenoaks had voted to keep its gas lamps when the conversion to electricity was first discussed in 1911. Since then the lighting of the town's gas lamps had been carried out efficiently by the public lighting superintendent, Mr Older and his staff.

Before this dissenting decade had finally drawn to a close there was one more matter of immense importance to be finalised — the route of the Sevenoaks bypass, its starting date and cost. A public inquiry, in September of that very warm year (1959), was notable for the heat generated by a succession of speakers. The westerly route was finally accepted, traversing from the Chipstead Road, south of Salter's Heath Farm, through Great Brittain's Wood, north of Dibden Lane, through Long Spring Wood, to the west of Hernewood and on to the Queen's Head cottages on Riverhill.

The cost was estimated at £2 million and a start — wait for it — was to be made within two years!

1958

Several farms in the Sevenoaks area are closed because of a new outbreak of foot and mouth disease.

January: Max Lock and partners are engaged to prepare a new plan for development of the town. The cost is 300 guineas.

New fluorescent-type street lights on 25-foot poles are approved.

The Rev Tubby Clayton, founder of the Toc H, addresses a large audience at Wildernesse Boys' School.

March: An early start will be made on Sevenoaks by-pass following the public inquiry next year.

New laboratories at Sevenoaks School are completed.

June: St Nicholas' Church restoration work is completed. The final cost: £32,000.

September: A violent storm hits Sevenoaks and district, a staggering 5.14 inches falling in two hours. Hundreds of tons of soil and rock close Sevenoaks railway tunnel and the branch line from Dunton Green to Westerham will be closed for days. Fire brigade receives 100 distress calls.

Vine cricketer Ted Collins takes five wickets in five balls against Bromley.

Dr A. Carnarvon Brown retires as medical officer to St John's Clinic. He has been associated with maternity and child welfare since its inception 44 years ago.

Bernard Barraud, who dies at Bayham Road, was the owner of Nipper the dog, whose picture appeared on His Master's Voice gramophone records.

Shoreham Place, once the happy home of the Mildmay family, was demolished by fire on the morning of Thursday August 13, 1959, after the then owner had failed to get permission to turn it into flats. A demolition company was entrusted with the work. Anthony, the last Lord Mildmay, was Britain's greatest amateur steeplechaser and he tragically drowned in the sea in 1950 at the age of 41. He rode for Peter Cazalet at Shipbourne and it was he who persuaded Queen Elizabeth and Princess Elizabeth to buy a racehorse. Shoreham Place, set in what were lovely gardens, had not been occupied for 10 years. It had fallen into decay and was considered a great hazard for village children.

In the early 1950s Sevenoaks staged its version of the Dunmow Flitch — one of Britain's oldest ceremonies — when a cured and salted side of pork was given to a couple who could prove that not once in a year and a day had they regretted marrying. The ceremony, which originated in the Essex town of Dunmow, was staged at Knole Paddock during the annual Royal Artillery Association fete. A mock court involving judge, jury and witnesses was set up and couples invited to give evidence to support their claim of wedded bliss. Among those taking part (and pictured above were Gordon Catling, (photographer), Bill Struthers (lawyer), Phil Sanders (bank manager) and Martin Hawkes (builder). They found a winner in the ubiquitous Billy and Alma Kay.

1959

January: Steve Smith of Shenden Way plays scrum half for England against Wales at Cardiff Arms Park.

Urban council clerk Mr Thwaites dies of a heart attack. He is suceeded by Arthur Davies.

Richard Robinson of the Royal Oak retires after 23 years as a councillor.

February: Police sergeant John Tritton retires after 32 years service.

May: A runaway lorry hits cars and crashes into the Kentish Yeoman pub at Seal. The driver jumps out just before impact.

May: Kent and England cricketer, Les Ames opens Holmesdale's new pavilion.

A tranquil scene of upper High Street as seen from the gates of Park Grange which had been left to Sevenoaks School by the Johnson family.

In 1950 members of Sevenoaks Riding Club (pictured here in Knole Park) were devastated by the news that their president, Anthony Mildmay had been drowned. The club was formed in 1949 by Barbara Waters and Elizabeth Franks and by the mid 50s had become the largest in Kent in terms of membership and attendance at shows. One member, Leonie Harris from Knockholt, was chosen to ride for Great Britain.

One name shone out like a beacon during the years immediately before and after the war — Sam King from Bow Petts, Godden Green, the grandson of a charcoal burner and a man whose passion for golf began before the Knole Park Club was laid out. Sam, who became the club pro, first played seriously in 1928, won several tournaments and was chosen for the British Ryder Cup team of 1937. He played a singles match and halved with Densmoor Shoot, then world open champion. He was picked for the Ryder Cup team again in 1939 (which was cancelled because of the war) and in 1949 when he lost at Grantham. In the 1950s Sam was living at Ide Hill with his wife and two daughters, teaching at Knole, where he is seen in our picture (left) with ace golfer Max Faulkner (right).

1959

James Richard, seventh earl Stanhope, leaves Chevening and 3,000 acres to the nation together with an endowment for £250,000.

June: The 1st Sevenoaks (Hicks Own) scout troop is presented with new colours in a ceremony in Knole Park.

The Rock and Fountain pub in London Road closes.

August: Shoreham Place, the former home of Lord Mildmay, unoccupied for 10 years, is demolished by fire.

More human bones are found on Polhill.

June 18 - August 13: Newspaper strike hits all local newspapers.

August: Vine cricketer Ralph Axten scores 189 against Court Court, the highest score on the Vine while a match is "still alive".

September: Botany Bay Bridge is to be rebuilt at a cost of £50,000.

October: An indoor cricket school is opened at Knole Paddock, Sevenoaks, by Lord Cornwallis who bowled the first ball to Kent cricketer Arthur Phebey. Much of the spade work has been completed by Ted Giles and the local AKCC committee.

Ernest Henry Evans, chief engineer to Sevenoaks and Tonbridge Water Company since 1932, dies aged 55.

December: James Kirkwood-Browne (Kirky), managing editor of the *Sevenoaks Chronicle* for almost 40 years, dies aged 67.

Frank King retires after 45 years as hairdresser in London Road, Sevenoaks. He started in 1914 when short, back and sides cost 3d.

Mr L.C. (Kim) Taylor, the 32-year-old headmaster of Sevenoaks School with his prefects. In his history of Sevenoaks School, Brian Scragg says that both masters and pupils alike were affected by Taylor's irresistible intellectual optimism.

Bypass, Beatles and blight
1960-1969

1960
January: Victor W. Froud is appointed editor of the *Sevenoaks Chronicle.*

February: Riverhead schoolboys Alan Colnet and Douglas Allan-King find part of a skull at the ancient burial ground, Polhill.

A small meat store is in use at Rye Lane, Dunton Green. The owner, Bill Davison says he has plans for more cold storage units.

April: Sevenoaks Urban Council, through its union, NALGO, seek a five day working week.

18 flats next to Rockdale are completed. The Old People's Welfare Committee now plans a day centre on the site.

Clive Russell-Vick of Wildernesse Chase is fined £50 for flying his 1929 German aircraft in a dangerous state. Examiners find 15 defects in the airframe.

May: The proposed Sevenoaks assembly hall will cost £70,000 members of Sevenoaks Preservation Society are told.

The urban council welcomes two new members, Sir John Dunlop and Paul Haydon, a Liberal.

June: Carl John Feldberg, one of the last men in Britain to manufacture fine harpsichords, dies of asphyxia by falling onto wood shavings on his workshop floor. He was 30.

With the Dordrecht link fading, Sevenoaks Rotary Club plans to link up with the French Rotary Club of Le Touquet.

August: Sevenoaks twins Tim and William Hoad, 18, crew together to win the British School's sailing championship.

Librarian George Bennett and H.A. Lampkin are the only two surviving officers of Sevenoaks Urban Council of 1920.

THE long-awaited, much-needed bypass did come in the 1960s but it was considerably longer than the two years promised before another amended route was approved by Kent County Council and Cementation won the contract for one of the most scenically attractive new roads in southern England. In the meantime it was a railway line that incited local people to let off steam. So much steam, in fact, that the issue reached both the House of Lords and the Commons.

In April 1960 the *Chronicle* reported that the branch line from Dunton Green to Westerham was to close. Next week this letter appeared: *"Those of us who use the passenger trains to travel on and for whom no equally efficient service is available are horrified to hear that plans are afoot to close our wonderful little railway line and are shocked by the general air of resignation which pervades your notice in last week's paper."*

Suddenly the people of Westerham, Chevening, Brasted and Dunton Green seemed to wake up. Minister of Transport, Ernest Marples, in one of his sweeping reforms, had decided the five-mile railroad through the fertile Holmesdale Valley was not paying its way and would have to go. In May a *Save the Westerham Flyer* campaign was launched followed by a petition. By June so many passengers were travelling on this once little-used service that the majority had to stand. As the list of those who opposed the closure grew and grew it was announced that Lord Stanhope, who frequently travelled on The Flyer from Chevening to Dunton Green on his way to London, would raise the matter in the House of Lords.

MP John Rodgers also opened an adjournment debate in the Commons but Mr Marples refused to alter his decision. He said: "I have walked the length of that line in dark glasses so no-one would recognise me. Believe me, it is not viable. In Westerham they have a use of adjectives which I have never experienced before and most of them are directed against me."

The railway line, promoted by local enterprise in 1881, closed soon after its 80th birthday on Saturday October 28, 1961. The Q-type engine pulling seven carriages left Westerham at 8.10 am. Among the passengers on this final journey was 82-year-old Jane Graves who, in her mother's arms, travelled on the first train in 1881. As the Flyer steamed through Brasted the name of the station, previously spelt out in stones, had been rearranged to read RIP. In time attempts were made to float a preservation society but that idea, too, was soon scotched.

Other ideas did not founder so dramatically. During the 1960 speech day, Kim Taylor, headmaster of Sevenoaks School, said he would like to introduce an International sixth form and a voluntary service unit. The latter followed a visit to the school by Kurt Hahn, the founder of the public school Gordonstoun,

1960

The £2m Sevenoaks bypass is given top priority by Ernest Marples. The route will run from Riverhill to Dunton Green.

Kent County Council rejects the Max Lock redevelopment scheme. It does not approve of a cul-de-sac to the east of Sevenoaks High Street.

1961

January: Chief Inspector H.A. Hosier becomes Sevenoaks' new police chief.

Ibbett Moseley and Card attempts to auction the Granada cinema building but bidding stops at £59,000 and it is withdrawn.

February: Sir John Dunlop tells members of St John's Ward: "I am an awfully poor man but I will gladly bet half a crown that the Sevenoaks redevelopment plan will start within four months!"

Sir Oliver Lyle, managing director of Tate and Lyle, of Kemsing, dies aged 70.

Kent cricketers Ray Dover and Colin Page agree to coach youngsters at the Sevenoaks indoor cricket school.

When Buckhurst Lane was widened in April 1961 two shops, Achille Serre, cleaners and the Chain Library had to be demolished. The building on the right shows the back of Timothy Whites and Taylors with the Holmesdale Tavern in the background. This is now the entrance to the bus station.

who spoke about the role of young people in society and how they could "arrest the decay of care and skill, the decay of enterprise and adventure and the decay of compassion". The Taylor scheme was adopted and volunteers stepped forward. VSU was born...

Two months later, in September 1960, the Granada died. Manager Mike Maynard told his staff they would no longer be required because "television and the modern trend towards canned entertainment was affecting the viability of the cinema". A few days later the Granada attracted its first full house for many years — not in sympathy at its demise but simply because the fittings were being sold at knock-down prices. There was a scramble for clocks, spotlights, carpets and especially tip-up seats for a tanner each. It was an undignified goodbye. Down on the Otford Road there was another. As Sevenoaks was now receiving its gas supply in pipes from Dartford the big holders had become redundant and the decision was made to demolish them. One came down immediately; the other two survived.

It was also in September that a large party of Sevenoaks residents, led by Sir John Dunlop, took part in a moving ceremony to commemorate the 200th anniversary of Sir Jeffrey Amherst's capture of Montreal and the capitulation of the French Government in Canada. They gathered at the famous obelisk and heard Chester Barratt declare: "To all Canadians this is sacred soil. During the war tens of thousands of young Canadians essayed a pilgrimage to Montreal House, the home of Lord Amherst, only to find

David Peacock's vision of Chevening Halt before the famous railroad was finally demolished.

Percy Reid, *Sevenoaks Chronicle's* reporter in charge of Westerham, is appointed president of the National Union of Journalists — the first country journalist to receive such an honour.

July: Thirty-five French girls, in Sevenoaks to learn English, say they don't like the local boys with long hair or the "Blousons Noire" — those with black leather jackets.

Sam King loses to California's Paul Runyon in the final of the Senior Professional world championships.

August: A Volkswagen car, fitted with special rudders and extended exhausts, drives across Chipstead Lake. The owner hopes the car will now pioneer journeys across the English Channel.

September: One hundred members of the Sevenoaks branch of CND join a protest in Trafalgar Square.

Sevenoaks Urban Council introduces parking fees.

October: Oliver Bonnett of Sevenoaks and John Boreham of Kemsing travel to Russia to supervise the laying of Marley tiles on the floor of the new congress hall in the Kremlin.

Oak Bank open air school, Seal — which opened its doors to under-nourished children in 1920 — is to close.

1962

January: The Munchery, a once-thriving cafeteria in the car park, is to close.

The Rev R.L. Travis, vicar of Sevenoaks Weald, refuses to allow the Weald Forgers the use of St George's Hall because their play, *Harlequinade* by Terrence Rattigan, is too sordid.

February: No waiting restrictions are introduced in Sevenoaks High Street.

it demolished. All that is left apart from the obelisk is the stable house where Captain Knight and his eagle Mr Ramshaw live, and the old summerhouse."

The Sevenoaks party who listened to the speeches on that warm late summer evening would have been surrounded by scores and scores of unfinished, but elegant, homes — for the Montreal Park development scheme was under way and much of Marlborough Crescent was still being carefully laid out by Salway Hill Estates. The land had actually been bought from the Amherst family in 1926 by Mr J.J.Runge, who had no intention of demolishing the house or building new homes but when he died, in debt, in 1935, his heirs sold the mansion and 160 acres (including Brittain's Farm) to Bernard Thorpe for under £40,000. Although it was in good condition Montreal House was taken down and sold with the land to Mr Fasey of Salway Hill. His ambitious plan for about 600 homes was thwarted by the war and building did not commence until 1953. By then it had been amended to 260 homes, each valued at approximately £10,000. (At the end of the century the same houses are changing hands for £350,000).

By 1961 the demolition men were also in Sevenoaks High Street. They bulldozed two timber-framed shops formerly occupied by Achille Serre and the Chain Library in order to widen the entrance to Buckhurst Lane and then turned their attention to Redman's Place between Barclays Bank and Eric Kemp the jewellers. Having flattened this little back alley, described by the Chronicle as "one of the older and more squalid parts of Sevenoaks", they took down a large barn used by one of the market traders for the storage of his fruit boxes. The builders would not have known that this was the site of a chapel opened by John Wesley in 1774 which served Sevenoaks well until a new Methodist chapel was built in Bank Street. A small memorial plaque was promised for the site.

Charlie, the 4th Lord Sackville, died at Knole in May 1962 aged 91 and a memorial service was held at St Nicholas conducted by the Rev Eric McLellan. He was succeeded by his batchelor son Eddy, the novelist, critic and musician who lived in Ireland and had no intention of "living at that big place in Kent". Before he died (in 1965) he wrote: "My cousin Lionel luckily loves the house and can put up with this and other features of the modern world, none of which I can abide." In fact Lionel, who was to become the 6th Lord Sackville, had already moved into a wing of the house with his large family. His brother Hugh joined him six years later.

It was the weather which made the news in 1963 for the snow which fell on Boxing Day night lay so thickly that lawns, fields and village greens were not visible again until March. Week after week, blizzard after blizzard, the *Chronicle* made reference to the weather and, as this Siberian winter entered its ninth week, said: *"There is still no sign of a let-up. Side streets are still encased in an armour of frozen snow as solid as the macadam itself. It is trying for us all. Even children, having exhausted the novelties of sledging, long to see the grass again. Business is slack, sport and social life has withered and elderly folk are suffering real privation — housebound, cold and bored. Sevenoaks, like a besieged city, is longing for relief."*

The great controversy of 1963 (apart from the weather) concerned the future of The White House, which stood opposite The Red House in Sevenoaks High

1962

John Profumo, Secretary of State for War confers the title Royal on the Armament Research and Development Establishment at Fort Halstead.

May: Peggy Fenner is chairman of Sevenoaks Urban Council.

Dr Gordon Ward, historian, philatelist, archaeologist, prolific writer and former general practitioner, dies at Oastfield Court, aged 77.

The Sevenoaks redevelopment plan is rejected by a Ministry inspector. Proposals do not take sufficient account of the present unusual architecural unity, scale and atmosphere of the High Street, he says.

The former Ormiston Hotel in Oak Lane is acquired by Sevenoaks School for its International Centre. It will accommodate 48 boys.

September: A memorial tablet to the Battle of Solefields is unveiled by Lord Cornwallis.

The Montreal summerhouse is not of sufficient importance to warrant a preservation order, the rural council is told.

December: The Rev Martin Heal is the new vicar of St. John's.

1963

January: News that the urban council plans to pay £7,000 and instruct a new firm of consultants to prepare a town redevelopment scheme, will be viewed with much misgiving by ratepayers, the *Chronicle* says.

April: Woods Garage and a number of shops on London Road, Riverhead are demolished to make way for a dual carriageway.

More than 5,000 people flock to a Conservative rally at Chevening to hear the Deputy Prime Minister Rab Butler, speak

Completed at last. Montreal Estate from the air.

Street. For many years it had been an antique business (Martin and Dolton) which moved from its previous site, later occupied by Woolworth, in the 1920s. Before he died Clifford Dolton sold the house to Rupert Samuelson of Godden Green, also an antiques dealer, who appealed, in February 1963, against the building's preservation order. There was immediate outrage. The urban council and the preservation society opposed the appeal and Sir John Dunlop told a public meeting that the White House was formerly two cottages and the Georgian front was added in 1810. It was listed Grade II along with The Chequers Inn.

A Government inspector, who presided at an inquiry, was told by an expert on Georgian architecture that the White House presented an imposing facade, was structurally sound and worthy of preservation. Mr Samuelson's team presented an opposite view. The inspector considered the case and, to the dismay of most of Sevenoaks, said the building was a warren of staircases and passages suffering from the ravages of death watch beetle and dry rot. "The preservation order", he said, "is not justified either economically or architecturally."

Some years later the White House was demolished.

1964 was the year in which everything, except the town redevelopment plan, began to come together. A start was made on the new maternity wing, a house in Dartford Road was converted into flats for the elderly, Christ Church Presbyterian Church was opened, work began on building the "much-needed" skyscraper office block at Tubs Hill — with all but a few "cynical *Chronicle* readers" confident that the 91,000 square feet of office space would be quickly snapped up by London businesses. And, to the delight of Sir Charles Pym, the former chairman of Kent County Council and Sevenoaks Rural Council who

Joe Russell was well known in local pubs, on a variety of racecourses and particular by those who sat in his barber's chair in Dorset Street.

The White House — 'preservation order not justified,' said the inspector.

had campaigned for a bypass since 1924, the ribbon was cut and work commenced. It was a bitter-sweet moment for Sir Charles for the route followed part of his beloved Westerham branch line and the track was immediately ripped up. A few days later the lovely Anchor Cottages, Hubbard's Hill, suffered the same fate.

So, at last, all was well with the bypass. Or was it? During one of his regular Monday morning meetings with the resident engineer, Mr John Shadbolt, *Chronicle* reporter Gordon Anckorn sensed the constructors were troubled although no official statement was issued. Gordon, then with 36 years' experience as a newspaper reporter, smelt a scoop — a scoop that may even earn a bob or two from the nationals. He began to dig around even more furiously than the giant earth removers on the site.

What he discovered was quite sensational. The land between Hubbard's Hill and Riverhill was slipping. The engineers had identified five major mud slides pouring into a vast underground lake containing millions of gallons of water. As work on the slopes overlooking Sevenoaks Weald was halted, geologists were invited to give more information. The fault in the escarpment, they said, was caused by the thaw which followed the Ice Age when landslides had first occurred. They said the bend in Riverhill dated from the days of the pack horse when travellers made a road round the clay outcrop which extruded from the hill. There was a massive geological defect along the southern slopes of the Greensand ridge.

It meant that the route of the bypass would have to be altered and landowners asked if they would release part of their land. The Hubbard's Hill bridge would have to be dismantled and re-erected further up the hill where the soil was stronger. Calamitously, the extra cost would be in excess of £1¼ million and

1964

Sir John Dunlop tells the town planning committee that the proposed Eastern Way relief road may still be 10 years away.

March: Gipsy caravans and 37 lorry loads of derelict car bodies are removed from Hosey Common. The rural council is told they must nominate an official site for the local gipsies.

April: Sandpits on the Bradbourne Estate may become the site for the council's new rubbish tip. Local residents protest.

The partly-clothed body of a Chinese woman is found in Shacklands Wood, Badgers Mount. She has been strangled.

May: Christ Church Presbyterian Church opens. The London Moderator, the Rev E.C. Lane, conducts the service.

the finishing date extended by perhaps two years.

Never mind, it was a good story for the *Chronicle* during a period in which the paper, now under the editorship of Vic Froud, was showing its campaigning disposition.

An example of this came with the death, from bronchitis, of a five-month-old gipsy girl at the illegal camp in Dry Hill, Sundridge. Minty Rose Smith lived with 44 adults in caravans surrounded by derelict car bodies and rubbish. The mud was so deep that the children could not leave their homes and water was collected from a polluted brook nearby.

The gipsy problem had plagued the area, and particularly the rural council, for years. 'Move them away' was the oft-heard cry. The *Chronicle*, appalled by the death of little Minty took a different view. *"Her death throws revealing light on the conditions in which she and hundreds of local gipsies live — conditions for which, to a large extent, public apathy and antagonism are responsible... Medical men are shocked; it is a disgrace to Sevenoaks and to the county of Kent."*

A public meeting, *The Gipsies and Us,* was arranged and 100 chairs laid out at St Nicholas' Church Hall. But more than 250 attended, including the residents of Dry Hill and the BBC. Chaired superbly by Canon Aidan Chapman of Westerham, the meeting passed a resolution urging every village to allocate a small site for a gipsy family and appealed to community organisations, schools and the newly-formed Voluntary Service Unit to help establish training centres so the gipsies could be rehabilitated before moving into council homes.

The gipsy encampment at Dry Hill Park, Sundridge, where little Minty Smith died.

1964

More than 150 mods and rockers beseige Bligh's Hotel and fighting breaks out near King's Hall. The police make four arrests.

Sevenoaks MP John Rodgers is knighted. He is currently deputy chairman of J.Walter Thompson and author of many books including a history of public schools in England.

July: Assa George Singh is jailed for life for murdering his Chinese wife the day after insuring her life for £10,000.

August: *Sevenoaks Chronicle* editor Vic Froud travels to Belgium with the local branch of the Old Contemptibles Association. They visit the sites where their comrades fell.

September: A by pass for the village of Ightham opens.

Sir Charles Pym, who has been proclaiming the need for a Sevenoaks by pass since 1924, cuts the ribbon to set work in motion.

Westerham's Black Eagle Brewery, where ale has been brewed for 300 years, is to close with 69 redundancies.

October: Rodgers wins the Sevenoaks seat with a majority of 13,000-plus but the Tory Government falls.

The Westerham to Dunton Green railway line is pulled up to accommodate part of the Sevenoaks by-pass. Anchor Cottages, Hubbard's Hill, are also demolished.

A Government Minister approves a site in Hever Lane, Edenbridge, as a permanent gipsy encampment.

December: The bells of St Mary's Church, Westerham peal in recognition of Sir Winston Churchill's 90th birthday. The Rotary Club toasts their honorary member.

Some months after the gispies had left Dry Hill Park, Sundridge and moved into a new site at Edenbridge, the **Chronicle** *went to see the Smith family to see how they were coping. They found old Amos confined to bed after a heart attack but still practising his skills on the violin. Amos said he had played the violin (and especially the melodeon) all over the world. He also said he'd never been out of Kent. The Smith family were happy in the new camp and told* **Chronicle** *photographer Alex Watson that they were sorry for the trouble they had caused.*

In June 1965, Mr Clemens, director of Messrs Pattullo and Vinson, announced that his firm wanted to re-establish the open market which had existed in Sevenoaks before the war when traders came from London and neighbouring towns with a diversity of wares. "It used to be a feature of our activities," he said. "We want to establish a happy hunting ground for housewives, browsers and collectors. A Petticoat Lane operation in Sevenoaks can flourish." And, of course, it did. Opening in October of that year on land re-levelled by Patullo and Vinson, the Sevenoaks Wednesday Market quickly became the envy of many similar towns in south-east England.

That was good news. So was the opening of the Sevenoaks Maternity Wing by Baroness Clementine Churchill who said: "It is a landmark in the history of Sevenoaks Hospital." On October 5, 1965, Susan Turner gave birth to Sarah, the first baby to be born in the wing.

By 1967 more and more young people in Sevenoaks were experimenting with marijuana (which slowed them down) and LSD (a hallucinogen). Sevenoaks CID had a busy time raiding parties and trying to nail the pushers. Senior schools reprimanded, or even expelled, those who took drugs. To the dismay

On June 24, 1966, a coach carrying 33 girls from Sevenoaks and Riverhead skidded on the wet road at Riverhill, plunged over a 15-foot embankment and overturned onto its side. The driver, Fred Hatward and the girls amazingly escaped with minor injuries. This picture shows Janice Lyne (head bandaged), Sarah Watts (with tennis racket) and Susan Clark leaving the scene of the crash.

1965

January: Sir Winston Churchill dies; Westerham discusses the possibility of a statue on the Green.

To help provide for heavy estate duty on assets left by Lord Sackville, a substantial part of the Knole art collection is offered to the Treasury.

Lord Stanhope threatens to sue the rural council if gipsies are allowed on his land.

March: The National Trust takes control of Chartwell.

April: George Bennett retires as chief librarian at Sevenoaks after 35 years in that post. His successor is George Lawrence.

Ernie Withey, landlord of The Chequers for 15 years, retires. Les and Marie Weeden are the new tenants.

of a few church leaders, and those who disapproved, the hem lines on mini-skirts became higher and higher. *Courier* newpapers, owners of the *Sevenoaks Chronicle*, sent a memo to the editors instructing them that girl reporters must not wear dresses which were more than two inches above the knee.

The *Chronicle*, taking full advantage of the existence of a lucrative teenage market, slightly changed its image and introduced a weekly Fashion Spotter, an attractive young lady, usually in a mini-skirt. It also began a regular weekly pop column with a top ten supplied by the record shops. When the Beatles came to Sevenoaks on February 3, 1967, a page of pictures was published alongside a full story of this "historic moment". That issue was a sell-out.

The civic issues, however, refused to go away and when Sevenoaks Urban Council issued an enforcement notice on Pattullo and Vinson ordering them to close the Wednesday Market until proper planning permission was obtained, housewives were furious. The *Chronicle* organised a survey of public opinion with a form on the front page. Hundreds replied and the result was 95.6 per cent in favour of the market and 4.4 against. One lady from Kippington said

1965

The gap in the High Street between David Grieg and Ackermans which has been an eyesore ever since the former shop (Youngs furniture) was destroyed by a bomb in 1940, has been replaced by a shop.

A 15-strong Sevenoaks delegation led by Sir John Dunlop visits Pontoise in France to help further the twinning arrangements which were inaugurated last year. Pontoise is an ancient French town on the River Oise which was occupied by the English during the 100 Years War.

June: Charles Robinson gives Ightham Mote to the nation.

Three girls, Carol Britton, 18 and Linda Groves, 18, of Sevenoaks and Patricia Smith 17, of Halstead die in a car crash near Hildenborough.

October: A Citizen's Advice Bureau opens in Sevenoaks.

Well-known Sevenoaks citizens Sir John Dunlop and Joe Boakes present Sevenoaks with a new coat of arms.

New industries are welcomed to the Vestry Estate on the Otford Road.

December: Audrey McMenamy of Hitchen Hatch Lane is barred from entering Sevenoaks Cattle Market because of the trouble she causes over "her concern about unnecessary suffering of animals and birds".

George Simmonds and his wife retire as Akela and Baloo of the 1st Sevenoaks cub pack.

1966

January: Several shops between Buckhurst Avenue and Locks Yard are still empty. When is the High Street redevelopment going to start, *Chronicle* readers ask.

When five local girls heard that the Beatles were due to make a television film in Knole Park they played truant from school, found a ringside seat and waited for the "fab four". Paul, John, Ringo and George duly turned up and gave each girl an autograph if they promised not to tell their friends. The girls then watched the first day's shooting for the promotional film due to be played on Top of The Pops to accompany the boys' new songs, Strawberry Fields Forever *and* Penny Lane.

For obvious reasons the girls refused to give their names but one of them said: "I fainted three times. None of us have ever had such a wonderful thing happen." Another said: "I don't care if my headmistress turns up. I'm not leaving. I will stay here all night."

In fact they went home, told some of their friends and found themselves next day among hundreds of boys and girls. The supposedly deserted hillside to the south of the house was a sea of straw boaters as pupils from Sevenoaks School joined those who were already there.

There was no mass hysteria which the Beatles usually seem to attract so they were able to continue with another day's filming. During the evening they ate in a High Street restaurant and were seen in a few shops.

1966

Gracious Lane, Sevenoaks will be a temporary link road while work on the southern end of bypass continues.

Edward Styles replaces A.C.R. Scully as district county commissioner.

February: Paynes Stores, a family grocer since start of the century, closes. One man, Walter Best, worked there for 50 years.

Scores of ratepayers are locked out of the council chamber as the urban council discusses, in private, a new plan for Sevenoaks town.

Small colonies of gipsies drift back to sites at Polhill, Otford and Rooks Hill.

Landlords of houses in Argyle Road, Beech Road and Victoria Road are told to equip them with baths, indoor toilets and hot and cold running water. One landlord, Hugh Outram says the rents will rise.

April: Peter Pearce (Labour) cuts John Rodger's majority in the General Election by 3,000.

Alex Cook retires after 40 years with the RSPCA.

Three traffic wardens start work on the streets of Sevenoaks.

May: Sevenoaks Preservation Society places plaques on all buildings of historic interest.

Chartwell staff say they are prepared for 50,000 vistors a year when home opens to the public in the summer.

A bid is made to turn Drill Hall, Argyle Road into a town theatre. The TA is due to leave next year.

Schoolteacher John Claudet becomes the first bachelor chairman of Sevenoaks Urban Council.

the market was making local traders improve their dreadful attitude and quality of service. Encouraged by this, Patullo and Vinson appealed and at a subsequent inquiry, which lasted only two hours, they were given permission to keep the market open. It was the turn of traders and the council to be furious.

No-one could fault Dorothy Parrott's devotion to duty. She represented the Conservative party on both the urban and county council, belonged to scores of local organisations, supported the Church of England and was loved by most people. But when she opposed the building of a new primary school, St Thomas' on land near her home in Crownfields, the Catholic community turned on her.

In fact Dorothy was in such trouble that the Tory party decided to nominate Anthony Wylson, a new candidate, for the forthcoming KCC elections and were rather astonished when Miss Parrott, who loved a good fight, stood against him as an independent. In the biggest turnout ever known in Sevenoaks for a KCC election, Wylson scraped home. Some time later building work on the new Catholic primary school began.

This story ran for weeks. On one occasion *Chronicle* reporter Peter Willoughby called on Miss Parrott for the latest news of her campaign not knowing that the Conservative agent, Lyndon Williams was hiding in the cupboard!

1968 was the year the urban council engaged, at an unbelievable cost, England's top traffic consultant, Professor Colin Buchanan to prepare a new town plan and road network. In a 60-page close-knit analysis of the town's problems he produced three alternative "solutions", the most revolutionary of which took traffic from the Tonbridge Road at Park Grange to the west of the High Street behind Rockdale, the Odeon and Argyle Road to join up with main road near the Vine. The other two were similar to those discussed many times before.

The *Chronicle*, sensing wrongly that the council would not engage someone as expensive and famous as Buchanan to prepare a plan that would be ditched, produced an eight-page supplement and sought reactions from various councillors. Eventually the Buchanan Plan joined the others in the council dustbin which prompted estate agents Jack Holt of Parsons, Charles Hodgins, and Humphrey Wickham of Ibbetts to issue a statement accusing the council of creating a Frankenstein monster which would loom over Sevenoaks for many years to come. They were echoing exactly the sentiments of Cr Hoad from a previous decade.

More positive news in 1968 concerned the decision to build a new social club, provide Lady Boswell with a new school, prepare a site next door to the Odeon for a new post office, open new flatlets at Rockdale and, thanks to the Boys Brigade, revive the town carnival. It was also the year that Sevenoaks by pass officially opened all the way with the engineer's daughters Pamela and Rosemary Shadbolt cutting the tape.

Two dramatic events occurred that year. In August a huge tanker overturned on the A25 by the Chipstead flyover and 6,000 gallons of petrol poured onto the road and then exploded. Mushroom clouds soared 300 feet in the air sending fire brigades racing to the scene from all directions. No-one was hurt.

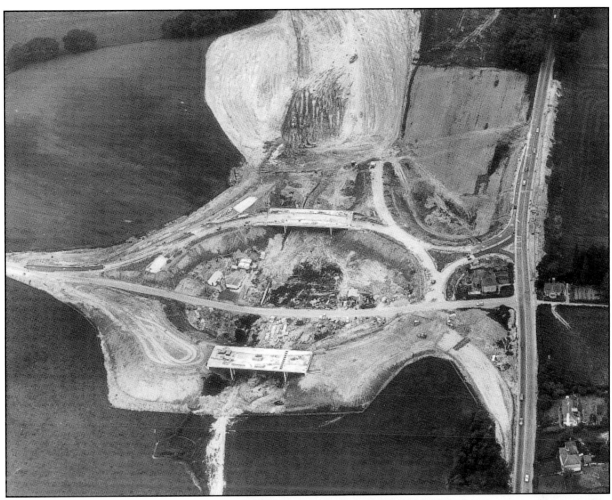

This aerial photograph of the bypass progress was taken by Alex Watson in June 1967 where the Morley's roundabout was taking shape. The landslip between Riverhill and Hubbard's Hill had already occurred and engineers were busy dismantling the completed Hubbard's Hill bridge and re-erecting it further up the hill. Notice, in the middle (right) Queen Anne cottages (formerly an inn) surrounded by roads. George Cheeseman who lived here with his mother said he would like to stay. He later changed his mind. Work on the by-pass began in 1964 and was due to be completed two years later. It took four years but the result was one of the most scenically attractive new roads in southern England. Right: The Bayley's Hill bridge which won a design award for its constructors, Cementation.

1966

June: Bandits throw ammonia in the eyes of two garage employees, Chris Smith and Miss J. Harrison and rob them of £700.

Riverhead primary school opens. Fred Poole is headmaster.

The famous eight bells of St Nicholas are retuned and returned. The cost is £4,450.

Three railway officials are beaten to the ground by iron bars as masked bandits escape with £1,500 of wages.

July: Charles Coupland succeeds the Rev Tom Jarrett as Minister of the Congregational Church.

An urban council dustman is given the tenancy of a £7,000 house in Pembroke Road. The urban council had planned to demolish it for an entrance to the car park.

Sevenoaks News editor, Donald Hooper dies aged 66. Vic Froud is appointed editor. David Pluck, 34, becomes new editor of the *Chronicle*.

Two caravans, towed by members of Sevenoaks Round Table, leave Sevenoaks on a 2,000-mile mercy dash to Turkey where thousands have died in an earthquake. Among those to make the trip are Roy Dickens, Bryan Richardson, Ray Jolly, Jim Davis and George Baldwin. Only one caravan manages to get through.

October: No 23 Eardley Road is identified as the house in which H.G.Wells lived and wrote *The Time Machine*.

November: Professor Buchanan is appointed to prepare a new traffic plan for Sevenoaks at a cost of £12,500. The press and public are excluded from the meeting.

The floods of 1968... 'must not be allowed to happen again'

A month later, in the early hours of Sunday September 15, a few spots of rain pattered gently onto rooftops throughout the district. The rain increased in its intensity and was transformed into a downpour of tropical proportions. It rained all night and all day Sunday and by that evening Kent (and Sevenoaks) was experiencing one of the most serious natural disasters of the century. Some 2,400 square miles had received as much as 400 tons of water per acre, fast-flowing flood water that embraced everything within its reach. The gentle River Darent, assuming all its ancient powers, could not cope with the sheer weight and speed of the water which quickly overlapped fields and roads and then homes. Westerham was flooded badly as were Brasted and Sundridge.

Chipstead Lake grew massively in size and the garden of a house called Hedgehogs was dramatically swept away. With it went a garage and a car and nearby lawns and fences. A state of emergency was declared in the village and an amphibious vehicle took more than 100 families to safety.

Still the rain poured down from a relentless sky, hissing and bubbling as it landed. By midnight on Sunday the Darent had completely covered the old stone bridge at Shoreham and was slopping against doors and windows. The bridge held firm but one at Otford was swept away. People brought out rubber dinghies and small boats but abandoned them as the torrent surged on. At Westerham the water came rushing down from the hillside on either side. Vast lakes were created in the areas around Pitts Cottage to the west and The Old House at Home to the east. The meeting point was Quebec Square where General Wolfe, his sword aloft, looked down on the enemy rapidly closing in.

Sevenoaks itself, 650 feet above sea level, did not escape. Rain gathering in the valleys of Knole suddenly burst through the ragstone wall and great waves gushed down Seal Hollow Road. In Mill Lane and lower-lying areas of the town, families waded chest-deep to rescue belongings. Dorothy Parrot, then chairman of the urban council, also waded in to give comfort to those in distress.

In Grassy Lane, in upper Sevenoaks, the water rose to 15 ft and families were rescued by neighbours with boats. Everywhere sewage spewed from blocked drains to form a sea of mud; trees and shrubs were torn from the ground.

Rescue centres were set up by the police, women's institutes and other voluntary organisations. Fire and ambulance services were overstretched but received valuable assistance from reservists. As 80 men of the Army Road Transport Corps worked all Monday night to erect a Bailey Bridge at Otford, the cry went out from all corners of Sevenoaks: "This must not be allowed to happen again."

For many weeks after the floods had subsided there was the heart-breaking work of mopping up, drying out and repairing and rebuilding. Many local people received Government aid.

1968 was one of the wettest years of the century and almost certainly contributed to an extraordinary event in January 1969 when a gaping 150 foot long crack opened in the road at Hanging Bank, Ide Hill, on the road to Edenbridge. The hole grew from 20 to 300 inches wide sending tons and tons of earth sliding down the hill from the garden of Mr and Mrs John Deed at Croachs. They were evacuated and so were their gardeners, Mr and Mrs George Bridger from their cottage.

Doctor Archer takes to a dinghy in Grassy Lane where water rose to 15 feet and many families had to be rescued by neighbours with boats.

To the rescue: The irrepressible Dorothy Parrott, chairman of the council in 1968, tucks the chain of office in her pocket, dons her wellies, picks up her skirts and wades into the floodwaters while a crowd of people look on in amazement. Her mission: to give a little assurance that all would be well to the beleaguered cottagers of Mill Lane.

1966

Patrick Mayhew, a barrister from The White House, Gracious Lane, is chosen as prospective parliamentary candidate for Dulwich.

December: Plans for a new Sevenoaks Services (or Social Club) are prepared. The architect is Arthur Cooksey.

1967

January: Morants Court Bridge which runs over the bypass at Dunton Green will have to be partially rebuilt because of a construction fault.

March: A Hurricane, piloted by Group Captain Tom Gleave and shot down in 1940, has been found in woods at Knockholt. Tom, who baled out badly burned, was a founder member of the famous Guinea Pigs Club.

April: Henry Phillips, engineer and surveyor to Sevenoaks Urban Council for 20 years, retires. Alan Bennett, 42, from Potters Bar, takes his place.

Hubbard's Hill will close for nine months to speed by-pass work.

July: The Salvation Army refuses to sell the decaying Sevenoaks Citadel in Cedar Tree Terrace to the Jehovah's Witnesses.

The Rev Leonard Lane commences his ministry at the Vine Baptist Church.

Yellow lines have appeared on roads in Sevenoaks, confusing many people.

August: Lord and Lady Colgrain of Everlands, Bayley's Hill, celebrate their golden wedding.

October: Former Irish international footballer Ray Brady and his wife Faith take over the Railway and Bicycle pub, by the railway station, from Nobby Clark, the man who donated the annual knock-out cricket trophy.

This is Seal Hollow Road on Sunday September 15, 1968. The rainwater which had gathered

in the valley of Knole Park suddenly burst through the ragstone wall and a great torrent swept down the hill.

Engineer Jack Hayton (fourth from left back row) and the staff of Sevenoaks and Tonbridge Waterworks Company at a Christmas party. The headquarters of the company was in Cramptons Road. These jolly people had also recently celebrated the 100th anniversary of piped water supply because it was in the mid-1860s that a team of contractors, digging the railway tunnel between Sevenoaks and Tonbridge, encountered so much water that a 120-foot well was sunk close to the tunnel at Oak Lane. A pumping station was erected, a reservoir built and water distributed throughout the town. In 1901 further wells were dug at Kemsing and new service reservoirs constructed at Solefields and Seal Chart. Two artesian boreholes were sunk at Cramptons Road in 1934 augmented by a further two in 1956. It was in 1948 that the Sevenoaks and Tonbridge Companies amalgamated. They were joined by Tunbridge Wells in 1973 when the West Kent Water Company was born.

1967

Plans for the re-organisation of secondary education in Sevenoaks are scrapped.

A new Hatton secondary school for girls is to be built on land at Bradbourne Vale Road for an estimated £166,000.

George Cheeseman and his mother who live at Queen Anne's cottage at the foot of Riverhill say they are not concerned by the fact that a traffic roundabout completely encircles their home. They like the idea of living on an island!

November: As a breathalyser is introduced for motorists who over-imbibe, two housewives set up a "drinkmaster service" taking customers home from pubs.

December: The Sevenoaks fatstock show is cancelled for the first time in 34 years because of foot and mouth disease.

As geologists studied this latest phenomenon a second crack, also 120 feet long, appeared on Bayley's Hill and more homes were in danger of "disappearing". Geologists said it was linked to the by pass slip of 1966. "The whole escarpment", they said, "has a high water table which tends to lubricate the side planes in the porous Hythe beds and then flow like liquid." After nine months of anguish the Bridgers and the Deeds nervously returned to start rebuilding their homes.

An atmosphere of uncertainty also hung over the town centre. With the rejection of the Buchanan report and no clear idea of what was going to happen traders began to move away and Sevenoaks took on the appearance of a ghost

1967

Vine cricketers vote against playing on The Vine on a Sunday.

1968

January: It is reported that Owen Aisher's (chairman of Marley Tile) salary in 1967 was £91,000.

February: Panda police cars make their appearance in Sevenoaks.

Richard Liversedge of Fawke Common takes part in the Olympic Games toboggan event at Grenoble.

March: Sevenoaks School headmaster Kim Taylor accepts an appointment with the Nuffield Foundation.
Dr Michael Hinton from Dover Grammar School takes his place.

Cricketer Colin Cowdrey returns to his home near Westerham having captained England to a series win in the West Indies.

Sevenoaks is a big bore, say teenagers. That's why we go to Bromley or Maidstone.

May: Sevenoaks School teacher David Howie has a plan to streamline the activities of all welfare organisations in the town.

The *Amherst Arms* is to be renamed the *Dog and Duck*. Riverhead residents are furious. The brewers relent and call it *The Riverhead*.

1969

January: A mystery oil slick kills 10 ducks at Bradbourne Lakes.

Sevenoaks Urban Council suggests building a tunnel under the High Street.

May: Freston Lodge school runs into financial trouble and will close. Headmaster John Claudet, former urban council chairman, leaves the area.

Chronicle photographer, Roger Tutt took this dramatic picture of the tanker which overturned by the Chipstead flyover in 1968. Although the by-pass had just been completed the area was still described as Chipstead corner.

town. The High Street was blighted by empty shops including Frank's, the former ironmongers, Wright's, the haberdashery store, Home and Colonial, one of the first of the chain grocers, Castle wine shop and Rallypoint. The White House and the six shops backing onto the Shambles were waiting for the executioner and Staples greengrocers had been taken over by Oxfam.

The decade ended on a tragic note. Adrienne Ferryman, Blind Horsewoman of the Year, was found dead at her home in Meadow Close of asphyxia after an overdose of barbiturates. At the time her husband Colin was having an affair with a 17-year-old girl groom from Bradbourne Riding Stables whom he later married. At an inquest in July the coroner recorded an open verdict.

Later in the same month 21-year-old Diana Davidson from The Butts, Otford, was found strangled at Paddock Wood close to the ground where she was watching her boyfriend play cricket. After a dramatic reconstruction of the tragedy, in which a young policewoman took the place of Diana, a 30-year-old unemployed farm labourer was found guilty and jailed for life.

1969

John Hill of Mount Field, Weald is the new Kent county council chairman.

The Ambulance station moves from Robyns Way to a new site in Moor Road. The cost is £60,000.

April: Bob Ogley, 29-year-old Sennockian, becomes editor of the *Sevenoaks Chronicle*.

Photographs of Apollo II, taking Neil Armstrong and his colleagues to the moon, are taken by Commander H.R. Hatfield of Clarenden Road, the country's leading authority on lunar photography.

Residents of Riverhead and Montreal Park are incensed by plans to transfer the famous obelisk to Amherst in Massachusetts. They tell solicitors for Earl Amherst that it is part of Riverhead's history.

August: Janet Webb wants permission to build a 30-unit hotel in Longspring Wood, Gracious Lane.

Work starts on the Tonbridge by pass.

October: 15 Sevenoaks Rotarians are hit by a mystery illness after their Friday lunch at Bligh's.

The Sevenoaks School Council wants to ban the biff. Jack Horncastle says his shop has sold the straw hat for most of this century.

Lord Sackville, chairman of the steering committee, announces plans for a Cheshire Home in Sevenoaks.

December: Canon Eric McLellan, rector for 15 years, leaves for a new post in Paris.

Vine and Holmesdale cricket clubs plan to join a Kent "super" league.

Elfreda Davies succeeds Miss Blackburn as headmistress of Walthamstow Hall.

This parade of shops was demolished in 1969. For young people the greatest loss was La Cabana, the popular Espresso Coffee bar, where they gathered in the late 50s and early 60s. Hundreds of romances blossomed in this building.

Canon Eric McLellan, Rector of St Nicholas' for 15 years.

Bernard and Peggy Fenner at home in St Nicholas Drive, Sevenoaks, in 1969. Bernard was an architect and Peggy chairman of Sevenoaks Urban Council during some of the most difficult years. In 1970 she won the Rochester and Chatham seat and took her place in the House of Commons, eventually retiring in 1997.

1970

January: Plans for a massive new telephone exchange by the Odeon car park will be a disaster, says officials of nearby Rockdale old folks' home.

February: Hughie Outram celebrates his 90th birthday. He inherited the High Street shop from his father, James, 40 years ago when it was largely a saddlers and harness makers. He first rode with the West Kent Hunt 75 years ago and owned many splendid horses.

April: The new post office, the third postal headquarters in Sevenoaks in 300 years, is opened by Dorothy Parrott.

The Rev Kenneth Prior from Hove, Sussex, a married man with three children, is appointed new rector of St Nicholas'.

Extra police stand by at Wildernesse School as controversial politician Enoch Powell addresses 1,200 people.

June: More than 50 Otford Road residents sign a petition objecting to a proposed new refuse tip. "We have put up with a refuse site on our doorsteps for 25 years," they say. "It is now someone else's turn."

Sir John Rodgers returns with a General Election majority increased by nearly 7,000 votes. Peggy Fenner wins the Rochester and Chatham seat. Ted Heath is Prime Minister.

Social upheaval and a heatwave
1970-1979

AND so to the 1970s, the decade of strikes and three-day weeks, of wage restraints and a growing disquiet in the workplace. A surprise election victory for Ted Heath gave blue-belt Tories cause for celebration in June 1970 but the feeling of hope did not last. Inflation soared, wages leapt and unemployment burst the million barrier by 1972. At the end of the decade it was nearer to two million.

The grim state of national affairs did not affect the Sevenoaks school building programme. In March 1970 the government gave the go-ahead for work to begin on an ultra-modern new Hatton in Bradbourne Vale Road. It cost £587,000 and 270 excited girls moved in four years later. Meanwhile Lady Boswells upped sticks from its home in the London Road (since 1818) and moved to Knole Paddock. The new building had eight classrooms, centred around a courtyard and could take up to 320 pupils aged five to 11. There was sadness at Walthamstow Hall on July 8, 1970, as Miss E. Blackburn retired as head after 24 years and a fighting spirit in Sundridge as 500 parents rescued Combe Bank convent from closure.

Schools gave hope for future generations but the state of the economy had many wondering exactly what sort of country their children would inherit. The three-day week, train strikes and electricity cuts bit hard at the beginning of 1974. Even the bakers went strike in December. However, a Dunkirk spirit prevailed. People wore warm clothes to the office and worked by candlelight. Firms tried to fit a five-day week into three days to ensure no staff were laid off and a spirit of cheerfulness prevailed throughout.

It was not the sort of climate in which to introduce yet another draft plan for Sevenoaks town centre but in March 1971 the urban council did just that. With Messrs Lock, Buchanan and other consultants paid off and dismissed, members now turned to their own officers. The new scheme had to have a name so the Chronicle dubbed it *The Bennett Plan* after the engineer and surveyor, Alan Bennett.

This one was little different from the others. A pedestrianised High Street, car park, offices and shops on land at Bligh's Meadow and, "most essential of all", a relief road called Eastern Way round the fringes of Sevenoaks School and Knole Park. KCC liked it; they

For sale — the Old Market House (or Skinner's Palace). Surely a future with more dignity!

1971

The "lock-up" rule applied to day boys who attend Sevenoaks School is abandoned. This means those seen out of their homes after 7 pm will escape corporal punishment.

January: Sevenoaks postmen, like those throughout the country, go on strike. They seek a 19° per cent pay rise.

February: Many Sevenoaks residents, particularly older people struggle to come to terms with decimalisation but the new system is soon accepted.

June: There is a national outcry as the world-famous "blackout board" at the White Hart, Brasted bearing the names of Second World War fighter pilots is sold for £1,000. Retiring landlady Kath Preston hopes it will stay in the district.

Census figures show the population of Sevenoaks to be 18,247. There are 21 larger towns in Kent.

August: Alan Tammadge, former wartime naval officer and a distinguished mathematician, becomes headmaster of Sevenoaks School following the resignation of Dr Michael Hinton.

It was in January 1976 that the news reverberated round Sevenoaks like a shock wave — "Have you heard Youngs is closing?" It was true. The finest store the town had ever known, then part of the Allders empire, was to cease trading at all three shops — the drapery department in the London Road, the men's outfitters opposite and the furniture/electrical store in the High Street.

S. Young and Sons was founded in 1780 by Robert Comfort, ancestor by marriage of the Young family and occupied premises in the London Road. In 1845, Stanford Young entered the business and was succeeded by Stanford J. Young in 1883. His son Alec joined in 1912 when the company was still using horse-drawn vans. In 1938, Alec opened the new furnishing branch in the High Street. He sold the business on his retirement in 1957.

pushed for the scheme to be built in 1974 but placed it on ice when the government said it would have to hold a public inquiry. That same year came the *Daws Plan* — with a supermarket and multi-storey on the same controversial triangle of land. This won approval at appeal and excitement mounted, especially among the traders. On and on it dragged until 1981 when it was finally rejected in favour of a new supermarket development at the old Post Office Yard.

Elsewhere the modern face of the town centre we know today was taking shape. Sevenoaks fire brigade moved to its new complex at Morewood Close in 1972 followed by the police and magistrates on the same site. The social club went up in 1975 and a massive new modern telephone exchange — the finest in the south-east — was built in South Park. The Post Office moved into its splendid new home and the 109-year-old Tubs Hill railway station building came tumbling down in 1977, a year before 10 traders clubbed together and bought Tubs Hill Parade for a cool £250,000. In 1978 Tesco opened its High Street supermarket on the prime site of Suffolk House.

There was one blip in this progress. S. Young and Son, the great department store, which had served Sevenoaks faithfully and well for 196 years, closed all three shops. This was a bitter pill. The town was stunned. How could it survive?

Made desperate by the growing number of bleak, cheerless, empty shops and the blight which they brought to the town centre, Sevenoaks Chamber of Trade paid for a full page advertisement in the *Chronicle* to announce that

1972

Mrs Dorothy Packman, headmistress and founder of St Hilary's School, Bradbourne Park Road, has retired.

Christmas: Sevenoaks firemen answer a 999 call within hours of moving to a new complex at Morewood Close. Police and magistrates are due to follow them into the site next year.

Bromley Borough Council buys the South Camp, the operational part of Biggin Hill airfield, for a figure believed to be £450,000.

Lord Astor of Hever is the new Lord Lieutenant of Kent.

Asians expelled from Uganda by General Idi Amin are accommodated in the disused airmen's huts at West Malling airfield before dispersal to other parts of England. Several Asians make their home in Sevenoaks.

Three Sevenoaks policemen and four customers of the Moon Palace Chinese Restaurant, Sevenoaks are hurt in what one onlooker describes as a "humdinger of a fight". Four men are charged.

1973

February: Marley millionaire chairman Jack Aisher and his wife, Eileen, are held up by masked raiders, one with a pistol, at their Toys Hill home.

Marley Tiles gives around £250,000 to Sevenoaks School for a new sports hall. It opens in 1974 and commemorates Marley's fortieth year in Sevenoaks but does not include the indoor swimming pool Alan Tammadge had hoped for.

June: Fifteen PTAs launch a monster petition to stop KCC going to a three-tier five-nine years old, nine-13 and 13-18 education system.

July: The Lord Chancellor, Lord Hailsham, is first to occupy115-room Chevening House, the stately home left to the nation by Lord Stanhope.

Combe Bank, the lovely school at Sundridge once run by nuns working for the Society of the Holy Child Jesus, which faced closure in 1972. After an emergency meeting attended by some 300 anxious parents, an educational trust was formed, funds raised and the school was saved. By the end of the century Combe Bank was flourishing with more than 400 girls in the junior and senior schools.

Bakers went on strike in December for a 66 per cent wage claim as galloping inflation gripped Britain and sent the cost of living soaring by 20 per cent. Thanks to the efforts of Plaxtol Bakery some loaves were available for those who queued.

1973

As mortgage rates rise to 10%, young couples cannot afford to buy in Sevenoaks even though prices are levelling out at £32,000 for a two-bedroom detached house in Oak Hill Road.

October: Sevenoaks Hospital celebrates its 100th anniversary. The Holmesdale Cottage Hospital opened in 1873 with only eight beds and one nurse.

November: "No Petrol" is the sign greeting motorists at Caffyn's Garage, Tubs Hill, as people start hoarding for fear of the war in the Middle East. Rallypoint report a surge in sales of lockable petrol caps then fuel rationing follows.

November: Bligh's Hotel is no longer to provide accommodation as 14 bedrooms close down.

1974

February: Tory MP Sir John Rodgers holds his seat in the General Election pushing Labour into third place.

December: A gallon of four-star petrol has increased from 42p in January to 72p.

Dandag's battle to save the Valley of Vision

Sevenoaks as a thriving trading centre, was "dead". A few days earlier executive members of the Chamber had spread themselves across the width of the High Street and walked slowly towards the fountain holding up the traffic. They then delivered a "strongly worded letter" to the urban council urging them to reconsider pedestrianisation and make progress with the town plan — particularly the clause which allowed for the construction of an Eastern Way!

The front page of the Chronicle was devoted entirely to the Traders' Revolt and the fact that four more shopkeepers had decided to quit, bringing the total to more than 20 empty shops. *"In a week of ill-feeling"*, wrote the *Chronicle*, *"there is a glimmer of hope for the future. It emerged this week that the giant supermarket chain, J Sainsbury, is searching for a suitable site within the town centre. This will act as a magnet to encourage other traders into the town."*

The date of that now-historic issue was Friday January 21, 1972. *"The town is dead. Long live the town,"* said the advertisement. *"No flowers please. No period of mourning. But let us all work together for a better future..."*

The arrival of the railways re-shaped Sevenoaks in the 19th century. Now motorways were to alter our outlook even more dramatically in the 20th. Dunton Green villagers were shocked to learn in April 1970 that their community would be sliced in half by the link road between the M25 and the M20 (later to be named the M26). The great consolation was that only two houses would have to be demolished and the traffic-congested villages on the A25 would return to the "peaceful times of yesteryear"!

Work began on the Sevenoaks to Godstone stage of the M25 in June 1975 and continued apace until 1977, when one 94-year-old lady brought the whole schedule grinding to a halt. Elsie Birkett's home, Laburnum Cottage in Dunton Green, was right in the path of the road (M26) and destined to be pulled down. She refused to budge.

Letters went backwards and forwards. The Department of Transport said if the cottage were saved it would lead to another round of public inquiries. In the end Miss Birkett bowed to the pressure and progress continued. The Godstone to Chevening section was finally opened by Norman Fowler, Minister of Transport, on November 14, 1979.

Miss Birkett was a crusader but not the only one. The Darenth and North Downs Action Group (DANDAG) launched a battle as well, this time to save Samuel Palmer's Valley of Vision by preventing the proposed Sevenoaks-Swanley link cutting a swathe through the lovely Shoreham Valley. A painting by Graham Sutherland sold in print form throughout the world and raised thousands of pounds for the campaign. By March 1978 the group had more than 1,000 members. They took their heavyweight protest to the Department of Transport headquarters in

It was in 1971 that Sir Desmond Heap of Oak Hill Road, Sevenoaks signed the contract for the sale of London Bridge to America. Sir Desmond was then Comptroller and Solicitor to the City of London — a post he held for a record 22 years.

This was not the first time that an articulated lorry demolished part of the railway bridge at Riverhead and nor was it to be the last. On this occasion, in November 1974, the road was closed for hours while the masonry was cleared and the busy commuter line above suffered an afternoon and evening of chaos.

1974

State school Wildernesse also becomes a centre of sporting excellence as a £1million complex with facilities for badminton, squash, netball, basketball, golf and cricket practice opens to the public.

April: Benefactor, former urban councillor and author of the quintessential history *This Pleasant Town of Sevenoaks*, Sir John Dunlop dies.

October: Ted Heath, who failed to win an overall majority in the February General Election, calls another and Harold Wilson's Labour Party wins by the narrowest of margins. Sir John Rodgers wins Sevenoaks with a reduced majority.

1975

Two years of work on the new £500,000 railway station at Tubs Hill begins. The old station, built in 1868, is pulled down to make way for more parking spaces.

London — on an eight-ton steamroller.

During the inquiry between September 1978 and March 1979 there were several small skirmishes. One man chained himself to a pillar in Swanley. The opposition claimed the inquiry was a *fait accompli* and pointed to a bridge close to the A20 at Swanley which had been erected in readiness for the road from Sevenoaks. The inspector, George Dobry, finally made his decision in April 1980. The route, by then amended to go over the North Downs, was given the green light.

The year of 1976 went down in history as the summer of The Big Heat. Sevenoaks sweltered. Tar blistered on the roads, the swimming baths, muddy lakes and rivers were besieged, tempers frayed, grass fires became more frequent and everyone had their own recipe for keeping cool. The long, rainless days stretched on and on.

The Big Heat began in May when, for the first time in the history of Sevenoaks, the use of hosepipes was banned. Local fairs and carnivals enjoyed record crowds, roads were jammed as thousands headed for the coast in search of respite from the heat, Knole Park Golf Club closed its parched course and local cricket clubs put down matting on their wickets. One dairy farmer was forced to sell his herd of 82 Jersey cows as the drought ruined his crop of hay

1975

February: John Simpson of Seal Hollow Road walks into Sevenoaks police station: "I've killed my girlfriend," he says. "Her body is in the car." Simpson is convicted of manslaughter and jailed for five years.

The Moorgate tube crash claims a Sevenoaks victim when the body of Charles Gale, a 23-year-old trainee accountant from Seal, is found among the wreckage.

June: Amid protests about traffic congestion on the A25, work on the Godstone to Sevenoaks section of the M25 begins bang on schedule. The Wrotham to Sevenoaks section of the M20, when built, is to be renamed the M26.

1976

Mock Tudor Donnington Manor opens as a 40-bedroom, £250,000 hotel complex in Dunton Green..

for the winter but there was jubilation in a Vine Court household when the occupants discovered an underground spring in the cellar.

Mother Nature at last relented and sweet rainfall kissed the earth in September, More torrential downpours in October brought the drought to an official close. At the West Kent Water Company hundreds of standpipes lay gathering dust. By the narrowest of margins Sevenoaks had escaped their use.

Health was another hot topic. The long-awaited pathology department at Sevenoaks Hospital was finally opened in 1976 — thanks to the League of Friends who had raised £5,300 — and there was good news for old folk when The Dynes, a £133,000 old people's home in Kemsing, was officially opened in February the same year.

There was more cause for celebration in February 1977 when the Leonard Cheshire Foundation's pioneer venture was completed. Keys to the £150,000 home for 10 disabled and handicapped residents on the shores of Chipstead Lake were formally handed over to the Rev Ian Ogilvie, chairman of the local committee. It was the culmination of seven years' hard work by hundreds of dedicated volunteers.

But, back in the town, our joy for the hospital was short-lived. In 1978 vans with loudspeakers toured the streets calling people to a public meeting to save the maternity unit. The Sevenoaks Hospital Action Group was formed to fight the Regional Health Authority's plans and mothers wrote to the *Chronicle* outlining their fears. There was even a deputation to the House of Commons.

A few Sennockians in the 1970s became caught up in IRA bomb outrages. Worst of all was the wounding of Stock Exchange secretary Joanna Knight, 26, of Pilgrim's Way, Otford. Opening the post one Friday a letter exploded in her face. She said: "I felt my face which was hurting like mad. There was blood everywhere, I felt for my nose. At least that was still there."

The district was put on a state of high

Prince Philip made his first visit to the then experimental wildfowl reserve at Redlands quarry in Bradbourne Vale Road in July 1970. Both men had sprained wrists. Accompanied by Dr Beeching, chairman of Redlands, and Peter Scott, director of the Wildfowl Trust, the Prince toured the reserve and later visited Dr James Harrison's home (Jeffrey's father) to see his museum of wild birds.

Lessons out of doors for the children of St John's Primary School. This was the long, hot summer of 1976.

Sir John Dunlop, former chairman of the Sevenoaks Urban Council and author of the book, **The Pleasant Town of Sevenoaks** *died in Kippington Grange in April 1974 aged 82. Sir John enjoyed a distinguished military career and was a leading military historian. He had a deep and lasting affection for Sevenoaks and for many years was its best known and most re-spected citizen.*

Cameraman Alex Watson joined the **Sevenoaks Chronicle** *in 1947 as the newspaper's first full-time photographer and, by 1999, had clocked up 50 years. Many of the photographs in this book were taken by Alex and his long-time colleague, Roger Tutt.*

Trousers and mini dresses for girls, long hair for boys. **Chronicle** *photographer Roger Tutt took this picture in Sevenoaks High Street in the summer of 1974.*

1976

March: The massive roundabout interchange junction for the M25 and M26 at Chevening and Chipstead is replaced with a new interchange placed as far as possible from the two villages. Traffic from the A21 will not be able to join the M26 Wrotham spur because the government has decided that the volume of traffic using such a connection will be too low to justify the high cost of additional roads.

May: Tories storm back into power in Sevenoaks District Council elections with a massive majority of 18 seats against combined opposition parties.

alert and post offices put a picture of a letter bomb on display for employees. Det-Insp Frank Powers said: "People must not relax for a minute... it could prove fatal. That might sound dramatic, but this is a dramatic business."

One hoaxer spotted an ideal opportunity for mischief. A man with an educated accent called the *Sevenoaks Chronicle* and told the receptionist he had planted a bomb in a school in the town. Every school in the area had to be evacuated.

Royal news was never far away from Sevenoaks in the 70s. Prince Philip visited the Sevenoaks Wildfowl Reserve at Redlands in July 1970 and returned two years later with the Queen to see an exhibition at Fort Halstead. Later, after much speculation, Prime Minister Harold Wilson announced in May 1974 that Prince Charles was to make his home at Chevening House. Villagers drank a loyal toast. Massive renovation work had been going since the death of Lord Stanhope, who had been anxious that Chevening should continue to be a family home and a worthy part of our heritage.

There were celebrations for the wedding between Princess Anne and Captain

In March 1979 the Labour government lost a vote of no confidence by just one vote. Among those casting a vote for the motion was Sir John Rodgers. By doing so he put a lid on his own distinguished political career, for the defeat of the Government meant a May election — and the retirement of Sir John after 29 years as the Member for Sevenoaks.

His replacement, Mark Wolfson, strolled home so comfortably that, with the help of new boundaries, he more than doubled Sir John's majority of 11,000 and gave the Commons one of its safest seats in the country.

Mark Wolfson is pictured above with his wife Edna and son, Julian. John Rodgers is with his wife Betsy.

Mark Phillips on November 14, 1973, and, in June 1977, the town let its hair down again to celebrate a damp Queen's Silver Jubilee. The more it rained, the more people enjoyed themselves — holding impromptu street parties. In Sevenoaks, the Round Table organised a carnival of some 40 floats and hundreds of youngsters decked themselves out in red and white.

On March 31, 1974 the Sevenoaks Urban and Rural Councils, which had looked after the town since the creation in 1894, were buried forever as the two combined to become Sevenoaks District Council with offices in Argyle and Oakhill Roads. Eileen Wickenden was the first chairman. Local government reorganisation also gave our first-ever town mayor in the shape of the well-known Cr John London.

The first meeting of the new district council was described by the *Chronicle* as a "shambles". Gordon Anckorn, the reporter who covered it, wrote: *It lasted from 7 pm until the early hours of the morning. It was noisy, unruly and the old chamber proved quite inadequate for the new authority. I was there to report proceedings but after six hours and a further day checking facts I found it impossible to give an accurate account of the meeting. There seemed to be two meetings going on at once. Mrs Wickenden was presiding over the official one and Cr Leslie Reeves, the other. More often than not Cr Reeves' business dominated!*

Cr Eileen Wickenden

The 1970s were famous for a new-found liberalism and one woman became synonymous with the campaign to keep television clean: Mary Whitehouse. Britain's self-appointed watchdog of moral standards made the rather unwise move of talking to Sevenoaks School boys in September 1973 on the controversial television showing of *Ulysses*.

She told sixth-formers: "It was the most obscene verbal material I have heard."

123

Dorothy Parrott, the lady who best epitomised Conservative Sevenoaks, died suddenly from a heart attack at Rene's hair salon in Sevenoaks High Street on July 13, 1978. Her popularity knew no bounds. Tributes poured in from colleagues, opponents and especially from those who had benefited from her extraordinary generosity.

Dorothy, who lived at Crownfields, South Park was larger than life in every sense. She loved the debating chamber and enjoyed many sparkling exchanges with the married couple who, almost alone, represented the then opposition, Liberals Paul and Pamela Hayden. She belonged to every organisation that mattered and was a benefactor to most. Soon after her death a memorial fund was set up which reached its target of £10,000 the following year.

John London, who became Sevenoaks' first town mayor in May 1974, is pictured below with his wife Meryl and children, Anne-Louise, Sally and James, who is now a councillor himself. Much of the administrative spade work during the difficult time leading up to reorganisation of local government was carried out by Cr Jack Portsmore.

The annual Point-to-Point at Yaldham Manor, Ightham was a feature of the Sevenoaks sporting calender in the 1970s and Chronicle *cameraman Alex Watson was ever-present to take pictures of the winners receiving their trophies. In 1973 there was a Foinavon-style pile-up and a melee of horse flesh appeared briefly before hundreds of astonished eyes. With a reflex that comes with almost 30 years experience as a photographer, Alex captured that dramatic moment.*

1976

July: Temperatures hit 95 deg during the hottest week since records were first taken.

Summer: Bulldozers move in to work on the giant Suffolk House supermarket scheme. George Sales, owner of a confectioners shop will have to move out. He has been in the High Street for 40 years.

November: Plaxtol Patisserie opens on Bank Street corner.

November: 24 regulars at the Prince of Wales pub in Seal celebrate a £65,554 pools win.

1977

January: A Piper Cherokee crashes at Bayley's Hill, killing a 16-year-old boy. Pc Chris Bradley spends many minutes speaking to him as he lies trapped upside-down.

One boy counter-attacked: "Experts have called this some of the greatest 20th century prose ever written." Another argued that the monologue was Anglo Saxon. A third said similar material could be found in Shakespeare.

By now Sevenoaks had a new MP, Mark Wolfson, who met his first challenge by campaigning with the *Sevenoaks Chronicle* to end the A21 "murder mile". A horrifying series of crossover accidents on the Sevenoaks bypass had claimed 11 lives in two years. The transport minister investigated and agreed to authorise central crash barriers. They were put up in June 1980.

The 70s ended the same way as the decade had begun as Sevenoaks found itself buried in the Winter of Discontent. In January the *Sevenoaks Chronicle* launched an urgent appeal for blankets as the temperatures slipped below zero and hypothermia threatened the lives of old people. The conditions worsened as the month dragged on. Commuters were without trains, schools closed down,

The Miss Sevenoaks competition was a feature of many past summers. Organised before the war by the Three Villages Carnival Committee and then in turn by the Chamber of Trade, Sevenoaks Variety Club and the Chronicle local girls would compete for the honour of wearing a crown and winning several attractive prizes. Here are the finalists in one of the last contests, held in the gardens of the White Hart pub at Brasted when the judges included Gloria Hunniford and Peter Skellern. As usual it drew a large crowd and raised a considerable amount for charity. Today, of course, such an event would not be considered politically correct.

the ambulancemen answered emergency calls only, Beeline taxis stopped running, panic buying set in and bus services were thrown into turmoil. The situation prompted Barry Morris, Australian reporter with the *Chronicle*, to publish a letter he had written to his mother in Australia. "As you have probably seen on TV, this country is engaged in its great winter sport — strikes. You may think that dear old Oz has seen its fair share of industrial action but the union boys over here put us in the kindergarten class."

The new Tory Government carried out its promise to slash public spending and directives were sent out to head teachers recommending that heating be drastically rationed in all schools.

It prompted one remarkable revolt to see out the decade. In Westerham, on October 23, 1979, rebel children led by senior pupils burned their books and walked out in protest against the cold. When headmaster John Coatman went into the playing fields to remonstrate, many returned but 50 to 70 stayed outside until a caretaker confirmed the heat was on.

1977

April: Government inspector Walter Wood overrules overwhelming public pressure for added slip roads on and off the M26 at Chevening. The extra cost of £2.4 million is not justified, he says.

May: 5 die in a horror crash joyride at Biggin Hill Air Fair.

August: Popular Sevenoaks librarian George Lawrence dies aged 57.

July: Fiona Topham from Otford is murdered while travelling in France. She is the third Otford girl in a few years to be murdered.

1978

February: Burglars steal former Kent and England cricket captain Colin Cowdrey's silver trophies among which are those he won during the Test against the West Indies in 1967/8.

April: Care Village, a home for 60 mentally handicapped residents, opens at Ide Hill.

April: News emerges that Lady Sarah Spencer, one of Prince Charles' constant companions, was suspended from West Heath, Sevenoaks, for drinking wine.

May: Tesco opens its brand new High Street supermarket. It boasts a bakery and extensive meat and vegetable preparation facilities.

May: Holmesdale Cricket Club members open their £31,000 pavilion. The old building was destroyed by a mystery fire the previous year.

July: Parents of children attending the new combined Sevenoaks Primary School threaten to keep their children at home in September in protest that neither the head of Bayham Road Boys' School nor the headmistress of Sevenoaks Infants' School have been appointed head of the new establishment.

Throughout the century Sevenoaks School has benefited from the generosity of many great friends such as Frank Swanzy, who presented the school with the New Buildings (or Swanzy Block) and Charles Plumtre Johnson whose gift of a large Victorian house called Thornhill (later Johnsons) enabled Sevenoaks to double its number of boarders. Now there was another — Jack Aisher and the Marley Tile company. Aisher Hall, the music centre, had been opened in 1967. In 1977 came the Marley Sports Hall which, along with the squash courts and girls' international house, was opened by Prince Charles. He is seen here with Alan Tammadge, headmaster and Lord Sackville, chairman of the governors.

1979

March: Edward Aldridge sells his cobbler's business where he has worked since 1928.

November: Norman Fowler, Minister of Transport, opens the M25 section between Godstone and Chevening.

The decade closes with a deluge. Householders along the River Darent watch in horror as two days of torrential rain see water rise to a height of 15 inches. Parts of Bligh's Hotel are flooded and sandbags come out at Shoreham.

In May 1979 Father Donnelly celebrated 50 years as a priest by attending a thanksgiving service at St Thomas's Church given in his honour. Among the hundreds who attended were pupils of the primary school, many of them pictured above. Philip Donnelly was ordained in May 1929. In the depressed years of the early 1930s he became a travelling missionary, looking after hop-pickers and 120,000 tramps who were on the road at the time. It was in this capacity that he came into contact with a tramps' hostel at Little Timberton, Shoreham, where he knew most of the men. He continued working with the tramps until 1946 when he was appointed parish priest at Sevenoaks and saw immediately the need for a Catholic school. He started St Thomas' in 1948, saw it grow into a school of 250 boys of all ages. In 1977, the new primary school was opened in South Park.

Joanna Knight, the Stock Exchange secretary who opened a letter bomb.

1980

January: Former Sevenoaks Chronicle reporter Percy Reid is made an MBE in the New Year's Honours List.

Straw Dogs, the film with a rape scene banned by Sevenoaks councillors eight years ago, arrives in the town's cinema, Focus, without a murmur of complaint.

In spite of highest-ever interest rates and sky-high house prices, 50 per cent of all mortgages are to first-time buyers. Parsons, Welch and Cowell have a three-bedroom detached house close to the station for sale at £59,500.

March: For the first time in its history the *Sevenoaks Chronicle* fails to appear due to countrywide action by the NGA print union. "We ask readers to bear with us during this extremely worrying period," noted editor Bob Ogley the following week as he struggled to produce three weeks' worth of emergency editions.

April: Plastic sack rubbish collection begins. The number of dustmen and dustcarts has been cut but a more efficient service is promised.

Hurricane, war and a sect scandal
1980-1989

THIS was the decade in which Sevenoaks became Oneoak, when a million trees fell overnight and utterly transformed our landscape, the decade in which the district mourned the tragedy of the 1987 hurricane. This cataclysmic event overshadowed much of what took place but there was so much more to remember: a Royal wedding between heir-to-the-throne Prince Charles and West Heath old girl Lady Diana Spencer; two devastating fires at a church and a school in Brasted, and another at a riding stables for the disabled in Sevenoaks.

There was disaster at Biggin Hill Air Show; a murder outside Bligh's Hotel. West Kingsdown man Kenny Noye was acquitted of murdering a policeman in his back garden but sent down for 14 years for his part in the £26 million Brinks Mat gold bullion raid.

The town welcomed Waitrose supermarket and new "battleship-look" council offices; an Ightham woman was killed in a mysterious parcel bomb attack; Sevenoaks School controversially turned coeducational and the town rejected the headteacher's offer of a new swimming pool.

Town church leaders were not afraid to stick out their necks. On March 15, 1980, Seal vicar Canon John Barnard, through the *Sevenoaks Chronicle*, attacked the decision to let Russia host the Olympic Games following its invasion of Afghanistan. The same month, the Rev Kenneth Prior, rector of St Nicholas' Church, labelled Monty Python's film satire on biblical events, *The Life of Brian*, "a cheap and nasty form of entertainment". The Rev Michael Shields, of St John the Baptist, Sevenoaks, was more forgiving: "It is in appalling bad taste but great fun," he said.

For many, especially those at Sevenoaks School at the time, the early 1980s meant one thing — Moonies. The first warning the religious sect was recruiting in Sevenoaks came from Ben Battle of Weald Road in March 1980 who claimed his 21-year-old son, David, a former Sevenoaks Schoolboy, had been brainwashed. He had become withdrawn, "zombie-like" and had dropped out of college. A year later Sevenoaks School master Casey McCann and school chaplain the Rev Peter Hullah "rescued" seven boys from the sect.

In an incredible tale that began in August 1980 with a phone call from the distraught parents of two brothers, the charismatic economics master took out a bank loan and flew to San Francisco to reason with the group that was "looking after" the boys. Meanwhile, the Rev Hullah brought pressure to bear at the Moonies' London headquarters at Lancaster Gate.

Casey McCann

Bejams freezer food centre is "delighted" as Sevenoaks District Council allows town centre shops to open on Wednesday afternoons, ending early closing day. Bookshops and jewellers have yet to be exempted from the new Shops Act and must keep to the old hours.

George Dobry, the government inspector who presided over an 18-month inquiry in 1978/9 into the Sevenoaks-Swanley route of the M25, rules in favour of the 8.6-mile route close to the A21.
It will follow the line of Polhill, then branch off near Shepherd's Barn Valley and travel to the west of Lullingstone Park.

DANDAG, the protest group set up to protect painter Samuel Palmer's Valley of Vision immediately appeals.

June: Lightning strikes the Main Road, Sundridge, home of 69-year-old Janet Tyler causing the television to explode in her face.

September: William Daws, building supplies and DIY department in London Road, Sevenoaks, closes in the face of competition from national chain stores.

November: Norman Fowler, Minister of Transport, and Mark Wolfson MP open the long-awaited £19m 10-mile M26 link between Wrotham and Sevenoaks.
Angry motorists call the Sevenoaks Chronicle and AA to complain it won't let them off at Sevenoaks. One even admits to doing a U-turn on the motorway!

December: Millie Sutcliffe, of Dartford Road, Sevenoaks and mother of the fifth Beatle Stuart Sutcliffe, mourns John Lennon who is shot today, aged 40, outside his house in New York.

Blind faith healer and leader of sect seduced women

Between them, the two otherwise ordinary school teachers convinced both boys and the Moonies that it would be better to let them continue their education.
Chronicle reporter Rosemary Urquhart, following Casey McCann's initiative, also found herself battling against a secretive religious sect, whose spiritual leader used mind control to seduce women. From 1979 she had been running stories in the *Chronicle* about The Christian Fellowship, a group formed 10 years earlier in Brixton by Kenneth Lock, a blind and illiterate storekeeper. Members claimed that in the early days Lock had been blessed with phenomenal healing powers.

Kicked out of the Brixton Pentecostal Church after women in the congregation complained about his "sexual counselling", Lock was invited to Sevenoaks to carry on his work in private homes. Funded by The Earmark Trust, which was run by Lloyds underwriter Charles Raven and his wife, Elizabeth, of Ightham, the fellowship grew. Gordon East, a former head teacher of Lady Boswell's, and his family moved into a house sold to the fellowship in Grassy Lane. They were joined by others, some of whom, like Mr East, relinquished their own homes to the trust.

But tales of divisiveness began to emerge and the *Chronicle* began printing stories of heartbreak and family splits. Relatives spoke about the "indescribable suffering" caused them by Lock. Mr Raven and his wife sued the paper's publishers, its editor Bob Ogley and reporter Rosemary Urquhart for libel in July 1980.

Lock died in June 1981 and the truth came out in dramatic style a year later at a mass meeting, called by Mr Raven, at Dunton Green village hall. Several women confessed they had had sexual relations with Lock. It confirmed relatives' belief that Lock directed his extraordinary powers of mind control to seduce women who either had no idea at the time what they were doing, or were convinced it was "the Lord's will".

Mr Raven said he and the fellowship had been deceived by Lock; they had no idea what he had done. He dropped his libel action, the fellowship disbanded and the *Chronicle* received many joyful phone calls saying long-lost wives, sons and daughters had returned to their families after years of estrangement.

Earlier, just six years after the then Prime Minister Harold Wilson had said Prince Charles would be making Chevening his country home, the country's heir to the throne announced, in July 1980, he would be leaving. Villagers, who had been hoping he would bring a bride to his 115-room mansion, were shocked and saddened. The Prince spent one and a half hours telling each member of staff personally about his decision, saying he felt it was wrong that he could spend so little time at such a grand house. A year later, in May 1981, the Government announced the house would become the official residence of the Foreign Secretary who was then Lord Carrington.

With a succession of national stories breaking in its midst the *Sevenoaks Chronicle* was enjoying these years and it was appropriate that, in February 1981, the newspaper should celebrate its 100th birthday by featuring four female staff in Victorian costume holding, at Hever Castle, an anniversary banquet and

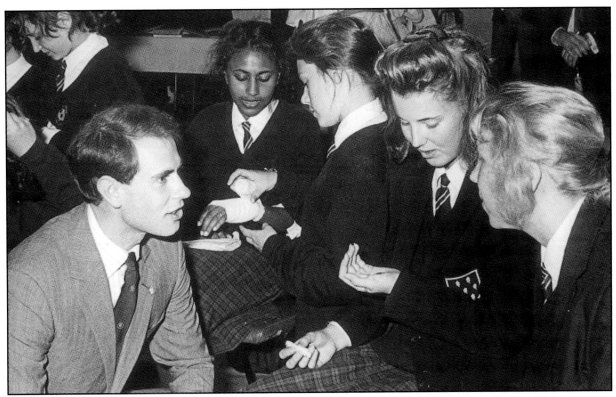

1981

February: Arsonists severely damage the music room and main hall at Wildernesse School.

May: Pensioner Percy Oliver of London Road, Dunton Green, vows to "wring Buzby's neck" after British Telecom mistakenly charges him for a staggering 35,000 calls.

May: *Sevenoaks Chronicle* reporter Chris Smith visits the Yorkshire Ripper trial at the Old Bailey. On a large table are a grizzly array of weapons – hammers, saws, screwdrivers and knives.

creating a holiday fund for people with disabilities. A year later there was sadness. The *Sevenoaks News*, now a midweek tabloid newspaper but regarded with great affection by many, appeared for the last time on February 17, 1982, having fallen foul of declining circulation and advertising revenue in the face of competition from its sister paper, the *Sevenoaks Chronicle*.

Two weeks later, Courier announced the launch of *Sevenoaks News In Focus*, an easy-to-read free community paper for the town and district with light news and features.

'Deadly' Derek Underwood, who lived at Gracious Lane, played more than 70 Test matches for his country and helped to win the final Test against Australia in 1968 with his 7-50, was made an MBE in 1981. However, he had found himself up to his eyes in controversy a year later (1982) when he joined the renegade 'England' tour in South Africa. The *Sevenoaks Chronicle* even received an anonymous letter threatening his family and others flouting the ban. It was handed to the police.

There were other sportsmen and women in the news. In April 1980 Paul Downton, the son of former Sevenoaks Vine wicket-keeper George Downton, announced that he was leaving Kent to play for Middlesex. In September that year he was selected as reserve wicket-keeper for England's tour of the West Indies.

Another Sevenoaks cricketing prodigy, Chris Tavare of Kemsing, was chosen for the England team in May 1980. In a golden debut he took on the fearsome West Indies attack virtually single-handed making an unbeaten 82. Tavare went on to become a most successful captain of Kent but lost his job when the county turned to Chris Cowdrey. Tavare then left the county for Somerset.

The Sevenoaks Chronicle *used colour pictures for the first time in its 99-year history to commemorate the visit to Knole by the Queen Mother on June 23, 1980. The National Trust held a garden party to celebrate her 80th birthday and decked out the Great Hall in blue, yellow and white flowers, all beautifully arranged by Sevenoaks Flower Club. Her Majesty also took time to visit Sevenoaks School and meet headmaster Alan Tammadge.*

Two days after the royal visit on June 25, 1980, a once-in-a-lifetime localised summer hailstorm pelted the town without let-up for 90 minutes. Four and a half inches fell at Sevenoaks School but outlying villages were hardly touched. Local meteorologist Peter Rogers said it was one of the most intense storms on record. It was also the nineteenth consecutive day in which it had rained — and that was another record.

In Grassy Lane residents saw three feet of water flood their homes. Manholes popped out under the pressure, Brittains Farm stream burst its banks turning Braeside Avenue into a river and pensioners at Rockdale watched as water cascaded into their kitchen.

In September 1980, news leaked that Prince Charles was dating former West Heath schoolgirl Lady Diana Spencer, then a 19-year-old kindergarten teacher. Five months later the two were engaged to marry and the school was thrust into the limelight.

Headmistress Ruth Rudge's study became an interview room for the world's media who wanted to know everything they could about the future Queen of England.

Miss Rudge remembered Diana as a "lovely, lovely girl" who excelled at fields sports and dancing. She was quite naughty with a wonderful sense of humour. She went into Sevenoaks one day, walked past the pet shop in Tubs Hill and bought a little kitten which lived in the cowshed — the sixth form dorm without anyone knowing for a week.

Penny Walker, wife of Riverhead vicar the Rev Chris Walker, taught Diana from the age of 14 and later engaged her as a babysitter. "She was the only girl I could really trust; she was instinctively maternal."

1981

June: Owen Aisher, chairman of Marley Ltd whose headquarters are at Riverhead, is knighted in the Queen's Birthday Honours list. Sir Owen's father founded the company in 1924 and opened the Riverhead factory in 1935.

July: Union Jacks and hundreds of yards of bunting decorate the town centre as Sevenoaks celebrates the wedding of Prince Charles to Lady Diana Spencer. Street parties are thrown at Queen's Drive, Lyndhurst Drive, Hillside Road, Chesterfield Drive, Crawshaw Close and Quarry Cottages in Sevenoaks

Schoolgirl Annabel Croft, 13 in 1980, was chosen for England's junior tennis squad to face the Americans in the Corona International. After a short but glittering tennis career Annabel later went on to star in Channel 4's series Treasure Hunt, a programme made famous by Anneka Rice.

In October 1982 DANDAG finally surrendered its bid to halt the Sevenoaks-Swanley M25 link after the Court of Appeal ruled environment secretary Michael Heseltine had not acted contrary to natural justice. In February the protesters, who included a QC as a member of Shoreham Society, had lost a High Court case. In this they had argued that plans for slip roads on the nearby M26 which would vitally affect the scheme were not made public until an 81-day public inquiry in 1978/9. The campaigners were told to foot the enormous legal bill.

As contractors got on with the work of completing the final link in the orbital route, Sevenoaks was hailing another dramatic feat of engineering. The raising of the wreck of Henry VIII's flagship, the *Mary Rose*, was the design triumph of Brasted engineer Ron Crocker. Showered with messages of congratulations,

August: The town's last blacksmith's, Terry's Forge in the Old Post Office Yard, is forced to close to make way for Waitrose supermarket. Smithy Bill Pearce, 64, says: "This is what's called progress, isn't it."

September: Richard Barker, former housemaster at Marlborough, takes over as head of Sevenoaks School.

A Saturday market which has been operating at Hitchen Hatch Lane since August must stop, says Sevenoaks District Council in a writ designed to protect town centre shops. The matter was not decided until Feb 1983 when the High Court ruled the council held the rights to a Saturday retail market in the town and not Pattullo and Vinson.

October: Bligh's Hotel cancels a male strip show after protestors label it immoral and pornographic in the *Sevenoaks Chronicle*. Women in the town retaliate with cries of sex discrimination and circulate a women's-only petition entitled 'Who stripped Sennockians of their rights?' As a result of this feminine outburst the strip show goes ahead after all – at Donnington Manor in Dunton Green.

More than 100 policemen, 19 cars, three motorcycles, tracker dogs and a helicopter descend on the Black Eagle pub at Badgers Mount to arrest IRA bomber Gerard Tuite. All they find are three Irishmen working on the M26 having a drink with barman Frank Wyer. "I thought they were filming an episode of Juliet Bravo," he says.

November: CB radio sets are like gold dust in Sevenoaks as they become legal from the first of the month. At £100 they are selling for 30 per cent more than their retail price.

Parents wait in fear for news of Falkland heroes

it was his protective cradle that lifted the ship from the bottom of the Portsmouth harbour where she had sunk in 1545. "The worst moment of all", said Mr Crocker, "was when the underwater lifting frame crashed down on to the *Mary Rose* protective cradle — my heart missed a couple of beats."

Families breathed a collective sigh of relief when news came through of the Argentine surrender in the Falkland Islands on Tuesday June 15, 1982. Many had endured weeks worrying about their loved ones. Now their sons and husbands were coming home.

One relieved parent was Mary Hart-Dyke of Lullingstone Castle whose son Captain David Hart-Dyke lost his ship, the destroyer *HMS Coventry*, to the Argentines on May 25. He was among 20 men injured. A further 20 were killed.

It had also been a desperate wait for Dorothy and Norman Shrubb, of Granville Road, Westerham. For 36 hours they had not dared to watch the television, listen to the radio or read a newspaper for fear that their son, Malcom, 28, on board the *Sir Galahad*, may have been killed in an attack by Mirage and Skyhawk fighter bombers at Bluff Cove. But the L/Cpl's name was not on the 57-name British casualty list; he was alive.

In another dramatic tale, two close friends took part in an attack at the San Carlos beachhead. Seal man Peter Wilkin, of the 45 Commando Unit, was peppered with shrapnel in the shoulder, arm and hands and sent home. But his pal Leonard Goldsmith, a Royal Marine in the same unit, survived the assault and went on to be mentioned in despatches for his bravery in taking out a machine gunpost at Two Sisters Ridge.

The 19-year-old from near Knockholt marched out from the place where Peter had been wounded, across 70 miles of open ground carrying a 110lb pack of weapons and ammunition. Two engagements later he and one other soldier were asked to brave continual artillery fire overhead and move forward into position to take out two half-inch machine gun emplacements which had 45 British commandos pinned down.

During his climb toward Two Sisters Ridge a bullet struck the webbing on Len's back but he pushed on and fired his anti-tank missiles at the gun emplacements. "When they launched the warheads, Len had 10 seconds to get clear," said his father, Derek. "He rolled over and put his fingers in his ears. The warhead went right over him." His colleague injured, Len helped him back down to safety.

Sevenoaks School's brilliant clarinettist, Emma Johnson, progressed through the heats of the BBC's Young Musician of the Year competition to the final in Manchester which she won with an exquisite performance of Crusell's Clarinet Concerto. Peter Woodward, director of music at Sevenoaks and Richard Barker, headmaster, were in the audience.

1982

Jan uary: Weald of Kent School in Tonbridge, attended by hundreds of Sevenoaks girls, wins a reprieve from the Kent Education Committee. Falling rolls had threatened its closure.

February: Charrington's bows to public pressure and agrees to remove the "bounty bar", "mutiny grill" and similarly-themed pub sign from Bligh's Hotel which, as every Sennockian knows, is named after a landlubber, not a seafarer, John Bligh who was a farmer and a brewer.

Sevenoaks travel agents are working hard to soften the blow to around 100 locals whose holiday plans have been shattered by the collapse of Freddie Laker's travel empire.

March: Swift-thinking 15-year-old Ann Rodger, showered by glass and beaten back by flames, sounds the fire alarm at Sevenoaks School for Girls. Some girls faint and become hysterical as they watch the blaze wreak £130,000 worth of damage to a teaching block.

April: St Nicholas' Church drops its plans for a £100,000 octagonal extension after the Sevenoaks Society and a newly-formed pressure group, the Friends of the Sevenoaks Conservation Area, successfully fight for environment secretary Michael Heseltine to call a public inquiry.

The number's up as £2.5m worth of telephone exchange at South Park gives us all a 4 in front of our five-digit phone numbers.

May: Nat West instals its first cash machine in Sevenoaks High Street, marking the beginning of the end of traditional face-to-face banking for all transactions.

December: International Stores supermarket, which opened in the High Street in 1913, is to close at Christmas in the face of competition from Waitrose.

Crowds stretch to catch a glimpse of the Queen as she walks down the front lawn at Dorton House School, Seal, during her visit in July 1989. Accompanied by headmaster Peter Talbot, she and Prince Philip toured the school before being shown the new college of further education which she officially opened.

Back in Sevenoaks, after more than 500 years as a male domain, the governors of Sevenoaks School set up a committee in May 1983 to consider the idea of allowing girls to join from year one. Heads at Sevenoaks Prep, Combe Bank, Walthamstow Hall, New Beacon, Solefields and Winchester House said the news had come as a "bombshell". There would be a reduction in places for boys, they feared, and it would hit other local girls' schools.

One month later the school and district council unveiled another plan: a new public pool on school land at the end of Solefields Road. Public money would pay for the £1m complex and 80 per cent of the running costs. In exchange, the school would provide the land and expect 12 hours of exclusive use, preferably some of it on Saturday afternoons.

The plan created a storm of controversy which ended with a referendum on August 18. Thirty-three people were appointed to man the polling stations and 18 to do the count. It cost £1,500 and resulted in an overwhelming 'no' to the proposal. In the end the council plumped for a new swimming pool on Buckhurst Field.

Meanwhile excitement was mounting among members and friends of the newly-formed Sevenoaks Theatre Action Group (STAG) who had been offered a site for a theatre in Old Post Office Yard next to the proposed Waitrose supermarket complex. Margaret Durdant-Hollamby, chairman of STAG, said she was "tickled pink" at the prospect. As a professional fund-raiser was appointed came an even more sensational offer from the Rank Organisation. "Would Stag take over the lease of the Ace cinema?" Mrs Durdant Hollamby said: "I had taken 17 years to get planning permission for a theatre and now, like the London buses, two sites come along almost at once."

January Sevenoaks motorists are told to "belt up" as new seatbelt laws are imposed.

Sevenoaks School for Girls has historian Elisabeth Blackburn as its new headmistress.

February: Lord and Lady Sackville-West are to be divorced soon after eight years' marriage. Lord Sackville, 69, marries for a third time, in December, and brings his new bride, Lady Jean Imbert-Terry, whom he has known for some 40 years, to Knole.

June: Mark Wolfson wins almost double the votes of his nearest rival, a Liberal Democrat, in the General Election. Third-placed Labour candidate Roland Gooding, a teacher at Valence School, loses his deposit. Nationally, Thatcher wins an historic resounding victory.

August: Jamie Simmons, 18, of East Sutton near Maidstone dies after being stabbed through the heart with a flick-knife outside Bligh's Hotel.

October: Sevenoaks Community Centre opens at Bat and Ball in what is hailed as a victory for ordinary people over town hall bureacracy, says town mayor Tony Branson.

December: Knockholt nanny Claire-Marie Neal relives the horrors of last year's Regents Park bandstand IRA bomb massacre as she receives a Binney Award for her bravery. Mistaken for a nurse because of her uniform, she was told to help the wounded.
She tore up her dress and petticoat to make bandages but the scene was awful.
Two soldiers died in her arms and another died as she tried to help him into the ambulance. "They were all calling for their mothers," she says.

1984

June: Teachers strike over a 4.5 per cent pay rise, sending 600 pupils home.

Stag Theatre is created with two cinema screens

In July 1983 after long, sometimes difficult, negotiations a deal was struck with Rank in which the district council would pay the entire cost of £250,000 for a 50-year lease on the proviso that Stag repay £100,000 within a year. *"The whole deal"*, said the Chronicle, *"is a remarkable coup for the council which has, at a stroke, provided more parking and a ready-built theatre while preserving the threatened cinema and its vital car park."*

Good news was soon followed by bad. On Monday afternoon May 21, 1984, a professionally-made parcel bomb packed with nails exploded in the kitchen of Ightham mother of three Barbara Harrold, 53. Wrapped with a red ribbon which acted as a detonator, it blew off her hand and inflicted severe stomach and head injuries. Six days later she died.

Officers at first suspected a link between her husband's connections with the arms industry and a terrorist attack but sources close to the family had always been suspicious of a man, Keith Cottingham.

They said he had sent her hate mail following a dispute over repair work necessary to the family's former holiday home which he had bought in Alicante, Spain. He left for Spain two days after the bomb exploded and was eventually arrested there for the illegal possession of arms and ammunition but Kent police failed to secure his extradition.

Det Supt John Hann made it his personal ambition in 1998 to bring Cottingham back but failed because the extradition treaty with Spain could not be backdated. Even TV crime-buster Roger Cook failed to persuade Cottingham to return when he confronted the frail 65-year-old with a camera crew in a Spanish market.

In July of the same year (1984) Sevenoaks School reported the strange disappearance of popular chemistry teacher, Willy Bleyberg, during a holiday on his own in Yugoslavia. An avid supporter of Amnesty International, speculation mounted as to why there was a delay of three days before the hotel reported him missing. Some feared he was incarcerated by the authorities for possible involvement with political prisoners. Some time later medium, Doris Stokes was called in by his wife, Anneliesse, and declared him dead on the side of a mountain.

On November 26, 1983 at Heathrow Airport, gold bars worth £25 million were stolen from the Brinks Mat security warehouse. Britain's biggest robbery was planned to the finest detail. Six men coolly broke through a formidable array of alarms, held up six guards inside and took an hour loading the three-ton haul on to a lorry.

Detectives suspected West Kingsdown millionnaire businessman Kenneth Noye had a hand in the operation and began to watch his every move at his home, Hollywood Cottage, in School Lane. They rigged up a video camera in a birdbox and staked out the cottage from a hide inside the grounds of a priest's retreat opposite.

Then, on the evening of January 26, 1985, Scotland Yard sent undercover detective John Fordham into Noye's back garden. Along with his colleague Det-Con Neil Murphy, he was well prepared in full camouflage dress and a

Keep your distance! During six minutes of carnage in a freak patch of fog at 6.05 am on December 11, 1984, 22 cars and lorries piled into one another on the M25, killing nine and injuring 10. It was Britain's worst motorway accident. So mangled was the wreckage, close to today's service station at Clacket Lane, it took firemen 1° hours to reach the middle of the blazing crash. "We were greeted by a wall of flame," said Sevenoaks fireman Tony Willshaw. "It was horrific, just pathetic, nothing we could do." Fireman Dennis Carey said the scene looked like a scrapyard doused in petrol and set alight. The road was not reopened until three days later.

Margaret Durdant-Hollamby MBE is the principal figure behind the revival of regular theatrical entertainment in Sevenoaks and the success of the Stag Theatre is testament to a vision that began in the 1950s when she was a young amateur actress with the Sevenoaks Players. Her campaign for a proper venue for theatre in Sevenoaks lasted 17 frustrating, years, until she found the right allies in the district council, the directors of Fraser Wood and then the Rank Organisation. The Stag Theatre opened in December 1983 with an auditorium for 455 patrons. In 1989 the board of Stag, led by Margaret, took over the running of the two small cinemas and in 1992 Sevenoaks District Council agreed to spend £1 million to refurbish the entire building. The final cost was nearer to £3 million.

1984

August: Controversy breaks out when the district council announces rubbish sacks must be left out on the pavement from December.

September: A bed saves a Sevenoaks couple from serious injury in the IRA Conservative Party conference bomb attack at the Grand Hotel, Brighton, in which four people die.
The four-poster takes the full force when the bedroom wall is blown in, burying Tory Jeremy Elwes and his wife Phyl, of Weald Road, beneath a mound of rubble.

September 30: If you want a last dip in Eardley Road swimming baths, the last ever ticket will be sold at 4 pm.

December: In just two weeks, as Band Aid rocks for starving Ethiopians, town charity International Christian Relief raises £70,000 for the thousands dying. Two years later 2,000 people crowd into Knole Park for the worldwide six-mile Sports Aid run.

1985

January: London Road clothes shop John Collier closes because it claims the town is not fashionable enough.

December: Nine hundred pupils gather in hushed silence for the memorial service of Gordon Peiser, 64, recently-retired headmaster of Wildernesse School for the past 17 years, who has died suddenly from a heart attack while on holiday in Eastbourne.

Sennockians are applying in their droves for British Gas shares.

1986

January: Sevenoaks School's new girls' boarding house set in a walled garden in the upper High Street is opened by Lady Sackville.

balaclava. But the two were not banking on Noye's three Rottweiler dogs which surrounded them. Murphy ran, leaping up on to the wooden fence and began beating it with his feet in an attempt to distract the dogs.

Noye, then 37, his wife, Brenda, and another man, Brian Reader of Grove Park, came outside. Noye stabbed Det-Con Fordham 10 times to death with a small white-handled kitchen knife but successfully claimed in court he had been acting in self-defence because he was frightened by the sight of the apparent intruder who he did not believe was a policeman. "May I thank you for proving my innocence. God bless you," he told the jury.

However, detectives subsequently unearthed 11 gold bars of bullion near his swimming pool and, in July 1986, Noye was given 14 years' jail for masterminding a plot to dispose of the Brinks Mat gold. The Old Bailey heard that Noye and two other men first smelted down the gold into unmarked ingots and then sold it to legitimate dealers for its market value. And, not content with their vast dishonest profits, they then charged 15 per cent VAT on the sales and pocketed it. Noye shouted to the jury as he was led away for sentence: "I hope you die of cancer."

Sevenoaks Hospital, which has always held a special place in the hearts of Sennockians, received a massive blow in the 1980s. News of its fate first broke through a document leaked to the *Sevenoaks Chronicle* in 1985. Its contents rocked the town: the Tunbridge Wells Health Authority wanted to close the Emily Jackson Wing, re-site the physiotherapy unit, close the maternity unit, take away its status as an acute hospital and stop overnight stays for surgery patients.

The town had already fought one battle, when the maternity unit came under threat in 1978. Now the town's paper was deluged with letters of outrage and, at the end of January, more than 600 people packed Wildernesse School hall to twice its legal capacity to voice their defiance.

By March 15 the authority had capitulated and cuts were postponed until further talks in 1987, its chairman Sir John Grugeon saying: "We have chosen to go for consultation rather than confrontation." But words were cheap and, in August 1986, the District Health Authority released a document for the closure of the maternity unit, plans which were confirmed by the end of the year. And on Friday, June 30, 1989, the Emily Jackson Wing closed.

There was little to distinguish the evening of Thursday, October 15, 1987 from any other that year. It had been raining all day and it was a cheerless, moonless night. A few Sennockians may have seen the weather forecast that lunchtime in which Michael Fish said: "Don't worry, there won't be a hurricane but we will have strong winds."

However, a small depression was already forming in the Bay of Biscay. Moving north-eastwards, from midnight, it deepened explosively as it headed towards Sevenoaks.

Those in their beds listened to the winds gain in ferocity. They blew harder and harder until, at 2 am, all hell was let loose. From then on, for four heady hours, the Greensand Ridge and Sevenoaks suffered blow after blow from great

1986

February: Nicholas Ridley, Secretary of State for Transport, opens the eight-mile Swanley-Sevenoaks section of the M25, five months ahead of schedule.

May: Triumphant customers of the Fox & Hounds, Toys Hill, save their pub from modernisation plans.

May: The radioactive cloud from the Russian nuclear plant at Chernobyl poses no risk to health and safety in the Sevenoaks area, John Newby, emergency services officer at Sevenoaks, says.

May: Sevenoaks' brand-new £700,000 library, museum and gallery is opened by Mark Wolfson MP.

June: Detectives investigate the possibility of arson as fire sweeps through a staff corridor at Walthamstow Hall Girls' School.

November: People are suffering from AIDS in the Sevenoaks Health District and the number will increase in the the next five years.

After years of controversy, Sevenoaks District Council demolishes the Argyle council offices and builds a new home bringing all the council's employees together under one roof. It cost 2.5m. Not everyone likes its design, some comparing it to a battleship, others saying it is prison-like, fortress like and "a cathedral gone wrong". However, for the first time since local government was reorganised in 1974, the district council's 280 employees are working in the same building.

1987

January: Freak snowfalls cut off many villages. In Knockholt a milkman walks an 18-mile round trip to his dairy for supplies then delivers his wife's baby at home.

gusts howling in at more than 100 mph.

Those huddled together in the countryside around the town were terrified. With a deafening roar, tree after tree came crashing down. Still in full leaf, the ground around their roots saturated by rain, one million mighty oaks, beech and ash trees gave way in the Sevenoaks district alone.

One tree nearly killed 12-year-old Rebecca Meredith of Little Vinesgate, Brasted Chart. A beech smashed into the house, splintered the upper storey and pierced the mattress of her bed. Luckily her father Paul, an ex-naval officer, had sized up the situation on a 5 am tour of the gale-swept garden. "Right, everybody run!" he had yelled and, with his wife, second daughter Hannah, 13, and two-year-old son Marcus, the family had fled to the relative safety of duvets at the bottom of the garden where they spent the night.

Others emerged next morning to a terrible sight. The landscape had literally changed overnight. Country roads were unrecognisable and impassable; everywhere was devastation. Roof tiles lay all about, overhead power cables lay like tangled spaghetti, trees were resting buried in roofs, and all around was the smell of crushed pine and beech leaf.

No one single sight represented the storm more poignantly than the fallen six oaks on Sevenoaks Vine. Sevenoaks had become Oneoak and the town hit the national headlines. Some viewers abroad were told we had been completely wiped from the map and there were prayers said for us in Jerusalem.

In Knole 20,000 tonnes of trees — 500 lorry loads — had been hurled to the ground. White Hart Bank, opposite the pub of the same name on the Tonbridge Road, was nearly wiped out; ancient beeches, more than 200 years old, had been simply snapped in two. Chestnut Walk had been hammered — a wide avenue of trees planted in Cromwell's time. Lord Sackville, 74, had dedicated the past 24 years of his retirement to the park. Somehow he slept through it all. He awoke, looked out of his window, and was utterly devastated.

Light aircraft at Biggin Hill had been tossed around in the wind. One plane flipped on top of another; three worth £20,000 each, were written off. Only one boy went to Wildernesse School on Friday. He called out to a member of staff: "Please sir, is there any school today?" No birds were heard in Sevenoaks for 10 days after the storm. Knockholt was cut off for three days by fallen trees

Kemsing basked in the glamour of Hollywood in June 1980 when some of the world's greatest film stars descended on Ronnie Norman's home, St Clere, Heaverham, to film the Agatha Chrtistie mystery **The Mirror Crack'd***. Here are three of the stars, Kim Novak, Rock Hudson and Elizabeth Taylor.*

1987

The body of William Choi is found in a shallow grave in a field in Ightham, on New Year's Day 1987. He had been hacked to death by a village schoolboy who said he suspected Choi of raping his girlfriend. Andrew Richens was sentenced to life imprisonment but in 1992 the Appeal Court reduces his conviction to manslaughter through provocation.

June: Margaret Thatcher is the first PM in more than a century to face a third full term in office backed by a massive parliamentary majority in the General Election.

1988

January: John Buckwell, whose family has run the Dorset Street coffee shop since 1861, hands over the running of the business to a firm from Tonbridge. He will look after his wife, Barbara, who is unwell.

March: More than 50 firemen battle to control a building ablaze in a town centre yard which threatens to spread to houses in neighbouring London Road and Bank Street.

June: The hurricane claims another victim as a 23-year-old New Zealander falls working on a damaged tree.

September: Rising cricket star Alan "Iggy" Igglesden of Westerham grabs the headlines with a career-best batting and bowling performance in the Brittanic Assurance Championship against Surrey. He scores 41 and then takes 6-34

October: Consultants commissioned by British Rail say they favour a high-speed rail link from the Channel Tunnel which would run past Heaverham, Borough Green, Ightham and Plaxtol, down the Bourne Valley. The demolition of homes and businesses will be necessary and local concern is growing.

This is Chestnut Walk in Knole Park, once an area of outstanding beauty, devastated by been knitted by time. Tops were plucked off and hurled away like litter. Oak and beech, salt-heavy atmosphere, the deer and their fawns had gone and so had the birds. Like the

the hurricane. Here the wind blew with such violence that it uprooted hundreds of trees, unravelling everything that had their roots more than 150 years old, were tossed aside. When dawn eventually came to Chestnut Walk, with a burning rest of Knole Park it was twisted and distorted by the sheer ferocity of the most powerful wind ever known.

Following the vandalism, seven mature oaks were planted by children in a second ceremony on The Vine. Here are the pupils of Lady Boswell's School.

and Dunton Green opened Donnington Hall as a community centre. In Sevenoaks, Riverhill was closed for more than a fortnight.

In the emergency control room of Sevenoaks District Council, chief executive Bruce Cova told his team these were the nearest conditions to a nuclear disaster they may ever see. MP Mark Wolfson cut through red tape to ensure the help of the army. Everywhere the Dunkirk spirit prevailed.

After the immediate recovery, Sennockians stumped up £70,000 towards the £129,000 Trees for the Future appeal which replanted 70 sites locally including Bitchet Green, Fawke Common, Seal Chart, Hosey Common and Knole.

But there was amazement when, just a week before the hurricane's first anniversary, drunken hooligans vandalised the seven oak saplings that had been planted by radio personality Gloria Hunniford, her daughter Caron Keating and town mayor Ann Dawson. *"This thuggery is worse than the wind,"* proclaimed the front page of the *Sevenoaks Chronicle* which, with the *Daily Mail*, bought more mature and resilient oaks as a replacement.

The late 1980s were renowned for a new type of music that revolved around drugs — the music of "acid house". Sevenoaks, hardly ever at the forefront of the youth culture music scene, suddenly found itself thrust into the limelight in November 1988 when police broke up one such party of 300 revellers in a derelict house in Pembroke Road.

The raid saw seven policemen injured and 13 arrests. The drugs haul from

Kent becomes one of the first counties to acquire an Air Ambulance. It took to the skies for the first time on December 21.

Christmas Eve: Ten horses die in a fire which sweeps through Bradbourne Riding School for the Disabled in the early hours despite the efforts of owner Peter Felgate and firemen. The blaze breaks out 25 years to the day after Mr Felgate founded the stables. It also destroys half his home. Richard West, 28, of nearby Betenson Avenue, later pleads guilty to arson and says he was high on drink and drugs.

Tony Branson — the man they called Mr Sevenoaks — was a former urban council chairman, district councillor, town councillor and three-times town mayor. He is pictured here with his wife Isobel on their golden wedding day in January 1987. Tony, an architect by profession, was a member of the Magic Circle and Sevenoaks Players. He died in May 1989 aged 80.

Bligh's — now council is accused of "dirty dealing"

that one evening also amounted to more than Sevenoaks police had recovered during the previous three years! But there were claims the police overreacted.

Waitrose supermarket might have been built fronting London Road at Bligh's Meadow if an alternative plan by builders' merchant owner Frank Daws had not been shot down in flames by Sevenoaks district councillors.

Mr Daws had offered Waitrose a similar sized store with a multi-storey car park on Bligh's Meadow as well as 18 shops and 30,000 sq ft of offices behind his own shop on the London Road. He had been planning his town centre scheme since 1958 and had organised the shopping complex around a new square with walkways linking it with the High Street, London Road and Bank Street.

However, as councillors rejected his scheme in favour of another by Tunbridge Wells firm Fraser Wood Properties to redevelop the Old Post Office Yard, a frustrated developer in the Daws plan, Christopher Collins, accused the council of "dirty dealing".

Bligh's was back in the melting pot and for the next four years the issue was rarely off the agenda as the District Council, the Town Council, Sevenoaks Council of Women, the Sevenoaks Council of Churches, Sevenoaks Society and hundreds of individuals made their feelings known about the future of this site.

Here is a brief resume of the muddled years which followed:

1985: A Dorking firm proposes an £8 million scheme for 40 shops and a car park on top of the shopping centre. Fraser Wood follows with an ambitious retail scheme. Sevenoaks Society writes to the government pleading for a public inquiry. The District Council throws the plan out. Too high, too big with access and highway problems. Try again, it says.

1986: The council agree to consultation with local groups. "We're going to get it right," they say.

1987: A revised Bligh's brief is published with a proposal that the bus station move to Buckhurst. Architects are invited to design a new scheme with 550 parking spaces and a public hall.

1988: A London firm of architects win a design contest and £40,000. They liaise with Fraser Wood Properties, joint owner of the site with the council.

1989: Council seeks compulsory purchase orders to buy up the rest of the land but Sennockians voice their fears. Sevenoaks Society conducts a poll and receives back 2,569 completed forms. "People do not like the plans," they say. "They want an open space or a town square, fewer shops and offices and residential units. Many fear the scheme will turn Sevenoaks into a second Bromley." Planning director Jeff Gaynor dismisses the poll. "The questions", he says, "are loaded."

The saga continues... The cost is mounting...

Four girls from the advertising staff of the Chronicle *help to dig out snowbound cars following the vicious blizzard which hit Sevenoaks in January 1987. Riverhill and Polhill were impassable and many people walked to Sevenoaks from outlying villages dragging sledges and wearing moon boots.*

St Martin's, Brasted, collapsed and the 17th century oak pulpit was destroyed as fire ravaged the Saxon church in November, 1989. The church bells were saved and then rung as a sign of hope after 50 firemen had left the charred scene. Villagers rallied round to rebuilt St Martin's and it now boasts many new features including a fine organ and a light and airy ambience created by a series of clerestory windows high in the roof. A youth was later charged with arson.

1990
January : Father-of-two Sevenoaks Pc Neil Attwood helps deliver a baby as police cover for pay dispute ambulancemen who are answering only 999 calls.

Sundridge responds to a plea by seven-year-old James Whatley and in two weeks collects enough toys and warm clothes to send a van and trailer to the children of Romania, now Communist dictator Ceaucescu has fallen.

April: Former chairman of Sevenoaks District Council and Westerham's lord of the manor John St Andrew Warde is new High Sheriff of Kent.

Crockham Hill youth hostel is to be sold to help the YHA raise £20m to modernise other hostels and provide "the creature comforts the youth of today expect". Former warden Kev Reynolds says it is a betrayal of the YHA's ideals.

Towards the Millennium
1990-1999

THERE seemed to be an almost perpetual hosepipe ban in the early 1990s. "Sevenoaks is suffering a drought 'of historic proportions' according to the National Rivers Authority," said the *Sevenoaks Chronicle* on July 26, 1990. "Ground water levels are lower than have been previously recorded, lower than 1976, and dropping. It would require six inches of rainfall just to moisten the top layer."

Crops had to be harvested early and sheep were beginning to break out in search of fresh pastures. Sevenoaks had survived the hurricane but one of the town's replacement oaks on The Vine could not withstand the water shortage. It died. Another was reported critical.

But more worrying still, the Darent was set to be labelled Britain's most at-risk river. Its flow in July 1990 fell to less than half its expected rate and by August entire stretches from Eynsford ran dry. The Darenth Valley Anglers' Consultative Association used electrodes to stun 500lb of fish. As they floated to the surface they were scooped up and taken to nearby lakes and tanks. It was worse the next year when the Darent dried up as far upstream as Chipstead and it was not until January 1993 that a £12 million package of measures was unveiled and eventually the river's future was secured.

Almost everywhere you looked in the early 1990s someone seemed to want to build a golf course, now a legitimate use of Green Belt land. Applications were made for Hewitts Farm, Badgers Mount; Nizels (a country house near Hildenborough); Pedham Place Farm, Farningham; South Ash Manor Estate, New Ash Green; Redlibbets, Fawkham; Austin Lodge Farm, near Eynsford; Panthurst Farm, Weald; Stonepitts Manor, Seal Chart and Valence Wood, Brasted. "Watch out!" warned a *Sevenoaks Chronicle* leader. "Soon we won't be able to walk anywhere without the danger of being struck by little white balls!"

Police arrested four prostitutes, one of them just 15 years old, in a raid on a brothel in Six Bells Lane, barely a stone's-throw from the parish church of St Nicholas', in September

Cracking up: In August 1990, Kenneth Lingham of Faulkners Hill Farm, Ide Hill, showed just how bad the drought had become. Cracks were five inches wide and three inches deep.

Former Westerham footballer and Wildernesse schoolboy John Salako, 21, is the toast of his home town. His team Crystal Palace beats Liverpool 4-1 in extra time in a huge FA Cup semi-final upset. Manchester Utd win the cup 1-0 in a replay.

June: Six months after the devastating fire which killed 10 horses at Bradbourne Riding Centre, the Princess Royal sees the stables back in action. At the same time Princess Anne, who is president of the Riding for the Disabled Association, is able to join in their 25th birthday celebrations.

August: Teenage Mutant Hero Turtle-mania hits Sevenoaks. Lorimer's rations its models of the hit US TV show.

The Rev Miles Thomson, rector of St Nicholas Church, announces a £2.1m project to create an undercroft.

September: An elderly man dies on the zebra crossing outside Amherst Medical Centre in London Road after being struck by a car police were trying to stop from fleeing a jewellery theft.

Sevenoaks is shocked to hear motorcyclist Ian Peters, 23, and his fiancee Alison Gibbons have been killed on their way home from the Kentish Yeoman in Seal. Their bike leaves the road near the Bucks Head in Godden Green.

Commuters who want to park close to Sevenoaks train station must wait up to four and a half years to be allocated a space in the two district council car parks. The council says it is "unfortunate" but there is little it can do.

Six beds are to close at Sevenoaks Hospital as the district health authority strives to save money.

A house of ill repute in Six Bells Lane

1990. For months officers had been watching from a Sevenoaks School teacher's house opposite the top of the lane. Following one customer home they discovered from his number plate he was a clergyman from north Kent. He went via the florist's before returning home to his wife! The house of ill repute had been advertised in the *Sunday Sport*.

Most working Sennockians commute to London. So when the 07:58 train smashed into buffers at Cannon Street, killing two passengers and seriously injuring 20 more, the town reeled at the news. The day was Tuesday, January 8, 1991, and the old slam-door service left Sevenoaks packed because the previous train had been four carriages short. When, 46 minutes later, it crashed, most of the 542 injured were from Sevenoaks.

The train had been cruising into the station at between just 8 mph and 13 mph when, for no reason an enquiry could establish, it hit the buffers and carriages five and six concertina-ed into one another. Commuters, standing shoulder to shoulder, were hurled down the length of their carriage.

Passenger Helen Croxford was trapped in the wreckage for over two hours after her foot smashed through the carriage wall. "I heard a crash and I felt as though I was being sucked back in the train."

A double-decker bus was commandeered to ferry 277 of the wounded to hospital; 33 were detained for at least one night. Slam-door coaches more than 60 years old did not meet international building guidelines. New stock would not have concertinaed.

Sennockians have always known themselves to be vulnerable to terrorism: so many movers and shakers live in the town and most travel to work by train, an easy target for a railway bomber. But bombs had been planted only in London stations — until March 1994. In that month a BR employee kicked what he thought was a sandwich box under the electric rail. It was a 1lb tub of Semtex complete with detonator that had almost certainly been planted the previous December when two coded warnings were received. Three months later a 3lb device hidden in a black plastic bag by the London Road bridge was destroyed in a controlled explosion.

Rail safety, train terrorism? There was even the infamous case of The Wrong Type Of Snow to keep commuters on their toes but who would have suspected there might be The Wrong Type Of Ticket?

In January 1996, erstwhile *Chronicle* reporter Owen Houlihan took up the cudgels for schoolchildren everywhere who, he discovered, were being charged more on the trains for travelling less.

An anomaly caused by fare zones meant that Sennockians would pay 90p less for a ticket to High Brooms than they would for the shorter journey to Tonbridge. So why not buy the cheaper ticket and get off a stop early? You'll be fined, said British Rail.

Amazed, Mr Houlihan put BR to the test — and picked up a £10 fine at Tonbridge. The story was irresistible to the national newspapers. An embarrassed BR later corrected its fares.

The Gulf War of 1991 was both distant and up close. For the first time satellite technology fed us pictures of Baghdad's battle with the bombs live into our living rooms. This was both immediate and yet removed, at times like a soap opera. "It's like the fourth of July," one CNN reporter cried as he watched the

November: Horror greets a private bid by Shanks and McEwan to turn a valley behind The Woodman pub, Ide Hill, into a 26-acre million-tonnes domestic rubbish dump. The Sevenoaks tip at Otford Road is almost full. Campaigners group rapidly and in July '91 the firm gives up.

Six beds are to close at Sevenoaks Hospital as the district health authority strives to save money.

December: Madge Leonard, 76, and her close friend Hilda Comer, 81, are hit and killed by a Bedford light van in Brasted High Street as they leave a pensioners' Christmas party. Poor lighting is later cited as a cause of the crash.

1991

January: The price of a season ticket to London rockets 10% to £1,336 per year.

March: Ide Hill's most officially vociferous resident, Speaker of the House of Commons Bernard Weatherill, announces he will hang up his wig and retire at the next election.

April: Tributes are paid to Colin Garner, former chairman and leader of Sevenoaks District Council, who has decided to stand down after 17 years.

May: The Tories lose Otford and their majority in the four town wards in the district council elections. The Liberal Democrats have a resounding victory.
Even in the parish elections Town Mayor Maurice Short loses his seat just 10 days before the end of his term to a man who did not even canvass or turn up to the final count.

June: Cybil, a black and white cat missing for two weeks from her Riverhead home, is found sooty but unscathed, trapped in a neighbour's chimney.

Sennockian's bridge destroyed in The Gulf War

tracer Ack-Ack bullets fly. But for our soldiers' parents it was a nightmare. Kemsing couple Peter and Gill Jones rationed themselves to morning and evening bulletins to avoid the speculation of live broadcasts as they waited anxiously for news.

The *Sevenoaks Chronicle* reception was inundated with gifts from Sennockians anxious to help our troops. Launched by Otford village reporter and landlady of The Bull, Sally Maycock, *News at Ten* cameras filmed the success of the town's appeal at the *Chronicle* offices.

Meanwhile, as peace protesters from Sevenoaks gathered outside the local Conservative Association headquarters on Vine Gardens, prayers were said in churches throughout the district. Kent and Sussex and Pembury hospitals also prepared to accept casualties.

Kemsing-born Rebecca Stephens became Britain's first woman to conquer Everest. At 7.41am UK time on May 17, 1993 she reached the summit ahead of her Sherpa guides and in a radio message said excitedly: "I'm on top of the world!"

Two men had a different perspective on the war. Kippington Road resident Alan Wilkinson saw on TV a Baghdad bridge he had built destroyed in a high precision bombing raid. And in February 1991, Chipstead RSPCA officer Jack Westlake returned from rescuing birds and wildlife coated in thick crude oil released by Saddam Hussein. He will never forget the smell, he said. "Looking north and south all you could see was black oil. I counted one dead bird almost every seven paces on one beach."

War also touched the life of Biggin Hill mother Theresa Paterson in October 1991 when she found a note from her 17-year-old son George. It read: "By the time you read this I will be out of the country." Thirteen days later, watching an evening news bulletin, she saw him fighting in the Yugoslavian civil war, in Croatia!

The early 90s saw recession and job losses. In June 1990, only two years after opening its head office on the corner of Suffolk Way and the High Street, Payless DIY said almost all its 235 staff were to go in a merger with Do It All. Then, in October, Marley made 49 people redundant at its head office in Riverhead and the following March, publishers Hodder and Stoughton announced 120 job losses at its Dunton Green head office. By now almost 2,000 people were unemployed in the Sevenoaks district.

The situation deteriorated. Five weeks before Christmas Greatness Brickworks closed and in July 1993 it was announced Hodder's would close altogether taking with it 350 jobs in a merger with Headline Plc. Later that same month Swiss Life said it would be closing its South Park offices making up to 70 staff redundant.

There were planning controversies too. In March 1990, Sevenoaks District

July: The collapse of the Bank of Credit and Commerce International (BCCI) leaves Shoreham man Paul Creswell, 47, out of work without redundancy pay.

August: An estimated 250 partygoers in 70-80 cars swamp One Tree Hill for one of the biggest bashes since the acid house craze. Moved on by police they head for a squat in Blackhall Lane, Sevenoaks.

October: Shoreham and Eynsford protesters pull the communication cord on a Sunday train service which no longer stops in their villages. By January the rail rebels win their battle.

Transport Secretary Malcolm Rifkind ends three and a half years of uncertainty by announcing the Channel Tunnel rail link will avoid Sevenoaks and district completely.

November: French's Dairies, Sevenoaks' oldest family milk company, sells out to Southern Co-operative Dairies blaming family ill health and the recession.

December: Tesco's decision to open its supermarket on Sunday provokes church protests.

Demolition men move in to pull down the old bus station in Bligh's, Sevenoaks.

1992

January: Amazed policemen stop a Reliant Robin travelling at 104 mph along the M20 at Wrotham. The three-wheeler, which normally struggles to make 70mph, has been souped up.

April: Knockholt half empties itself as 500 villagers pack out Wildernesse School hall to demonstrate against a proposed 16-pitch KCC gipsy site at Randles Lane. They win their case

Multi-storey in Suffolk Way — 'No', says Sevenoaks

Council chairman Cr Colin Garner attacked his own council for its plans to build a dry ski slope at Greatness Park. By September an ice rink had been added to the £3.8 million scheme but councillors were unhappy with the cost and scaled down the scheme in November, before it was eventually scrapped.

And one bright idea to solve the town's parking problems had more switches in the storyline than almost any other printed in the *Chronicle* in 1993 — the multi-story multi-storey. First Sevenoaks District Council revealed it wanted to build a multi-storey in Suffolk Way. Then over 1,300 people signed a petition begging councillors for a change of heart. Would pressure prevail? No. The £3 million scheme was approved. A public meeting was held which unanimously called for an end to the "monstrosity" but it was only in November, almost a year later, that the beleaguered councillors gave way, shelving the idea to cheers and applause from an overflowing public gallery.

Schools were scarcely out of the news in the 90s. Charismatic Casey McCann, who rescued pupils from the grip of the Moonies in the early 80s, left Sevenoaks School to be head of the prestigious St Paul's in Brazil in June 1990 just as Mark Pyper, registrar and organiser of the Sevenoaks Summer Festival, left to be head of exclusive Gordonstoun, the public school where Prince Charles was educated.

At the same time, headmaster, Richard Barker unveiled his glass-topped entrance gates. Instantly they were labelled machine gun posts, goldfish bowls, even glass cases for "the greenhouse effect". Even worse - there were more similarly-topped constructions on the lawn behind the oldest building, School House. Mr Barker said these were "pavilions" for boys to sit in and contemplate matters while looking out at Knole House. But few in the school seemed to like his idea. "They're hideous," said one sixth former. "Everyone thinks so."

Cr Colin Garner who retired in 1991 after 17 years on the district council.

In September 1996, Tommy Cookson, 53, took over as head of the school. "Education is for life," he said. "It should not be narrowly vocational but an enriching experience." The forward thinker followed this philosophy to its natural conclusion and, to great national interest, announced in March 1999 the school would be ditching A-levels in favour of the International Baccalauréat exam.

About the same time, Bradbourne School head Lynton Karmock-Golds was defending herself over news that 15 of the school's 33 teachers would be leaving at the end of the summer term. In a two-page letter to the *Sevenoaks Chronicle*, the former head of English said he had never seen a staff so demoralised since the head had taken over 10 months earlier. Mrs Karmock-Golds answered: "We want staff that are up to speed" which did not please some of those leaving.

What were you doing when you heard the news that Diana, our popular Princess of Wales, had died? Few will forget that moment, on Sunday, August 31, 1997, when, for a moment, the world stood still. First we suffered disbelief then an overwhelming sense of loss throughout the nation. Many Sennockians joined the pilgrimage to Kensington Palace where flowers stretched out in a

Is it your house?
I'm really sorry

Shortly before this crash, 10-month-old Jessica Minnis had been playing in the front room of this wrecked 17th-century cottage in Seal. The date was August 1994. The lorry was a fully-laden 32-tonner heading into the narrow section of the High Street.

Cutting equipment can be seen on the roadside but firemen are having to wait while paramedics stabilise the driver's condition. His first words to the owner were: "Is it your house? I'm really sorry." He was trapped for two hours but escaped with a compound leg fracture.

There were two other big lorry smashes in the 90s and amazing escapes in each of those too. In October 1990 a Romford driver died as his beer truck careered into two 500-year-old cottages but luckily no-one was at home at either 225 or 223 Main Road, Sundridge. And in 1996 a 15-tonne lorry demolished the front of Crockham Hill post office where two hikers had been standing just moments earlier.

✳ In July 1993 on the day Princess Alexandra visited Care community for people with a mental handicap, a 52-seat school coach parked outside nearby Ide Hill school slipped its brakes.

It hit a parked car, ploughed through gardens, returned to the carriageway, smashed into two parked cars, finally coming to rest in the ragstone wall of a house.

March: Brasted Chart property tycoon Malcom Potier is thrown off the Scottish island of Gigha he bought for almost £6m to use as a holiday home. The Swiss bank that was owed money for loans secured over the island and other properties in the central belt of Scotland sent Sheriff's Officers to the island to officially seize buildings there.

Potier beat the likes of Mick Jagger to buy the island which has just120 inhabitants.

April: Knockholt half-empties itself as 500 villagers pack out Wildernesse School hall to demonstrate against a proposed 16-pitch KCC gipsy site at Randles Lane. They win their case.

Sitting Tory MP Mark Wolfson romps home for a fourth consecutive General Election victory, polling more votes than his four rivals put together.

A mystery vandal is conducting a campaign of terror against elderly residents in Overdale, smashing windows, slashing car tyres and breaking into garages.

May: Sainsbury opens its Otford Road superstore. With 650 free parking spaces a regular bus service and Sunday opening, High Street Tesco and Waitrose suffer an immediate downturn in profits — Tesco by 28 per cent.

Talks are under way to demolish Tracks, the pub at Bat and Ball, to make way for a car showroom.

Sevenoaks School for Girls is the latest school to opt out of local authority control.

Children belonging to town dentist Tim McKenzie escape a fire which rips through their farmhouse in Toys Hill.

July: Fire guts empty listed Emily Jackson House, the geriatric wing of Sevenoaks Hospital closed in June '89. Next year it becomes a private nursing home with 59 beds.

The death of Diana

vast carpet of condolence, their scent at times overpowering. Many also took the train to London for the funeral — a strange day, first almost holiday-like in atmosphere, then suddenly sombre and upsetting as the funeral cortège and guard of honour passed down The Mall. Back home, the High Street, at 11 am on a Saturday morning, was as quiet as a mouse.

To Sevenoaks, Diana was more than just their princess. She was also an old girl of West Heath School, the former bright and bubbly youngster who loved children and dancing, had showed talent as a pianist and then set the town on fire when her engagement to the future King of England was announced.

Shrine near Buckingham Palace, the day of Diana's funeral

Ironically, that black Sunday was also the day West Heath closed under a cloud of mystery and confusion surrounding a sudden financial crisis coming from supposed falling pupil numbers. Parents rallied round but a last-ditch rescue package failed. What would happen now, people wondered? Rumours abounded of developing the site for executive homes, a hotel, a health spa? Sennockians wanted something different, something fitting. After all, Diana once said she had spent some of the happiest days of her life here.

So, on October 16, 1997, the *Sevenoaks Chronicle* launched a campaign to save the school and turn it into a centre for emotionally damaged children. "It is what Diana would have wanted," wrote the newspaper, and the town agreed. Perversely the Diana Memorial Fund refused to buy a building "for sentimental reasons" and Mohamed Al Fayed stepped in with £2.5 million. The New School at West Heath now gives emotionally disturbed youngsters, may be sexually abused or bullied and who exclude themselves from school, a second chance at life.

For 21 years Dr Anne Rodway was a highly respected partner with the Amherst Medical Centre Practice. In October 1991 she was expelled — her colleagues claiming that, at the expense of her patients, she had been spending too much time researching breast cancer and a pioneering breast screening service at Kings College Hospital, London.

Dr Rodway set up in practice on her own in her home, the Chantry House, in the Upper High Street but more trouble was to follow. In July 1998 her new practice with Dr Paul Landy at South Park was dissolved and, in October 1998,

1992

Raw sewage and stream water floods 18 homes in Watercress Drive during thunderstorms which see the heaviest rainfall in 12 years. At least two people are taken to hospital during the three-hour night-time ordeal, one of them a 14-year-old boy who develops a skin rash and begins vomiting.

October: Diana, Princess of Wales, makes an unscheduled visit to Sevenoaks Age Concern. A pensioner comments on how beautiful she looks. "It's only the make-up," she replies.

November: Rector of Sevenoaks the Rev Miles Thomson regrets the decision of the General Synod to allow women to be ordained. He believes "in a team of both men and women - under male leadership."

December: Former Sevenoaks schoolboy Cmdr Tim Laurence, who used to live in Copt Hall Road, Ightham, is to marry Princess Anne. He was a day pupil from 1968-72 and is described as a fine sportsman.

Fierce opposition greets a plan to create a landfill site just south of Morleys roundabout, next to the A21.

Former Sevenoaks building society manager and Rotarian David Fountain is jailed for life for murdering his fiancee.
Fountain, 41, strangled Deanna Kapalka after a row and set fire to his car with her body in the boot. He had wanted to die with her but rolled out of the car when he could no longer stand the heat.

Skipper Edward Styles, well-known Hicks Own scoutmaster, dies.

Pollution of the Darent

she served him with a writ which hinged around the former partnership as well as joint ownership of the £1m building. The two went head to head in the High Court. Dr Landy hailed it a victory after the judge ruled his opponent would have to meet the bulk of all legal costs.

Meanwhile, in June 1999, her son, Steven, faced massive legal bills after his firm lost a courtroom battle with Eurovision pop star Gina G who said she had not been paid her fair share of her top 10 hits.

In January 1992 the River Darent in Sundridge was polluted with thousands of gallons of diesel in a vendetta against a farm owned by the former High Sheriff of Kent, Westerham landowner John Warde. A tractor was gutted the same night at Force Green Farm off Westerham Hill and 1,400 litres of milk were half-emptied over the floor and the rest contaminated with bleach.

Hats off to our Doris. In May 1990, 85-year-old Doris Zobel received a special community service award from Sevenoaks Rotary Club having collected nearly £40,000 for charity over the years. Two years later she received a British Empire Medal. Miss Zobel's charity pitch was outside Peter Dominic's and she always wore striking hats. Well known in Sevenoaks she dedicated her life to teaching English, music and Pitman's shorthand.

The 1990s will be remembered for two high-profile deaths. The first, in 1995, was the murder of Diana Goldsmith. She was kidnapped from her home in Argyle Road on January 25 1995 after dropping her three children at school. Her car was found at Lakeside Shopping Centre and police dragged the lake. Two years later, in March 1997, the 44-year-old's body was found buried in a garden in Bromley. The police began gathering evidence. In a bizarre scene, a temporary court was set up at the hospital bedside of her former boyfriend, district councillor Charlie Hatt. "I hope my evidence will help justice prevail," he said. Charlie died of cancer a few days later.

Michael Fitzpatrick, the former son-in-law of Diana's ex-common-law husband, power shower millionaire Derek Goldsmith, admitted conspiring to murder Diana and burying her body. Meanwhile, Ian Colligan, a friend of Fitzpatrick's, was accused of the actual murder and hung himself in prison.

Then Derek Goldsmith himself was brought to trial. It was alleged the former Aqualisa shower boss of Crockham Hill had paid £20,000 to have Diana killed because she had been granted custody of their children.

But on May 11 1999 the judge ruled the prosecution's case was unsafe and flawed. Derek Goldsmith walked free, cleared of any involvement in Diana's death.

Det Supt Dennis McGookin, "disappointed that this matter was not put to the jury", was also given charge of the decade's other major inquiry: the death of Stephen Cameron. This so-called "road rage" stabbing on Sunday morning,

Sevenoaks District Council spends nearly £80,000 beating Tesco's bid for a Riverhead superstore at a public inquiry only to later lose at an appeal.

February: A poisonous gas leak at Vestry Estate sends 13 to hospital.

William Hughes, lifelong footman and butler to the Sackville family of Knole House, dies aged 81. He has waited on seven millionaires and others including Queen Mary, the Duke and Duchess of York and the Queen Mother.

February: Dr Phillip Razzell of the town medical centre lashes out at a "two tier health service" which is denying one of his patients a hernia operation. Tunbridge Wells Health Authority has had to cancel all non-urgent operations because it has once again run out of money.

Comedian Chubby Oates and Lord Harris of High Cross join Sevenoaks commuters to defy Network SouthEast's recent smoking ban by lighting up on the 08:24 Tonbridge to Charing Cross service.

March: Amherst Practice doctors are devastated to learn that householders in Riverhead are refusing to sell them land left to the village for allotments. They eventually rebuild their London Road surgery in St Botolph's Road.

March: Dunton Green woman Julie Rumsey becomes one of Kent's first female firefighters.

One of the first women doctors in Sevenoaks, Dr Jennifer Daniel, dies at 88.

Who was the driver of the Land Rover Discovery?

May 19, 1996, had stunned the nation. Stephen, 21, died cradled in his teenage fiancée's arms on the M25 interchange near Swanley, a few hundred yards away from his home. Danielle said he had become embroiled in a stand-up row with another man in a Land Rover Discovery. Stephen had everything to live for after setting up his own electrical engineering business and proposing to his 17-year-old girlfriend on Christmas Eve.

There were other deaths, too. The 90s saw the trial of John McCarthy for the alleged murder of Peter Gibbs, who had been shot outside McCarthy's home, in Brasted Hill Road, on August 18, 1989. McCarthy was tried and acquitted because the Crown's case, once a key witness went missing during the trial, rested on the evidence of a man who was serving 18 months for dishonesty. It would be dangerous to rely on this man's evidence, the judge told the jury. The absent witness, John Corbett, a 29-year-old car dealer from Mount Pleasant, Biggin Hill, was later jailed for three months for contempt of court.

Then there was the tragic case of former racing driver, Ightham villager and father-of-three Nick Whiting. He was kidnapped and murdered in June 1990 by men who burgled his garage in Wrotham Heath and stole five high-performance cars. Police combed nearby woodland and searched with a helicopter before his body was found in Rainham Marshes a month later.

Evil killer Karl Watson, 29, was jailed for life in December 1993 for brutally stabbing to death his mother's wealthy lover, John Shippey, of Rectory Lane, Ightham. The police investigation into Shippey's death revealed him to be a romeo fraudster who had stolen £800,000 from his company using it to fund a millionaire lifestyle with a string of mistresses.

At the centre of the two inquiries: Det-Supt Dennis McGookin with (clockwise from top left) Derek Goldsmith, Diana Goldsmith; Stephen Cameron and Danielle Cable.

In November 1990 snobbery among parents at Combe Bank School, Sundridge, was vigorously denied after an inquest into the deaths of two little girls and their mother who drove them off the cliffs at Beachy Head on June 23. Millionaire chairman of Testers, the Land Rover centre at Edenbridge, Michael Kentis told the inquest his wife was upset over clashing birthday parties at the school, but her mother said she may have also been suffering from post-natal depression.

In August 1991 a bizarre death saddened the town. Just three small scorch marks on the front of Piu Fong Lam's clothing showed where she had been struck and killed by lightning during a thunderstorm, as she walked home past The Vine cricket ground from a shopping trip in the town. Passers-by, 15-year-old Andrew Charters and his father Shoreham Pc Bob Charters did all they

1993

Sir John Rodgers Bt, Conservative MP for Sevenoaks 1950-79, dies at 86. He enjoyed a long and distinguished career in business and politics.

Freeman Hardy Willis shoe shop closes in Sevenoaks High Street due to the recession. The Woolwich takes its place, moving from the Market House.

Highways inspector Peter Holland retires. Responsible for placing the Maroon at the Remembrance Sunday Parade, no-one will forget the occasion when one was placed upside down. It exploded leaving a large crater on the Vine and showering local dignitaries with mud!

May: Kent County Council becomes a hung council for the first time in its 104-year history. The Tories keep all local seats but Cr Ronnie Norman wins by just 63 votes.

The Milk Race with a cavalcade of support vehicles passes along the High Street, Sevenoaks, on the way to the finish in Tunbridge Wells.

June: The first doctor to live and work in Kemsing, Dr Robinson, retires after 31 years.

Thousands take part in *Celebration '93*, Diana Edwardes' son et lumiere presentation in Knole Park. The pageant depicts the district's history and celebrates the 40th anniversary of the Queen's coronation.

August: Estate agent Barbara Harrington escapes three gun-wielding soldiers-turned-armed robbers in Penn Lane, Ide Hill. She reverses back up the lane with one man on her bonnet and another banging the window with his gun. They had planned to use her as a hostage while carrying out a post office raid.

Dig deep: That was the message from Sevenoaks rector Miles Thomson to his flock when he annnounced the only way to provide St Nicholas' with the extension it so badly needed was to bury it underground — at a cost of £2.1million. Parishioners began fundraising and work began in August 1993 with an exploratory dig by the Oxford Archaeological Unit. They traced the church's origins back to the time of the Crusades and beyond. The church soon hit controversy when it began to exhume human remains but it pressed on, excavating 1,200 tonnes of sand. In June 1995 The Rev Thomson and his determined administrator Brigadier Ian Dobbie celebrated the project's end. The undercroft now boasts a meeting room, creche, kitchen, refectory and bookshop.

could to resuscitate her, but the 49-year-old mother-of-three from Bradbourne Vale Road died.

In June 1995, two pensioners died and more than 60 fell ill, 26 of them so seriously they had to go to hospital, after contracting salmonella poisoning from a Meals on Wheels strawberry mousse made with contaminated raw eggs.

Politics has always been a good talking point and never more so than when the *Sevenoaks Chronicle* received a phone call in February 1996 from someone giving their name as Alan Clark. Yes, it was *the* Alan Clark. He wanted to be Sevenoaks' next MP - could he have a chat with the editor to find out a bit about the character of the place? When the paper broke the story, few welcomed the interest of an outsider whose main claim to fame, aside from blowing the whistle on the Matrix Churchill affair, was his philandering. A reader wrote the following week. "If Alan Clark should ever be adopted as the local Conservative candidate may I suggest that the Stag Theatre should present as

September: A car negotiating the new traffic calming chicanes in Brasted High Street, smashes through the front door of the White Hart pub hurling four customers across the room and over the bar. Landlord Ian Young labels the chicane "ridiculous".

The first phase of the Stag Theatre's £2m refurbishment sees a 1930s art deco-style Plaza Suite opened.

A saucy seaside postcard sent from Brighton to Oak Tree Cottage, Weald almost 70 years ago is finally delivered still bearing its Penny Red stamp with King George V's head.

September: The Rt Rev David Bartleet, Bishop of Tonbridge, retires after 11 years in the job. The Rt Rev Brian Smith takes over in November.

October: Otford cyclist Dave Wellman is made a Freeman of the City of London for his many charity rides which have taken him the length and breadth of Death Valley and 500 miles from Kathmandu to Mt Everest in Nepal.

October: Tim Barr-Smith bids to reopen an historic airstrip in Sundridge but ultimately fails.

Crowds turn out to witness Jennie Churchill, great grand-daughter of Sir Winston, marry merchant banker James Rappart at St Mary's, Westerham.

Kemsing woman Teresa Debenham kills herself and her two young children by setting fire to the family car.

November: Princess Diana lookalike Giselle Goldich of Seal is at the centre of controversy after posing in a *Daily Mirror* spoof dressed as Di in a leotard at a health club.

Sevenoaks sailor Ian Walker us proud in August 1996 when he brought home a silver medal from his 470 class races at the Olympic Games in Atlanta. Tragically he lost his sailing partner John Merricks in a road accident in October the following year when the English team's Land Rover 12-seater overturned in Italy. Middle distance athlete Kelly Holmes kept us equally on the edge of our seats during the Olympics but a stress fracture in her left leg put told to any medal and the Games ended in heartbreak for her. However, despite her injury, the star of TV's A Question of Sport, who always finds time to help out with local sporting and charity events, still competed in the 800 and 1500 metres events.

soon as possible *Lock Up Your Daughters."*

It was Michael Fallon, an ex-schools' minister, who finally won the right to stand in what was to prove a colourful General Election. In the run-up to the May 1997 poll, the former Speaker of the House of Commons, Lord Weatherill, chaired a Great Election Debate. Organised by the *Sevenoaks Chronicle* and held in the Sevenoaks Community Centre, all six candidates attended, including a member from the yogic flying Natural Law Party who accidentally knocked a glass of water over a harassed-looking Mr Fallon. Then, Sevenoaks transsexual Natasha Crist publicly backed him and insisted on joining the campaign trail. Mr Fallon, of course, won his seat but the shine of his victory was more than dulled by the nationwide result — there had been a Labour rout under the leadership of Tony Blair.

Then — what a Christmas present: *Fire stations face the axe*, read the headline on the 1996 festive issue of the *Sevenoaks Chronicle*. Politicians at County Hall had decided that the only way they could balance their budgets was to make sweeping cuts. The Liberal Democrats blamed Government underfunding. The Tories blamed Liberal Democrat mismanagement of the county's affairs.

Either way, Sevenoaks' second fire engine and part-time crew were to be cut and Seal station closed altogether in an effort to wipe £4.8 million from the brigade budget. Library hours were also to be slashed and adult education, among other services, would be hit.

Sennockians had rarely been so angry. "This is our safety we are talking

CCTV could be up and running in the next three to four years in Sevenoaks.

December: A truck full of readers' gifts is taken on a two-day journey to Croatia by *Chronicle* reporter Matt Graydon.

November: The idiosyncratic Len Nye dies —and with him Ide Hill's vintage petrol station.

December: An appeal to build a hydrotherapy pool in Sevenoaks closes after reaching its £100,000 target. It is expected to open in February on the site of the old Vitasan clinic in South Park.

1994

August: Sennockian Mark Dalton sets up a relief group for cholera-struck refugees of the terrible Rwandan civil war.

September: The *Sevenoaks Chronicle* does away with its broadsheet format after 113 years and switches to a compact size. Editor Eve Fuller stresses the newspaper will keep its traditional values of honesty and integrity in all its reporting.

September: World walker Ffyona Campbell strolls through Ide Hill, Sundridge and Badgers Mount on the final leg of her journey.

October: Two trains collide head-on on a fog-bound section of single track at Cowden, killing a husband and his wife, the two drivers and a guard.

1995

February: Rock and biker venue the Frog and Bucket closes at Ide Hill despite a "Don't Let the Frog Kick the Bucket" campaign.

May: The Tories lose 14 seats and control of Sevenoaks District Council. Labour gains 10 seats, the Liberal Democrats nine.

Fire crews saved after angry campaign

about," people cried at a packed public meeting at Sevenoaks Fire Station. Gloria Hunniford joined the growing campaign, then the firemen threatened strike action. By April brigade officers and unions had found savings from elsewhere, by cutting five senior posts, fire safety civilian jobs and personnel allowances.

Seeboard sparked a storm of protest too when, just before Christmas 1998, it said it would charge a hard-up 78-year-old widow £15,500 to connect her remote home in Seal Chart to mains electricity. Her husband, a diesel fitter, had died of cancer and the generator he installed had packed up. The massive bill forced May Richards, whose income was just £73 per week, to live a Victorian lifestyle using candles for light and a wood burner for heat. The Duchess of York, pledged thousands to help her but two months later it transpired cash-strapped Fergie could afford only £1,000. To cap it all, her replacement petrol generator was stolen in February. "Who could be so mean?" asked the *Chronicle* in its leader column.

The town's first "superpub", Wetherspoon's, was due to open on October 19, 1999, bringing to a close a long battle by local pub landlords and police to stop

September 1998: Sevenoaks TV and radio celebrity, Gloria Hunniford, makes a weekend of it with the stars as she marries millionaire hairdresser Stephen Way at St Peter and St Paul Church near Hever. Cliff Richard and Barbara Windsor are among the celebrity-studded guests.

Actor/pop star Jerome Flynn of Brasted Chart is mobbed by teenage girls at Ide Hill fete. His recording of *Unchained Melody* with Robson Green spends eight weeks on Top of the Pops.

July: Care in the Community is slated after an agoraphobic of Granville Road is found surrounded by excrement and flies after being shut in her room for two and a half years.

September: Fire in six classrooms and the staff room ruins 15 years of work for Bradbourne School teachers.

October: CCTV cameras go live in Sevenoaks.

November: Neighbourhood Watch leader Jon Pritchett walks free from court after shooting two burglars at his Borough Green warehouse.

December: VSU and Sevenoaks Almshouses are awarded £192,000 by the National Lottery.

1996

February: Roger Perkins fulfils a childhood dream and becomes editor of the *Sevenoaks Chronicle* as Eve Fuller leaves to head up the *Hexham Courant* in Northumberland.

March: A mother of two Sevenoaks school pupils sells a spore from Sir Alexander Fleming's original penicillin mould to pay for her children's education.

May: Two wooden classrooms burn down at Riverhead Infants' School which is desperate for a new site.

August: Former Sevenoaks *Chronicle* editor Vic Froud dies, aged 82.

Cattle market closes and a tradition ends

chain owner Tim Martin from winning a licence. Readers of the *Sevenoaks Chronicle* provided its name The Sennockian. Other suggestions had included The Michael Fish after the TV weatherman who wrongly assured viewers there was not going to be a hurricane in 1987.

As this book went to press, Knockholt residents were waiting for the verdict on Sevenoaks Pc Paul Careless who had pleaded not guilty to dangerous driving. His patrol car was in a crash at the top of Star Hill on January 9, 1999, which seriously injured four young people, putting the driver into a coma.

The youngsters were driving to a party in Sundridge, the police car, it has been alleged, was rushing to a non-emergency call in Knockholt where youths had been reported driving a car on the village green.

Sevenoaks firemen spent more than an hour cutting coma girl Rachael Edwards from the wreckage. She had been travelling in a convoy with three other cars which continued unawares to the party. Arriving there they wondered where she was. A friend set out to look for her and came across a police road block at the foot of Star Hill. In a sad twist of fate it was understood he was so shocked by the news that his car crashed off the road as he left the scene.

Sevenoaks' cattle market at Hitchen Hatch Lane closed for good on Monday, August 2, 1999, to make way for new offices set to employ 1,200 people working for BT. It ended a tradition dating back to AD780. It is sadly poignant this should happen five months short of the new Millennium and just as our beef is allowed back in Europe, wrote the *Sevenoaks Chronicle*. The popular Wednesday retail market was relocated to Buckhurst car park next to the new bus station on September 15 but there were fewer stalls because of its limited size.

As Sennockians toast the New Year and contemplate the past century of news, many will ponder with amazement how long one particular issue has rumbled on and — even more amazingly — how it was finally resolved in the very last year of the Millennium. That issue? Bligh's!

The decade kicked off in typical style with Sevenoaks District Council being accused of "blatant propaganda" in publicising results of a "biased" survey into the proposals. The saga dragged on and on. Anchor stores that weighed anchor and left the scheme included Marks and Spencer, Allders and even Argos, the catalogue store ("not very Sevenoaks," said some). Land was compulsorily purchased despite last-minute opposition by 11 councillors, then SDC decided to buy Bligh's Meadow from Fraser Wood Properties giving it control over what was built. The scheme was actually going to enjoy a summer start in 1997. But then there was a petition, then nine out of 10 opposed it in a *Sevenoaks Chronicle* voteline, then traders made a last-ditch bid to stop the scheme and finally it fell short of tenants.

Although they lost Argos, developers Centros Miller requested another chance to get enough tenants for a watered-down scheme. They failed. In January 1999, they were given the boot by the council for failing to sign up enough traders. Bligh's would be developed piecemeal instead and Ironbridge Estates and Morrison Developments were given the contract to build a precinct with shops, housing, car parking and a community hall. Work began on September 13, 1999.

Do you remember that Sevenoaks urban councillor who prophetically accused his colleagues of "creating a monster" that would torment the town "for years to come?". By that, we believe, he meant five or six years. In fact, it was 48!

1997

September: A petition is launched to save Sundridge Hospital. It will fail to change the decision.

November: The town's first Liberal Mayor, Dorothy Peirce, dies, leaving her body for medical research.

November: Sevenoaks Rugby Football Club announces ambitious plans to build a new £1.5m floodlit ground in Dunton Green.

1998

February: Sevenoaks is put on the rock'n'roll map as The Beatles' 60s escapades in Knole Park earn it a place in the guide *Cool Britannia*.

Chronicle photojournalist Mark Davey exposes sex-for-sale massage parlour in Crampton's Road, Sevenoaks.

March: Jason Andrews, 14, has been regularly abducted by aliens since his fourth birthday, claims his Borough Green mother in a book.

April: Foreign Secretary Robin Cook dodges the paparazzi at Chevening House by tying the knot with his mistress at Tunbridge Wells register office.

July: Refugees from Kosovo, the war-ravaged enclave of former Yugoslavia, smuggle themselves to Sevenoaks in the back of lorries.

October: Sevenoaks referee Paul Alcock makes national headlines after Premier League star Paolo Di Canio pushes him over.

December: McDonald's opens at Otford Road, six weeks ahead of schedule.

1999

January: Talk Radio boss and former *Sun* editor Kelvin MacKenzie of Knockholt is refused entry to Knole Golf Club.

Going, going, gone! Sevenoaks market's association with Britain's colourful agricultural past is legion. Reputed to have started in AD 780 it was finally condemned to death by British Telecom's plans to put an office on the site. Here for centuries red-faced farmers, smallholders, horse dealers, butchers and poultry farmers came to chat and bid before retiring to the Sennocke (later the Farmers) or Railway and Bicycle. Photographs show sheep in the famous pens and (below) children, who were placed there by the evacuation officers 60 years ago.

1999

February: Former Met police officer Det-sgt Brian Weeden of Sundridge is one of those criticised in the Lawrence Inquiry report, for the delay in arresting suspects. He was in charge of the investigation into the racist murder of Stephen Lawrence.

March: Popular Chipstead footballer Dave Dougan dies from a brain haemorrhage after going up for a corner with a mass of players in the Sevenoaks Charity Cup semi-final.

The West Kent Hunt closes after 270 years as it merges with Old Surrey and Burstow.

April: Work starts extending Sevenoaks Swimming Centre to include a four-court multi-sports hall, health suite, gym and aerobics studio.

May: Brands Hatch boss Nicola Foulston wins back the Formula One Grand Prix for 2002.

August: The Government orders an inquiry into why thousands of Kemsing and Plaxtol residents lost their mains water supply for up to five days during the hottest weekend of the year.

Sevenoaks Police Station is set to be sold off and a smaller beat bobbie shop opened in the town centre, 28 years after the High Street station closed.

Ex-Kent and England fast bowler Alan Igglesden from Westerham is recovering from a brain tumour.

Sevenoaks 2000. Alex Watson's aerial picture shows modern Sevenoaks still endowed with ple... leisure complex and, remarkable as it might seem to all the sceptics, a start has been made ... in part to the financial climate and council uncertainty but most of all to the insistence and ... gratefully but also of countrymen who never want to leave it. It boasts one of the finest deer ... and always will, as a physical barrier to the metropolis beyond. Othe...

despite the loss of so many during the great storm of 1987. Next to the swimming pool centre, work continues on the new
's development. Of all the civic issues during the century this one has dominated. Its lack of progress has been due,
tion of Sevenoaks residents that the council must get it right. Sevenoaks is principally a town of commuters who return to it
gland, one of the oldest cricket grounds, a fourteenth century parish church and the magnificent North Downs which act,
ches and lakes and farmland adorn Sevenoaks. The great house of Knole crowns it.

SEVENOAKS CHRONICLE

FRIDAY, OCTOBER 23, 1987   19p

Hurricane special: souvenir edition

- 26 teams of men plus private contractors were employed by the council
- 10,000 faults on telephone lines were reported
- 5,000 trees fell on the lines in Southe

Sevenoaks' heritage destroyed in night of disast

OUR DARKEST HOU

THE loss of six of the seven majestic oaks which stood on the Vine captured the national imagination and came to symbolise the irreparable damage to the wooded landscape of Sevenoaks and district

Woodlands devastated and villages cut off

SEVENOAKS will not look the same again in our lifetime. In the dark hours of last Friday morning the town's trees and woodland, nurtured through centuries, were devastated by hurricanes which swept through Kent at speeds approaching 100 miles an hour

injured. Power and telephone lines, water and gas supplies were cut, and many homes are still without water or electricity one week later. Entire villages were cut off from all outside contact.

. All major roads into the town were blocked on Friday, and many are still closed. Riverhill, the town's major approach road from the south, was expected to be opened today, after seven days non-stop cutting by teams of council workers and private co

majestic oaks which stood on the Vine cricket ground captured the national imagination.

The trees were part of an-

REPORTS by Fiona MacLeod, Andrew Rayfield and Rachel Turner.

PICTURES by Alex Watson, Roger Tutt and Michael Knights.

the White Hart, probably planted by the third Duke of Dorset in the early 18th century, which were replaced by Lord Sackville

Communications by road or telephone were enormously difficult

Police have been faced with a rash of minor accidents as drivers are becoming more frustrated with each day of single-track routes and long detours.

Praise for the public's patience and understanding has come from all the public services. Mr Bruce Cove, chief executive of Sevenoaks District Council said that the public had generally been very understanding, and both British Telecom and Seeboard local offices, coping with thousands of calls each day, said that customers had reacted